Traditional Family Values

Life, liberty, and the pursuit of happiness. Perceptiveness, interconnectedness, and community. These are the core principles and essential beliefs of Witchcraft.

If you've ever been curious about the Old Religion but were unsure where to begin, this is one book you must have. Written with the solitary student in mind, *Green Witchcraft* provides an excellent overview of basic Wiccan practices.

Wicca is a vital, satisfying alternative to mainstream religion. Positive and life-affirming, the way of the Witch is one of herbal remedies, environmental awareness, and ancient magic. Use the rituals and spells in *Green Witchcraft* to bring about personal harmony with the cycles of nature.

Based upon the insights, personal anecdotes, and observations of a third-generation Witch, *Green Witchcraft* is a unique blend of ancient folkways, family traditions, and modern techniques. Here are the fundamental elements of Witchcraft open to all who would learn.

About the Author

Ann Moura (Aoumiel) has been a solitary practitioner of Green Witchcraft for over thirty years. She derived her Craft name, Aoumiel, to reflect her personal view of the balance of the male and female aspects of the Divine. Her mother and grandmother were Craftwise Brazilians of Celtic-Iberian descent who, while operating within a general framework of Catholicism, passed along a heritage of folk magic and Craft concepts that involved spiritism, ancient Celtic deities, herbal spells, Green magic, reincarnation belief, and rules for using "the power."

The Craft was approached casually in her childhood, being experienced or used as situations arose. With the concepts of candle spells, herbal relationships to magic, spiritism, reincarnation, Rules of Conduct, and calling upon the elementals and the Divine already established through her mother's teachings in particular, she was ready to proceed in her own direction with the Craft by the time she was fifteen. In her practice of the Craft today, Aoumiel has moved away from the Christianized associations used by her mother and grandmother. She is focused on the basic Green level of Witchcraft and is teaching the next generation in her family. She took both her Bachelor of Arts and Master of Arts degrees in history. She is married, has a daughter and a son, and is a certified history teacher at the high school level.

To Write to the Author

If you wish to contact the author or would like more information about this book, please write to the author in care of Llewellyn Worldwide and we will forward your request. Both the author and publisher appreciate hearing from you and learning of your enjoyment of this book. Llewellyn Worldwide cannot guarantee that every letter written to the author will be answered, but all will be forwarded. Please write to:

Ann Moura
(Aoumiel)
c/o Llewellyn Worldwide
P.O. Box 64383 Dept. K690-4
St. Paul, MN 55164-0383, U.S.A.

Please enclose a self-addressed, stamped envelope for reply, or $1.00 to cover costs. If outside the U.S.A., please enclose an international postal reply coupon.

GREEN WITCHCRAFT

FOLK MAGIC, FAIRY LORE & HERB CRAFT

ANN MOURA

(AOUMIEL)

1997
Llewellyn Publications
St. Paul, MN 55164-0383, U.S.A.

FIRST EDITION
Fifth Printing, 1997

Cover design by Maria Mazzara
Illustrations by Nyease Somersett
Book design, layout, and editing by Rebecca Zins

Library of Congress Cataloging in Publication Data
Moura, Ann (Aoumiel)
    Green Witchcraft: folk magic, fairy lore & herb craft / Ann Moura
(Aoumiel).—1st ed.
            p.   cm.
    Includes bibliographical references (p.   ) and index.
    ISBN 1-56718-690-4 (pbk.)
    1. Witchcraft.   2. Herbs—Miscellanea.   3. Magic.   4. Fairies.
 5. Ann Moura (Aoumiel).   I. Title.
BF1572.P43A58   1996
133.4'3—dc20   96–16406
                                                              CIP

Publisher's note:
Llewellyn Worldwide does not participate in, endorse, or have any authority or responsibility concerning private business transactions between our authors and the public.

    All mail addressed to the author is forwarded but the publisher cannot, unless specifically instructed by the author, give out an address or phone number.

Note: The herbal usage in this book is not recommended as a substitute for proper medical care. Please use herbs within the guidelines given and heed the cautionary notes regarding poisonous and otherwise dangerous herbs. The publisher assumes no responsibility for injuries occurring as a result of the herbal usage in this book.

Llewellyn Publications
A Division of Llewellyn Worldwide, Ltd.
P.O. Box 64383 Dept. K690-4
St. Paul, MN 55164-0383, U.S.A.

Other Books by the Author

Dancing Shadows: The Roots of Western Religious Beliefs (as Aoumiel)

*Balance in Darkness: Working with the Dark
Aspect of Divinity* (forthcoming)

This book is dedicated to the memory of Wanda Lee, who after a sudden illness passed into the realm of the Lord of Shadows on March 24, 1993. This lovely lady had the gift of divination with Tarot cards and gave me the push I needed to write about the Craft. She encouraged me to reach for my star and to do what I really wanted.

Take your rest in the loving care of the Lady and the Lord, dear sister, and blessed be.

Contents

1

The Green

It is my intention to discuss the Green elements of modern Witchcraft and neopagan practices as well as relate those elements to my own Craft practice and the bits and pieces of Iberian-Celtic tradition handed down to me from my mother and her mother. My approach is both historical and personal; my interests lie in history, and I would be untrue to myself if I discarded history (which is so great a part of my perspective on life) in any presentation of Craft practices. My family associations with the Craft did not come through formal training or through recognized tradition, but by observation, activities, and verbal guidance.

Much of Craft practice has been softly muffled through its passage over the generations. It has only been in recent decades, with the formalization of Witchcraft traditions, that practices have been created to preserve oral traditions that otherwise might have faded. I am very grateful for the Gardners and the Bucklands and all the other writers of the Craft who have worked so diligently to preserve an ancient religion. My purpose here is to show the underlying thread that appears to run through most traditions and relate it to the ancient historical past, while also presenting insights as to how this thread weaves its way through three generations of my family, and is now entering the warp and weave of a fourth.

This does not mean that I know all there is to know about any one tradition—I don't. I am a solitary practitioner and have been for over thirty years. My information on traditions comes from reading about them and keeping current with the Craft through newsletters and other pagan publications. I correspond with a number of Wiccans, some with coven traditions and some who are solitaries, and I have found that some issues are repeatedly addressed, which I will bring out in this book. I have found that there are terms and there are *terms*, which means that words like "tradition" can lose their generic, mundane inference and be seen as representing a formal school of the Craft. I shall avoid using this particular word except in its accepted Wiccan form whenever possible. The generic version will be substituted with words like "custom" or "practice." Another word that sometimes carries negative inferences is "Aryan." From the historian's point of view, the Aryans were a people from the Central Asian areas that extended as far west as the Ukraine who were absorbed some three thousand years ago into the cultures they conquered. Any connection of Aryans with twentieth-century Nazis or modern racial, ethnic, and religious bigotry does not figure into this writing. The Aryans as a separate people simply don't exist anymore, although their heritage, like that of the Dravidic people of the Indian subcontinent, can be found throughout the modern world.

My own practices involve elements that appeal to me, but do not reflect an endorsement of any one tradition or practice. To be fair, many pagan usages recognized as belonging to a particular group are really older, common practices formalized by that group. To use a circle is not to be a Ceremonialist any more than to call upon Brigid is to be a Roman Catholic. Circles are a custom that pre-date Medieval Ceremonialism by many thousands of years, and Brigid was a Goddess long before she became a Christian saint. Just as old Pagan temples and holy sites are recognized today as Christian ones—from Lourdes to Notre Dame—the ancient beliefs underlying the modern ones cannot be claimed as a possession of the modern with any sort of historical validity. The four directions, the elementals, the center of the spirit, the five-pointed star, the star in the circle—all these are primal images that go back ten to twenty thousand years with no formalized Wiccan or Ceremonial tradition. Yet it is due to the Ceremonialist and modern Wiccan traditions that these ancient symbols and usages have not lost their meaningfulness. Most of the images of the Craft and Ceremonialism can be found lurking in the dark recesses of modern mainstream religions like Judaism, Christianity, and Islam, but it took the neopagan movement to pull these out of the shadows and back into a primary focal point.

I tend towards a pragmatic approach to the Craft and all religion in general, which does little for "faith" but a lot for connection with the universal powers of which we all are a part. The idea of an immanent Dual Deity makes faith unnecessary and contact an easier proposition. This is all part of being in tune with the energies flowing around us and recognizing that we and the energies are one. The communication is ongoing and does not have an "off" switch.

It is my impression that human unity with the life force was the normal state of affairs prior to the great Aryan expansion of 2100 B.C.E. It was with the need for leaders and followers in a warlike culture that the newer religions came about and created a need for deities to enforce a ruling class and a warrior class, with a priesthood to stand between the masses and the elite. The power of the priesthood was not in arms but in spirit, and over time, this drew the spiritual connection of the common folk away from their oneness with the universe and into the priestly caste. This spiritual power has been at constant war with the temporal (political) power ever since. This is the source of friction between prophets and kings, popes and kings, preachers and government officials—who really rules the people: the political, legal rulers or the spiritual guides who communicate with God?

With the resurgence of Pagan practices in modern times, the clergy class has come under the threat of a significant loss of power. Secular humanism and neopaganism go hand in hand, and these are targets of religious propaganda and hysteria in the modern world—the Salem mentality of our times. Political aspirants have and will continue to ally themselves with leaders of the clergy in order to gain power and dominion. One faction feeds upon the other: clerical ministers become powerful through media exposure to large numbers of ordinary people by supporting a political personage, who gains power through media exposure to large numbers of ordinary people by soliciting the support of the clergy. Thus we see Nixon and Billy Graham, Kennedy and Cardinal

O'Connell, Bush and Pat Robertson, and so on, united in purpose to control the governance of Americans. Independent thinkers are generally ignored or vilified without such political pairings.

My basic goal, then, is to reunite the individual with the energies of the universe through the various exercises of Wiccan traditions and Ceremonial magic. My personal approach is not one that can be pinned down to any one tradition; I have borrowed what I wanted and discarded as I saw fit (and still do). Although I am not a member of a specific tradition, I use a variety of practices found in different traditions because they aid in my union with the Divine. I use a few elements that are not generally (or at all) recognized in formal traditions, yet I have traced these from my mother and grandmother to what were once common concepts still identifiable in myths and stories. It is not my intention to offend or discredit any tradition, but I cannot ignore customs with which I have grown up or those that I feel have become a concern to many people in the Craft. These matters will be explained as I progress so that the practical side is weighed with that of belief.

I consider it important for individuals to have information made available to them so they can make informed decisions. People sit on a jury during a trial, hear all the evidence, and then are required to make a decision. Just as people are trusted to decide on legal matters, people should be making rational decisions on matters of the spirit. We have minds; we may as well put them to work in conjunction with our spirits in order to be a whole, functioning being. Just as the Lady and the Lord are One, my perspective is that we should be united within ourselves. Our minds can work with our spirits to give us a connection with the energies of the universe and with each other.

Green History

My use of the term "Green" as the core element of Witchcraft is derived from various sources that are easily identifiable in modern Paganism. Green is the color used to describe the nature worship and herbal usage that has been a part of humanity from the earliest times. Green relates to the Lord and Lady of Greenwood, the Primal Father and Primal Mother, the Earth Mother and the Lord of the Wildwood. The Celtic and Gaelic peoples used this color to denote the earth spirits, fairies (or *faeries*, which I don't use as it is associated in some literature with fey, ill-fated), as can be noted in a variety of legends in which the mere mention of the color gives away the nature of the person involved. I highly recommend Katherine Briggs' book *An Encyclopedia of Fairies* for an excellent analysis and compilation of fairy motifs, legends, and anecdotes.

Green was an important color for the people of the British Isles, who maintained specific rules for making and using green dye. Men could participate in the labor of plant cultivation, but other parts of the dyeing process were only to be done by women. The proper natural shade of the color was the result of a long, involved procedure that could have been part of a ritual (see *The Witches' Almanac*, 1992-93, Pepper and Wilcox, pp. 88-89, for some fascinating details gleaned from Briggs, Lady Wilde, and others). If not properly created, the color was considered unlucky. One takes great care when working with the colors of the Other People, but no matter how well the material is dyed, the Scots consider it an unlucky color that should only be worn by someone attuned to the earth and the Craft of the Wise.

While fairies figure into the Green elements of Witchcraft, this is not the same as the fairy or elf traditions of Wicca. The ancient origins of Green Craft practices are easily identifiable in aspects of today's various traditions of Witchcraft (or Wicca), Ceremonial magic, and a variety of practices frequently lumped together under the label of neopaganism. In these Pagan expressions, the Green factors form the foundation upon which the more recent ideas and practices have been layered. This solid base level is primarily derived from what constituted the "Old Religion" as it existed before the innovations of political deities, authoritarian dogmas, designated priesthood, complex rituals, and degrees of initiations.

In the Norse/Teutonic systems (often identified as "Aryan" in the historical sense of the term), the base level is labeled Green, with the additional "higher" levels of Red and unified Blue and White becoming the primary focus of worship and practice. The identity and function of the deities occupying these various levels, however, gives evidence to their actual origins and purpose. Green belongs to the Lord and the Lady (*Frey* and *Freya*, literally translated), with the Lord representing abundance and fertility and the Lady representing peace and love as well as vast powers of magic. Red belongs to the Warrior (Thor), representing strength. The upper level is shared between White, belonging to the Lawgiver (Tyr) representing societal law and order, and Blue, belonging to the Ruler (Odin) representing paternal chieftain power, magical power (runes), and magical self-sacrifice. These same deities appear in other Aryan religious structures (with different names, however).

5

The Lady is able to travel upward to the realm of Odin, and she supposedly taught her magic to him, the practical effect being that the newer deity of Odin has usurped the position of the Green-level Lord in the northern system. A deity of rulership was created some 4,000 years ago to equate the political reality of communal living being replaced by a ruled society; hence, the deities of the Red, White and Blue levels are relatively newer innovations specifically designed (or evolved) to authorize the new political situation. As Edred Thorsson in *Northern Magic* describes, however, it is the Green level that is the true Witch level.

I traced the Northern levels back through time in my book *Dancing Shadows: The Roots of Western Religious Beliefs*. While the new deities of the Warrior, Lawgiver, and Ruler can be found as early as 4,000 years ago, the oldest known religious practices of humanity came from a people called the Dravidians living in the Indus Valley. Their religion dates back 30,000 years, transported over the millennia by seafaring merchant folk to form the core of Pagan systems throughout Europe.

The Dravidic people still exist as a distinct ethnic group in India today, and their practices reflect much of what we tend to label as European Paganism—the concepts and even the names are recognizable. The Dual Deity of the Indus region, the Dravidian (rather than Hindu) Shiva (or *Isha*) and Shakti (or *Uma, Danu*) can be seen from the perspective of dating, migrations, and trade routes as the forerunner to the European duality of the Lord and the Lady—the Horned God of love/fertility/wildlife and the Goddess of life/death/ rebirth—which formed what later became known as the Green level (base) of the Odinist (*Asatru*) tradition. The Green level reflects the earlier religion before the establishment of a warrior class and a ruling class, and before the need for the creation of political deities to authorize the power of rulers through a clergy class. It was the latter that resulted in people's separation from their deities, which led to the subsequent pattern of the remoteness of God as reflected in modern mainstream religions.

It is significant here to understand that when I write about the Green style of Witchcraft, I will be using deities that have become part of the Aryan-based Vedic Hindu tradition but which pre-date even that ancient religion by tens of thousands of years. It is not a matter of mixing pantheons to use both Shiva and Cernunnos, for example. Cernunnos' origins are from the Dravidic Shiva who is depicted in Indus Valley archeological finds as horned, surrounded by animals both wild and domestic, and symbolizing fertility and love, teaching and blessing in a yogic position. Cernunnos, seen on the more recent Celtic Gundesrup cauldron, is also seated in a yogic posture, horned, and surrounded by animals with one hand raised in blessing. This is the deity brought to Europe by the Celts, who themselves are of Dravidian heritage, being a people driven into Europe and the British Isles (by way of the Iberian Peninsula) from their home in Lydia because of the expansions of the Aryan tribes from 2000 to 1000 B.C.E. I have placed a further discussion of religious development in Appendix A.

In my practice of the Craft, I have tried to be as close to the Green customs as possible, and I find that this does not involve set litany, stylized prayers or rituals, required vestments and accouterments or dogma. From my conversations with other Witches, both traditionals and solitaries, and from my readings of other people's practices, I have deduced that this practice of not conforming to a style or format is common. This Pagan approach was part of what spurred the Protestant Reformation to move away from the elaborate pageantry of Catholic ritual—codified and adhered to without room for improvisation and without the need for understanding—and back to a simpler expression of religion.

It is no coincidence that the ceremonies of Catholic Rome were discarded by the Germanic peoples, who had a stronger rural Pagan heritage and practice. The Catholic vestments, formalities, and design of the altar all come from the Roman Emperor Diocletian, who ruled as a god and was duly worshiped as one. The Catholic Church merely appropriated Diocletian's ceremonies and labeled them Christian after the old emperor retired. The Pope has become the emperor of religion. John Romer gives a fascinating analysis of this evolution of religious practice in his video presentation *Testament*.

The Connection of All

The Green-level Witch does not require detailed instruction on approaching the Divine because the Witch and the Divine are connected as One. The Green Witch performs only those rituals that appeal to the individual's point of focus, being as elaborate or as plain as the mood dictates. With many people who practice a natural Witchcraft there is a sense of cheerful anarchy along with profound belonging, for the Witch is not a steward of the earth, the Witch *is* the earth. What the earth is, a Witch is—be it part of the solar system, the galaxy, the universe, or more—we are an integrated part of All. As was stated in the television series *A Practical Guide to the Universe*, we are all made of stardust.

By being part of the earth in all of its manifestations, one is then both pantheistic and animistic. The planet is like Cerridwyn's cauldron, and we are part of the stew bubbling inside. Sometimes we rise to the surface, pop, and return to the soup to intermingle and rise again. The forms of creation are always changing, for change is a sign of life and not something to be feared. Science recognizes, as the ancients did, that energy is immortal, which is a view at odds with the central message of Christianity—believe in Jesus' immortality or die. But even this dogma is confused, as the Scriptures state that non-believers will actually live forever, only in a lake of fire and/or the torments of hell (a place curiously named after the Norwegian Goddess Hel, ruler of the Norse Underworld, where everyone went after death to rest before rebirth).

In the Green level, life is an immortal energy. The Goddess' message that we do not "die" is what the Judaic religion tried to suppress two and a half thousand years ago in its story of the Tree of Life (a Dravidic theme). For students of religion and cosmology, it is common to say that the Goddess represents matter (Mater; Matri; Mother), and the God represents energy (Spirit; Fire; Father). He is life, and she is the form that life takes; the one requires the other for definition. This is the nearly 30,000-year-old heritage of Dravidic Shiva and Shakti. It is the mainstream rejection of matter in favor of energy that throws people into conflict with their very existence. Denial of our unity of body and spirit projects a self-loathing element into the new religion that curbs one's enjoyment of life by imposing artificial restrictions, making death preferable to life.

For the human species, hatred for the material container of the spirit, the body, is suicidal. Much of society's wars and psychological problems can be traced to the separation of people from the joy of life through unity with the Goddess and the God. Indeed, early Christians, including the revered St. Augustine, taught that all sexual union was evil, having children was evidence of committing sin, and all people should be celibate to be worthy of the Kingdom of God. Augustine kept a mistress for most of his priestly life, however, postponing baptism in the belief that he would then be forgiven. Interestingly enough, the fate of "bad" King Herod—a painful death from intestinal worms, seen as a sign of God's punishment—was the same death experienced by St. Augustine, yet he is called holy. The result of people actually

8

practicing what early Christianity preached, however, would have been the end of the human species. That is why modern calls to espouse "Christian family values" are historically humorous—it was the Roman Pagans up through the fifth century C.E. who denounced Christianity as being detrimental to family values (Tacitus). I recommend Will Durant's highly readable *History of Civilization: Part IV, The Age of Faith* for anyone looking for a start in studying religious history.

The connections found through the Green elements of the Craft place the practitioner of the Craft in harmony not only with the Lady and the Lord (who are seen as equals), the earth, the stars, and the universe, but also with other life forms and the elementals. The four elementals are more than the personification of earth, air, fire, and water; more than the symbols of colors, directions, seasons, and aspects. They are the real entities of powers that the practitioner can invoke for assistance. They are part of the Goddess and the God, but in the same way that many Christians find it more comfortable to work with the Son of God or with saints, many Witches find they can work better by directing their focus on the elemental powers of the Dual Deities. Because these are aspects of the Lord and Lady, two are seen as relating to each Deity; earth and water to the Lady (matter), and air and fire to the Lord (energy). I see in this a deeper significance.

There are those who see the elementals as unknowable forces without personality—as a "what." My view is that since I am made up of parts of them, and I am a "who," so are they. I call them my kith and kin: earth is in my body, air moves my breath and stirs my intellect, fire is the spark of energy within me and my passion, and water is in my bodily liquids and my emotions. I have learned through contacts with other Witches that I am not alone in this viewpoint, so perhaps it is an undercurrent in Witchcraft today that is simply not well publicized.

My own approach to the elementals, as developed from the pantheistic heritage of my mother and her mother, is one not found in most traditions as far as I can tell. My subsequent studies indicate that my mother and grandmother, both Brazilians of Iberian-Celtic descent (with a surname that is a Celtic god), passed on a perspective still practiced in the modern derivation of Dravidian and Vedic religions known as Hinduism. Witchcraft of European heritage contains aspects of the Dravidic culture as it was spread through a series of migrations, the most recent wave being the Gypsies (initially assumed by Europeans to be Egyptians but subsequently recognized by historians as being from India, with one branch traveling through Egypt and later into Spain

The connections found through the Green elements of the Craft place the practitioner of the Craft in harmony not only with the Lady and the Lord (who are seen as equals), the earth, the stars, and the universe, but also with other life forms and the elementals.

circa twelfth century C.E., and the other through Eastern Europe), and I consider both the pantheistic and animistic qualities to be part of the relationship with the elementals.

By becoming connected with nature and the universe the Witch can expect to have new, meaningful experiences from which to gain insights, which is one reason it is a good idea to keep a journal for dreams and visions. From one such inspiration, I saw that the elementals are as "personal" as the forces that are the Lady and the Lord—the connection between the God and the Goddess and the elementals is too wonderful to be summoned or banished. While I had been pondering over whether or not I should incorporate that tradition into my own practice, my conclusion was that this was not right from my animistic perspective.

The Law of Return

Within the traditions of Wicca and all forms of magic practice there is a Law of Return. In Wicca this is usually called the Law of Threefold Return, meaning that whatever magical power is sent out returns threefold, but my mother and maternal grandmother taught this concept to me more equitably. "What is sent comes back," my mother told me on numerous occasions. This is a Green element found restated in mainstream faiths as "doing unto others as you would have others do unto you." I am more inclined to accept an equivalent Law of Return as its appearance is more frequent in a variety of sources, throughout various belief systems and Greek philosophies. The original emphasis was not so much on being a good neighbor and obeying civil laws as it was a warning to not indulge in magic to harm others. From this comes the traditional Witches' Rede, "If it harms none, do what you will," which I have added to my Green practice because of its appropriateness and its widespread use in Wicca. The Law of Return had always been the main guide for my mother and grandmother, and the logic of the two are the same. You do not want to harm others because what is sent comes back, hence you would be harming yourself.

A Religion and a Craft

As Marion Green points out in her book *A Witch Alone*, Witchcraft is both a religion, with a reverence of the Lady and Lord (rather than a faith in them, as their immanence makes belief unnecessary) and a

11

Craft, with magic spells, charms, and the use of herbal knowledge. In mainstream life, the law of Pagan religious practice has become related to civil injunctions and is presented as ethics, while the magical power itself has became the possession of the clergy to distribute on behalf of the people under the right conditions and with proper compensation.

This leads to another aspect of the Green customs of the past: magic was not performed for monetary payment. If a person gave a donation of their own accord, that was acceptable, but the Witch rarely asked or demanded something in return. The Green heritage indicates that an exchange would be made to "secure" the magic, like giving a gift to receive a gift in fairy legends. Instruction was another matter, but not considered the same as a professorship at a school. The "student" was actually a "seeker," and it could have been a hindrance to another's spiritual development to require payment, except perhaps as an apprentice's service. Things have changed, however, and the ideal of the village Witch with one apprentice, or performing magic and receiving tokens such as food and materials, is not realistic today. The number of seekers is enormous and the expense of training would be prohibitive. The Craft is truly learned through intuition, so the more experienced Witch can only offer the benefit of that experience for the seeker to accept or discard. In the end, it is the seeker who must connect personally with the Lady and the Lord. Learning, however, is an unending road.

Solitary or Communal?

For the most part, the Green elements of the Craft are seen in the path of its ancestry as a solitary practice, although it had communal elements and can be covened and overlaid with nearly any tradition. The aspect of personal union with the Divine does not lend itself to dogma, however, and any coven focusing on the Green elements would have to provide for variations in approach. When Wicca was "re-discovered" early this century, the idea was initially promoted that there had always been covens of Witches practicing their craft in an underground environment. Later, when it was difficult to defend Margaret Murray's theories of continuous practices, it was postulated that the Wiccan tradition was never passed along and that anything calling itself Witchcraft today was basically someone's fabrication. These are ideas that are known among practicing Witches, have been written about in a variety of books and articles, and in some instances have given rise to controversy within the Pagan community. Paganism has many sects and denominations, just like Christianity, Judaism, and Islam, and some are very defensive about their heritage. From the pragmatic viewpoint, this is unnecessary.

The Grandmother Heritage

I have heard people ask what to do to become a "real Witch" and this is troubling to me. The traditions that have relied on a chain of initiations (Gardnerian and Alexandrian, for example) have been presented at times as being more "legitimate" for their ties to Gardner, while the so-called "Grandmother Heritage" became tied to Murray's erroneous conclusions and became accepted as basically fraudulent. Yet to accept a narrow view that makes the heirs of Gardner's particular variety of Wicca the only "true" Witches is to pretend that there were never any Witches elsewhere in the world or to retain a myopic view limited to Europe. Again, this could be considered a matter of terminology. For some, the word Wiccan does not mean the same as the word Witch, but the definitions are still hazy and it may be that something will be worked out over the next few decades. I have no trouble with the idea of being a Witch, but I do not yet see myself as Wiccan, unless I use the words interchangeably.

What has perhaps added to this confusion is not that there is no "Grandmother Heritage," but that it has been misunderstood by the people who write about coven-oriented Wiccans. It has been my experience that there are indeed two kinds of "Grandmother Heritage"—one in which the grandmother (and/or grandfather) practiced folk arts without regard to the religious conventions of the land, and one in which the grandparent practiced the Craft within the confines of those religious conventions. Much of the Green elements of the Craft survived two thousand years of Christian oppression by being integrated with the prevailing religions or by non-acknowledgment. Spell work was done without payment, with no civil laws involved and only tokens exchanged, like a barter system outside the realm of taxes and bureaucracy.

In my own family background, my maternal grandmother was known as an herbalist and a healer in her region. She was consulted even when medical doctors were available because she was known to cure even the most hopeless of cases with her herbal remedies. The payments she received were things like chickens, fruit, and odd jobs around the house and yard. Often there was only gratitude. She was sought after for charms, cures, "the power" and advice, but no one called her a Witch and she functioned quite comfortably within the folk traditions of the Catholic Church in Brazil. In her case, there was no element of Afro-Brazilian *macumba* (a Brazilian type of Santeria); instead, she drew upon her Celtic-Iberian roots from Portugal and Galacia (in northwestern Spain). Not surprisingly, I find the writings on Celtic Witchcraft most meaningful to me, but I include the Dravidian connection. My mother also related to the Dravidic Shiva; due to his aspect as teacher and healer, she gave her brother a small Shiva when he went to medical school.

The non-aboriginal people of the United States have mostly lost touch with their Pagan roots simply by not being exposed to them for two centuries. This is particularly true for those of European descent. The religious culture of Christian America is rather lackluster compared to that of Christian Europe. How many people in America understand Morris Dancing, Jumping the Bonfire, Maypole dancing, the Green Man, the Fool's Parade, or any number of other Pagan traditions still held in Europe and the British Isles within or parallel to a Christian context? There are no standing stones to relate to (like Avebury or Stonehenge), no multiple thousands of years of pre-Christian European-based history, mythology, and landscapes, and no ancient ancestral caverns, burial mounds and artifacts for the European-descended American to influence American religious practices.

I feel a sense of loss over this distance between American Witches and their European heritage because even if a person studies and learns about these things, the culture was not "lived." What is attractive about the Craft is that the expression comes from the experiences and feelings of the practitioner. For example, it is fine to learn Celtic (all knowledge is a delight), but there is a difference between learning Celtic and growing up Celtic in Wales.

Even in Europe, the Celts are an elusive people. Other cultures, be they Roman, German, Norse, or Saxon, have worked so diligently to eradicate rival ethnic Celts over the centuries that today, Europeans of Celtic descent can only piece together what was once Celtic. Today the places in America where the Pagan heritage is strong are those areas where the folk ways of isolated ethnic groups have been largely undisturbed, such as in the Celtic practices of people of Irish and Scottish heritage in the Appalachian Mountains.

Another aspect of the solitary "Grandmother Heritage" that makes this influence hard to assess is the lack of formal training for the solitary compared to that experienced by modern covens. My grandmother (and there are other Witches who have had similar experiences) never instructed anyone on herbal cures, spells, or charms, but used them in her daily life when the need arose. Family members simply picked things up through being exposed to the actual practices. My own mother passed along some of the spells and guiding principles, but I know there were many spells which are lost to me that she forgot or never used because there was no need.

Although my mother considered herself a Catholic, for her the Catholic Church was a connection to the Pagan past, with the anointing oils and sacred magics of the priest motivating her attendance at Mass in her later years. Despite all the Catholic rhetoric about sin, heaven, and hell, she still believed fervently in spiritism and reincarnation—ideas that would have been considered un-Christian if she had spoken carelessly about them. So for many modern solitaries, the heritage has always been there, perhaps evidenced by unorthodox customs coexisting with Christian practices.

The Green elements of the Craft are like the "Grandmother Heritage"—quiet and not flashy. There are aspects of the Old Religion that have moved into the mainstream such as the Christmas tree (a relatively recent Christian development), mistletoe, holly, and so forth, some of which were illegal only a couple of centuries ago because of their Pagan connections. Today this trend of incorporating Pagan practices is even more manifest in people who see themselves as Christian but also accept New Age ideas. Crystals, herbs, candles, and meditation move easily into a Christian setting.

Coming Home

For many modern Witches, the sensation of coming home that is found in Wicca is partly due to a personal acceptance of the intuitive process that brought the older heritage back into prominence. For a successful transition, the baseless fears induced by mainstream faiths for the purpose of controlling their members must be discarded, and the individual must be opened up to the power of the Goddess and the God. The deities of Wicca are not the punishing political deities of conventional religions. When the Witch talks of a loving God and Goddess, there are no lists of laws, dietary demands, dogmas, worship formats, or even "witness"-type acknowledgments required. There is but one major rule to remember: "what is sent comes back."

The most frequently used Green materials are herbs and other natural objects (flowers, sticks, nuts, rocks, shells, et cetera), candles, and invocations. Also used are oils, inscriptions, string, fiber cords, feathers, and natural cloths like wool, cotton, and muslin (which is simply a stronger cotton). These are sometimes stocked as part of a magic supply, but frequently the items are procured from one's surroundings as needed. The Lord and the Lady will always provide what you need to work a spell, from the words to the ritual to the materials used therein. You will learn through experience to trust them for your needs.

Another item found in Green usage is a forked staff, or stang. I have had many over the years. We move around a lot, and I have always found a nice staff awaiting me in my new location. This is something that I use while living in an area, and which I leave behind as belonging there when I move away.

Only recently has this changed, and the manner of this change was meaningful to me. I am currently in an area that I like very much, but I will be moving again to what should be my permanent home. When I first arrived here, I did indeed gain a staff right away, but when I realized that I would be leaving here to finally settle in another place, I began to think about taking something of the spirit of this area with me. There were some tall beautiful trees in the neighborhood, many of which have now been cut down. As I walked near a pile of tree trimmings, I realized that the stack of debris was full of strong, straight, neatly forked staffs. Now I have permanent stangs for everyone in the family, and the individual decorating of each stang is a ritual that personalizes the staff while allowing us to take part of the spirit of this region wherever we go. In a way, I have been given the last vestiges of trees now gone, and the stangs will remain connected to the Lord and Lady through attendance in rites and Craft work. These stangs can be used as natural altars in outdoor rituals or simply as walking staffs. When indoors, mine carries some of my tools: feather, cord, pouch, and seasonal wreath.

Craft Connections

The deities of the Green level of the Craft are the Ancient Ones of human history, with names that have flickered on the edges of our awareness for two thousand years, and yet, they are nameless. Many popular names for the Goddess and the God abound in the Wiccan community, derived from various heritages. The names include Cerridwyn, Cernunnos, Hecate, Herne, Danu, Lugh, Parvati, Shiva, Kali, Hades, and many others from the Near East, the Far East, Europe, Africa, and the Americas. But the Oldest of the Old is the Great Mother and the Great Father, the Lord and the Lady who figure in creation and destruction, the beginning and the end, and also renewal and rebirth.

While many modern traditions of Wicca incorporate elements of Ceremonial magic, with the accompanying Kabbalah and lists of angels, arch-angels (and their demonic counterparts), realms and levels, these aspects are unnecessary to the Green experience. There is instead an open communication with the Ancient Ones, and as you practice this dialogue, your powers will be enhanced through use. Tools of the trade are the familiar ones; for example, the kitchen witch of modern times is close to the Green elements of the Craft. It is unnecessary to follow a particular pattern of activity in the conducting of ritual because the emphasis is on individuality. People of today do not need to emulate what they may believe to have been the behavior patterns of the people of a few centuries (or millennia) past to know what feels right. Sometimes the approximation of forgotten customs can enhance one's work, other times it is a detraction. Only the practitioner can decide what should be used or discarded.

In the past, for example, swords were only held by the nobility; the moors were certainly too cold and damp for naked circles, especially in a time when disease was a dire threat to survival; and people were for the most part illiterate and not regulated to calendars in things of nature but to the changing of the seasons as they actually occurred. Calendars of Roman heritage were re-designed by the Church to institutionalize conformity in behavior. In modern times, pushing aside the inhibitions of orthodox religions may be aided by naked dancing, or drawing a circle with a sword may add to the individual's visualizations. It is always a matter of personal choice.

The folk who practiced the Green level of the Craft were the common people who lived close to the earth and knew the cycles of nature as they revolved in the weather and growth patterns. Their implements were from nature or from their country existence, and their ritual robes would have been the same as their daily wear or their festival dress, if they were fortunate enough to possess such a thing. They kept no written litany because they were illiterate, and they passed their

Craft ways along through a variety of myths and everyday practices. In *Buckland's Complete Book of Witchcraft* there are many options offered, with the acknowledgment that the practitioner of the Craft may pick and choose among the elements to formulate a suitable path. In this respect, it is an excellent source book for some of the varieties of approaches to the Craft.

A Symbolic Union

I have heard from a number of women who have asked whether they must have sexual relations with a coven leader in order to be a "real" Witch. This is another controversial aspect of the Craft that I feel needs to be discussed simply because it is not something that can be ignored. The idea of having to engage in sexual relations with a coven leader has the undesirable effect of linking Wicca with Christian cults like those of Jim Jones or David Koresh (wherein girls as young as eleven and twelve years old were turned over to these men by their dominated parents to be sexually initiated and impregnated by the cult leaders) but that is *not* what Wicca is about. People are constantly being warned in various Pagan publications against the potential for domination, control, and ego-mania in the coven situation. Once again, if something feels uncomfortable, it is not appropriate for you. Witches are not cultists, but individualists, and any time you find a coven environment that denies the power of the individual, you may be well advised to seek elsewhere for companionship.

For those who wonder if sexual energy produces magical results, the reality is that it is a hit or miss situation that will vary with each attempt. Human sexual psychology is immensely variable, not only between couples, but between each encounter for the individual. Sexuality is so personal and intimate by nature that the only person who truly knows how things went is the one who experienced it. But for a couple to have sexual intercourse aimed at one purpose, each person must fully depend on the other not to lose concentration or stray in the mental imaging, and how many can honestly attest to that? It might work, but then again it might not. Rhiannon Ryall in *West Country Wicca* states that in her childhood, the coven members believed that if the woman being initiated got pregnant, she did not handle the magic properly. So besides an unexpected (and perhaps unwanted) baby, the woman is blamed for messing up the magic and made to feel like she is an incompetent Witch. This attitude is debasing to women and is simply another way of asserting male dominance in what should be a religion of balance. The chances of pregnancy depend a lot on the internal cycles of the woman, which have nothing to do with effecting magic for distribution at a gathering (as suggested by Ryall). The risk today of AIDS and sexually transmitted diseases (STDs), let alone the possible psychological damage, must be weighed against the expected gains. With monogamous pairs who care about each other the chances for success are much higher, and a lack of success would be less likely to cause psychological harm.

The Etruscans performed sexual unions in the presence of others without concern and enjoyed watching one another after banquets, according to Greek writers (who found such behavior disgraceful). Public copulation was perfectly acceptable, and the men did not know or care who fathered the children in a marriage—but their society no longer exists (Massa, *The World of the Etruscans*). Who is to say that the so-called immorality of the Roman emperors was not an attempt to return to the Etruscan heritage that pre-dated the Romans? Yet societies do change and we are not separated from our culture, so a coven approach to sexual magic might result in more pain and unhappiness than power-raising. It would seem reasonable, then, to relegate such magic to married or recognized couples.

So what is the history of the Great Rite? It was the symbolic union of energy and matter that was later replaced with the transubstantiation used today in the Christian Eucharist. The translation of the Unity of the God and the Goddess into a human physical union originated with a marriage between the High Priestess and the secular king who ruled for a year and a day. Merlin Stone (*When God Was A Woman*) and Joseph Campbell (*Masks of God* series) both offer insights into the way this practice developed in different cultures, particularly in the Near East. The public witnessed this union of the sacred and the secular leaders and believed that this would ensure the fertility of the land and the people for a year. At the end of that time, the king was executed as a willing sacrifice, and his role became that of the Sacrificed God, with his body and blood being distributed about the fields of the realm in a ceremonial holy communion. Indeed, this is the ancestor of the Christian sacrament of the same title, to be reborn as the corn (this being the European word for grains, especially wheat or oats; "corn" as maize is an American plant) that sustained the people.

It is important to remember, though, that this was an institutionalized public performance relevant only to the point in history where it appeared. Modern Witches do not perform blood sacrifices, nor do they burn or strangle messengers to the gods. Likewise, they do not perform a sexual union before the whole national community—and the word "national" is vital. The ancient event was not confined to a small crowd of select membership, like a coven, nor to a private area set aside from a small gathering (an option offered by some covens), but before thousands of onlookers as part of a civil ceremony. The spectators themselves then participated in feasting, sexual unions, and general celebrating. This was a societal event.

The application of sexual union to Witchcraft is more Ceremonial than Wiccan in heritage as it came from the later time frame of an instituted priesthood. This occurred when the power of the female lead of religion was overtaken by Aryan priests, with the priestesses becoming the generational tool by which a permanent secular king (or pharaoh) gained his throne legitimately through marriage (see Stone). For the practical Witch, the Great Rite is performed when the knife (athame) is lowered into the cup during ritual, so while the first is a national event out of context in a coven, the second is a personal and symbolic event suitable for either private or coven ritual. The symbolic union of male and female is for the happiness of both, and anyone who is uncomfortable with the idea of having sexual intercourse with a coven leader is certainly correct to not do so.

In reality, there are only a few covens that require sexual union in order to acquire the highest degree of initiation, so this is the exception rather than the norm. The Green Witch experiences the Great Rite through personal union with the Lady and the Lord. The use of "degrees" is a practice derived from Ceremonial magic orders and need not be applied to Witchcraft. As Marion Green states, you either are a Witch or you are not: no degrees are involved. The actual sacrifice of the king became obsolete and was replaced with the symbolic ceremony, so there is even less point in reviving in part the practice that even the ancients discarded in total.

The Key to Green

The central Green element of all Craft expression is the Goddess as undying, threefold, and associated with the earth, the moon, and the living (sacred) waters, and the God as undying, threefold, and associated with the earth, the sun, and the sky. As God of grain and solar phases, he is also the willing sacrifice who "dies" and is "reborn" in the Goddess in the yearly cycle of the seasons. God the Father, God the Son, and God the Holy Spirit is that concept of the Trinity dating back some 30,000 years to Shiva as the Threefold God. He is both the seed and the eternal energy of life.

"Green" is a somewhat generic term, then, for the elements that can be found in herbal, natural, traditional, or family traditional Witchcraft, and it has great flexibility and variety. The Green elements can be adapted to those Ceremonial aspects you find appealing, and it forms the foundation level of the Odinist tradition (which is very restrictive on what elements are acceptable—Kabbalah and Tarot not being used, as an example). The key to the Green facet of Witchcraft is to be attuned to nature and the natural forces surrounding you.

Green Festivals

The Green-level festivals are centered around the solstices and equinoxes. Marion Green calls the other Sabbats "White festivals," relating to events in the lives of the Goddess and the God, but really the solar Sabbats also relate to events in their life-myth, and the whole of the eight Sabbats can be seen as one continuous, mystically overlapping story. As a child, in my family the changing of the seasons—spring, summer, fall, and winter—were noted along with All Hallows Eve and Harvest Home, so two of the traditional eight Sabbats were ignored— Imbolc in February and Lughnassadh in August. I have since included these two for many years in my own wheel of the year, because I have found a relevancy for them and they make my year complete.

Since the seasons of plantings and harvests vary depending upon where you are in the world, the eight Sabbats are, from a practical sense, centered on the quarters and the cross quarters as they relate to the central myth of the God and the Goddess. I label the solar festivals as the quarters and Lesser Sabbats, with the cross quarters being the Greater Sabbats at the mid-points between, but I have seen these labels interchanged in various combinations in my readings of different Wiccan traditions. Some covens only celebrate four of the Sabbats, others trade off leadership roles between the High Priest and the High Priestess according to Sabbat. It is basically a matter of preference. Each Sabbat is worthy of attention for attuning to the earth and the universe, but I have skipped Sabbats from time to time and know this is common among other Witches. Sometimes the celebration comes a day sooner or later than the normal timing, which can work because the Craft is not dogmatic nor possessed of an orthodoxy. The individual's input is vital.

Personal Power

As you study the Craft, make your own interpretations and your own variations. There are no precise spells or recipes, but those given here are tried and true formulas that have achieved their goals. Each Witch must make a change of one sort or another to personalize any spell adopted from another's spellbook. The tables of comparisons can be manipulated in any way that feels appropriate to you within the overall format. An important thing to remember is that magic takes place between you and the deities you invoke. It is personal, and you create your own sublime power.

2

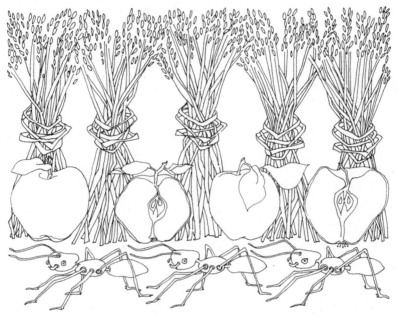

Basics

The Sabbats of Wicca are fairly consistent no matter what the tradition. There are the quarters (the lesser Sabbats) of the solstices and equinoxes, and the cross quarters (the greater Sabbats) of the midpoints between the quarters; although some traditions freely adjust these terms, the sequence remains fairly uniform. In my own application, the terms "lesser" and "greater" are not used for the Sabbats, while quarters indicate the Sabbats of the four seasons, forming the Solar Cross in the wheel of the year. Some Wiccan traditions celebrate only four of the eight Sabbats, and as I was growing up, we observed six (but with their mundane names rather than as "Sabbats"). In addition to the accepted eight festivals, there is one other that is sometimes used—the annual festival called Twelfth Night. For those who observe it, this is generally a day set aside for use only when it is needed for a Naming Day. It need not be celebrated every year, although you may use it to reinforce the power of your Craft or working name.

To envision the progression of the Sabbats, it is easiest to think of the year as a circle, or a wheel, with eight spokes. Starting at the top is Yule, the winter solstice, which generally falls on December 21 (almost any calendar will have the solar phases clearly marked as "First Day of Winter," "Spring," "Summer," and "Fall," so any variance to these dates can be easily found for your correction). Moving right leads us to Imbolc, which is February 2, although some Witches celebrate it on the eve of February 1 (rather like some Christians go to church on Christmas Eve, others on Christmas Day). Next comes Ostara, the vernal (spring) equinox on March 21. This is followed by Beltane on May 1 (May Day), then Litha, the summer solstice (traditionally called Midsummer) on June 21. The wheel of the year progresses now to Lughnassadh on August 1, which, like its opposite on the wheel, Imbolc, can be celebrated on the previous eve—in this case, July 31. Mabon follows as the autumnal equinox on September 21, and the last Sabbat of the year, Samhain, is celebrated on October 31. The year begins anew at this point for many Wiccan traditions, and the wheel turns onward to Yule.

Twelfth Night and Other Celebrations

It is easy to see how the celebration of the New Year could vary from one tradition to another in the old days before the Christian calendar unified it all. For many people, Samhain was the end of the old year, being the last Sabbat of the year. But then Yule was the day the sun began its trek back to the earth, so it was also appropriate to see Yule as the last Sabbat of the old year and the beginning of the new year. January 1 is merely a compromise as the midpoint between Yule and Twelfth Night, which the Christians appropriated as Epiphany, the day the three Wise Men located Jesus and recognized him as Christ (a type of Naming Day occurring about two years after he was born, yet they show up at the crèche scenes anyway). Marion Green states that in earlier times this was a day for bringing children into the community of adults through a naming ceremony, which relates to the naming of the God. With each community the God's name would be different, and perhaps revealing the name to the child in a puberty rite was part of the ceremony.

In the old tradition, the God was from birth to Naming Day simply, Son, the Son of the Mother, or Mabon. In a community Twelfth Night is celebrated annually, but with the solitary Witch this is unnecessary.

The indication, then, is that a Green element such as Naming Day only be used when someone, either the individual Witch or a family member such as a child who has reached the age of puberty (generally between the ages of twelve and fourteen), is brought formally into the Craft and chooses his or her Craft name. In modern Wicca, this is a Rite of Passage. It really does not matter when you decide to commence New Year, but I have always used December 31 because this is part of the cultural society I live in (coming from the Norman/Scottish Hogmanay Day), and it was how I was raised. The purpose of religion should not be to set people apart from others, but to celebrate and honor the gift of life.

Sprinkled around the calendar are other days that can be marked with any degree of ceremony you desire, be it the simple lighting of a candle or incense before an image to a fully developed ritual. These days include April 14 as Mother Goddess Day, May 18 as the Feast of the Horned God, August 20 as the Marriage Day of the God and the Goddess (coming after their union and her becoming pregnant, as was traditional for people in times past), September 23 as Ishtar's Day, and November 27 which doubles as Parvati's Day and Triple Goddess Day. There are any number of *Goddess' Book of Days*, *Witches' Almanacs* and *Magical Almanacs* to peruse that will give information about a variety of holidays throughout the world for you to pick out your favorites—the above are a few of mine. I generally use an almanac and like to mark a new calendar with all the holidays for the upcoming year as part of my Yule ritual. Calendars for all the family members are always a Yule gift in my home.

The Life-Myth and the Sabbats

The Sabbats are integrated with the life-myth of the Goddess and the God. This requires an understanding of the allegorical nature of the myth, for the deities will sometimes be two different beings at nearly the same time. This is usually explained as how the Goddess is changeable—going from pregnant mother-to-be at Mabon to the crone at Samhain to new mother at Yule—although this means that she is crone and pregnant at the same time, mythically speaking, and young again at Imbolc. In the God's life-myth, he impregnates the Goddess with himself in summer, "dies" in the fall, and is "reborn" in winter. At the same time, he is the King of Shadows at Samhain, and the Holly King (Santa Claus) at Yule who is displaced by the Oak King (or New Year's baby) at winter solstice—banished by himself, as it were, with the dark of winter aspect giving way to the Sun God aspect as "Light of the World." Somehow, it all comes together and evokes a sense of rightness with the world and the orderliness of life's cycles.

Yule [*Yool*] (December 21) is when the Goddess gives birth to the God (a familiar tale from which Christianity evolved one of its major holidays). This is a time of rebirth, and candles are lit to welcome the God who is the returning sun of the winter solstice. Gifts are given (especially to children) by the departing Holly King as he rides his solar sleigh, pulled by the eight Sabbats personified as reindeer, through the sky at Yule Eve. He was called Old Nick by the Pagan Norse, was usurped by Christianity and turned into a sainted bishop named Nicholas, and is recognized today as Santa Claus (while "Old Nick" became a name for the Devil—the Pagan horned god of nature). This is the holiday that Pagans and Christians can both relate to as a holy time and a sacred birth. My Catholic mother and grandmother focused their adoration on the Virgin Mary, and the birth of the "Light of the World" had the greatest appeal. The winter solstice celebrations were held on December 25 rather than on December 21, demonstrating how smoothly Pagan observances were blended into the Christian religion over time (our tree never had an angel on top, however; it was always a five-pointed star).

Imbolc [*Em-bowl/g*] (February 2) is a time when the Goddess recovers from the birth, rejuvenated, and the God is a spirited youth. It is a time of purification and dedication. This is one Sabbat we never celebrated as I was growing up, the four seasons being considered primary.

Ostara [*Oh-star-ab*] (March 21) is the vernal equinox, when the God and Goddess walk the fields causing creatures to reproduce. The first day of spring is inspiration for renewal and creativity, translated into Christian belief as the resurrection of life from death—the seed buried in the ground now begins to move back into the world. For my family Easter served the same purpose as Ostara, with the annual romp of the Easter Bunny and the celebration of renewal with fresh spring flowers, particularly tulips, crocuses, lilacs, and hyacinth (we never used lilies).

Beltane [*Beel-teen* or *Bell-tayn*] (May 1) is when the Goddess and the God unite and is a celebration of fertility and healing. We celebrated May Day with flowers and flower tokens (anonymous gifts of small nosegays, tiny baskets of flowers, and flowers stuck in the crevices and crannies of porches, walls, and fences).

Litha [*Lee-thah*] (June 21) is the summer solstice, although referred to as "Midsummer." It is the peak of fertility, used to celebrate love, health, purification, and dedication. In my childhood, this was merely Summer.

Lughnassadh [*Loo-nahs-ah*] (August 1) is when the God impregnates the Goddess with himself, and is the feast of bread and time of transformation. This is the other Sabbat we did not celebrate when I was a youngster.

Mabon [*May-bone* or *Mah-boon*] (September 21) is the autumnal equinox when the God prepares to leave and the Goddess rests. This is celebrated today as the Harvest Home feast of Thanksgiving, which was moved to the November time frame in the nineteenth century by President Lincoln even though the Pilgrims celebrated it in September. While we noted autumn with shopping for new warm clothes, Harvest Home was transferred to Thanksgiving. We did not indulge in solemn prayers, but celebrated the abundance of the earth with a loaded table and wine for everyone.

Samhain [*Sow-een*, or the American *Sam-hain*] (October 31) is when the God departs and the Goddess mourns, but knows he will be reborn at Yule. This is a time of celebrating the mysteries of death and of contacting spirits. The Catholic Church adopted this celebration with an All Hallows Eve Mass and calls the following morning All Souls Day. Although there are Protestant churches that consider Halloween Satanic, they could be viewed as biased against Catholicism as much as anything occult, Wiccan, or even Satanic, as Catholics also keep it as a holy day. The Christian deity of evil is not part of the Witch's pantheon. Instead, the dark and the light are seen as a balance of positive and negative energies—every yin has its yang.

The images of the Sabbats are more meaningful when you keep in mind that in some of the Sabbats the Goddess is the earth and the God is the sun, while in others they represent the cycles of the spirit: life, death, rest, and rebirth. With or without the imagery, however, the Lady and the Lord can be successfully invoked and will respond to those who seek them. The names of the Sabbats as given here are typically found in Wiccan traditions, but are of a generic Celtic heritage. Mabon and Litha are considered newcomers to the celebrations of Witches in names if not in practice, according to Marion Green. Today, I use all eight Sabbats and the typical Sabbat names, but as a child, the names we used were simply winter/Christmas, spring/Easter,

May Day, summer, Harvest Home/Thanksgiving, and Halloween. In this way, our celebrations were attuned to the Christian community in which we lived and occasionally participated.

Modern Issues for Celebrating Sabbats

The modern Witch needs to reconcile the mythic presentation of frolicking deities with the realities of the cycles of the earth. People know today that the seasons will change and the order of nature will proceed whether or not someone celebrates a Sabbat, so the individual must decide what relevancy the Sabbats have in the modern world. Just as I know of families who stop celebrating Christmas after their children grow up and leave home, and others who enjoy getting into the holiday spirit year after year, there are Witches who do not always feel in the mood to celebrate a Sabbat. Intuitive feelings, personality and worldview play an important part in how a person greets the turning of the wheel.

For my immediate family, the Green Sabbats (Yule, Ostara, Litha, and Mabon) are celebrated as a time for uniting with the ebb and flow of the sun's energy as manifested during the solstices and the equinoxes. These are times for recharging individual batteries, just as the earth does, while moving through the cycles of planting and harvest. The other four, the White Sabbats, are times for internal realignment and feeling at one with the earth and the cycle of life itself.

Imbolc, then, is for self-cleansing and for the purification of our surroundings in preparation for spring. This is when we work on restoring our balance, re-dedicating ourselves to our Craft, and performing an internal housecleaning that rids us of unproductive and undesirable feelings, habits, and concepts. It is a time for self-assessment and re-direction. This is the rest of the spirit between lives. As my practice evolved away from Christian influences, I found Imbolc very meaningful to me as a time to reaffirm my path.

Beltane brings a sense of complete renewal and the joy of budding new life when the earth is at the height of its springtime—I always bring fresh wildflowers into the house (daisies are my favorite). Now is a good time to assess your physical and emotional health. This is the union of spirit and body.

Lughnassadh is the first harvest of the grains, the Bread Festival, and is a time for well-being celebrated by acknowledging the earth's abundance. Now is also a good time for renewing your commitment to the protection of the earth's resources. This is the spirit alive in the body and enjoying life on earth. We enjoy picking berries and baking blackberry pies for this Sabbat, and eat fresh multigrain bread and drink blackberry wine. This special day is now part of my wheel and makes my calendar complete, but my parents never made any fuss over August except for my birthday. While there are Catholic holidays covering all the ancient Pagan days of celebration, with Lammas on August 1 to recall the imprisonment and miraculous escape of Saint Peter, and Assumption Day on August 15 to honor the Virgin Mary ascending to heaven, my mother and grandmother did nothing to note these.

Samhain is when your spirit reaches out to disembodied souls (I like to consider the notion of Cerridwyn as the Great Sow being a misinterpretation by the modern British of the word "Soul," for when it comes to visualizations, there is an immense difference between sow and soul), instinctively recognizing that we are all of the same essence and making the same passage through life, death, rest, and rebirth. There is no fear of the dead, but loving connection instead, and this is why the Goddess and the God are seen as rulers of the Land of Shadows, or the Summerland. At Samhain, we greet the spirits passing to the shadowy realm. We bury apples or pomegranates in the garden as food for the spirits as they travel to their rest, and sometimes we set out a Mute Supper of bread, salt, apples, and cider for our departed friends and relatives whose spirits are invited out of Summerland for a visit. Carved and lighted pumpkins light their way to our homes. This is the death of the body and the passing of the spirit from this life into Summerland for rest and renewal. Some years this holiday becomes at least as hectic as the Yule season and we do not have time for all the observances, but we enjoy it to the fullest of our ability.

Different Ways of Celebrating Sabbats

Throughout all religions, recognition of Green events are well-known and serve as focal points in their particular litany. By any name and with any mythology, the solstices and equinoxes are celebrated worldwide. The only difficulty with this is that some religions have become strident in demanding that their particular litany is the only "true" one. Witchcraft, however, involves much more than the sum of its Sabbat mythology—it is a way of life that can exist perfectly well without the formal celebration of a single Sabbat, and perhaps that is why some covens limit themselves to the four Greater Sabbats.

Common celebrations include Yule as Christmas or the Festival of Lights (Hanukkah); Ostara as Easter or Passover; Litha as the time of weddings and the June bride; and Mabon as Harvest Home, Fall Festival and Thanksgiving. The other four Sabbats are still incorporated into Christian and secular calendars by other names as well. Imbolc becomes Groundhog Day, when we look for signs of spring or six more weeks of winter. Beltane is May Day, and is greeted with May baskets or simply the desire to fill the house with the first flowers of spring or begin planting in the garden. Mother's Day is a means of celebrating the goddess aspect of motherhood in women and is a May festival that lends itself as a further expression of Beltane. Lughnassadh is Lammas on the Catholic calendar, and is a time of summer picnics with bounteous food, fresh breads, pies, and cakes. In the countryside the farming community still observes the bread festival without calling it as such, celebrating after the crop is brought in. This is the time for fairs and rodeos. Samhain remains as Halloween, a sore point with many Fundamentalist Christians who refuse to celebrate a day honoring the dead, and so have tried to ban the holiday. Yet the Catholic Church has special Masses for the Dead on All Hallow's Eve and All Souls' Day, and many people enjoy the atmosphere of mystery and closeness to the Underworld and the Otherworld inspired by this time of the year.

A Personal Journey

From my experience growing up, the Sabbats were not celebrated as rituals of Divine lifestory events. Instead they were earth-centered, forming a special feeling for the time of the year and for the sensations of the earth as we moved through the yearly cycle. I have danced around the Maypole as a school activity and gorged myself on the blackberry pies of Lughnassadh simply because the wild berries were in season and we went out and picked a bucket of them. My own children have had the indescribable pleasure of picking their way through the wild tangles of berry bushes, competing with birds for the plumpest berries, and fending off spiders who strung their webs across the sprawling arms of the bushes to catch unwary insects—all for the reward of seedy blackberries the size of thumbs, filling pots and pans for me to bake into pies. Without a formal ritual, robes, and tools, the Sabbats are honored by doing and by living them. Through experiencing the Sabbats, we invoke the elementals and become united with the earth and with the Lady and the Lord.

This gives a clue as to how those who are not sure they want to abandon their Christian upbringing may still look to their Pagan roots and expand their Christian perspective to include pre-Christian, Green-level practices. Since the holidays are virtually the same, it may be that over time one might move away from the newer expression and closer to the earlier one. My mother and grandmother were not "churchy," and I was not raised in strict Christian spirituality. I rarely attended a Catholic Mass, and actually spent an occasional Sunday in a variety of Protestant churches. I experienced the Lutheran and Baptist church view by spending my first two years of formal education attending a Lutheran elementary school, where learning catechism was as important as any other study, and later by attending a Baptist church in high school. Out of curiosity and an interest in the varieties of Christian beliefs, I have also attended services in Methodist, Episcopalian, and Presbyterian churches, sometimes with my mother, other times alone, or, on special occasions like winter solstice and spring equinox, with my husband and children when they were little. These were social events for the children where they could be involved with other children in festivities and egg hunts, but as early as first grade, each had recognized that the ideas taught at such gatherings were contrary to their own sense of self worth and connection with nature. They are content with family gatherings and gravitate toward friends with open minds and hearts.

The family of my childhood celebrated the cycle of life independently, yet on the fringes of the societal framework. By the time I was fifteen, however, and had been questioning the meaningfulness of Christian doctrine to myself and how my family related to the Christian holidays, I realized that the groundwork for the Pagan heritage had been quietly and firmly laid. My personal explorations into a deeper connection with Witchcraft were greeted with interest by my mother, who then supplemented my studies and offered her perspective on what I was picking up. Her emphasis was on spiritism and channeling, but even so, she still considered herself Catholic.

After I embarked on my path as a seeker, my mother used to tell me she envied me for being strong and not feeling the need to conform. I am pleased today that my children are not growing up under the constraints of a religious system I cannot endorse, but might feel is imposed by societal convention. My mother continued to attend Mass until she passed on; however, the book on her bed table that she read from nightly was not the Bible, but a book of spiritism as revealed by a master

31

My own children have had the indescribable pleasure of picking their way through the wild tangles of berry bushes, competing with birds for the plumpest berries . . . all for the reward of seedy blackberries the size of thumbs . . .

spiritist in Brazil. Neither she nor my grandmother could say very much about the Bible, or even the Catholic sacraments—it was always like a foreign territory to them—but they could talk at length about spiritism, reincarnation, the powers, and contacting the Others for help.

I used to find it humorous that because I had been exposed to various religious patterns over the years, my mother would depend on me for Bible information even when I was a child. I remember her amused smile when I recited Lutheran catechism for her or told her about the Bible stories I had learned. She was very tolerant even of the religious fervor of my Baptist friends, and never indicated outwardly that she did not agree. She was always pleasant and amenable to other people's religious or political positions, so that any churchly visitor left feeling a convert had been made to their particular point of view. But she never was swayed into any kind of fundamentalism or rigid view, and remained detached from churches and dogma all her life.

These days, after making my own spiritual journey, I celebrate the eight Sabbats for the enjoyment I derive from them and for the feeling of closeness to the Lady and the Lord. The rituals are comfortable, and I have collected many items over the years that I use in my ceremonies. Although I keep a magic box for many of my supplies, I also place some of the ritual tools in plain view around the house. My whole living area is part of my circle of magic and infuses the house and my family with warmth and familiarity.

Studying history was a major step towards breaking the grip of conventional religion for me. This step was important because I wanted to know what the relationship was between the Christian faith my family had lived on the fringes of and the Pagan practices I had experienced, sometimes with my mother, in an atmosphere of seclusion. When I could see images in cards, foretell the future, and engage in spell workings, I had to be circumspect about who knew about my activities. Even so, there were times when fellow students and friends considered my views and maternally-encouraged activities as not quite acceptable. As time went on, it became more a matter of associating with people of like mind rather than being on the edge of heresy and damnation. One benefit of getting older is being freer to pick your own friends.

Once a historian learns the truth about the beginnings of modern faiths and the derivations of the modern myths, it is fundamentally impossible to remain a "believer" in any sense of the word. Many famous people, from Arnold Toynbee to Joseph Campbell, have started on a quest for knowledge and understanding only to be amazed at the results. I should not have been surprised when the same happened to me. For some, the response has been a mild refutation of Judeo-Christian beliefs, or a case stated for relinquishing "faith" as obsolete and an enforcement of ignorance. For me, perhaps because I had the additional perspective of religious teachings applied to women as second-class humans, the result was anger. I was furious to discover that people have been lied to for two thousand years, and enraged that people considered me odd for having Green knowledge. I was incensed that fictional characters of the Bible were not only taken from pre-existing, non-Judaic sources, but that they were still appearing in history books as real-time persons involved in real-time events. But anger is unhealthy, and rage only leads to headaches, so I write and hope to reach at least a few people.

As a teacher, it is a delicate matter to present history to teenagers unfamiliar with anything outside of the familiar church rhetoric. I try to teach a balanced, non-judgmental course in which all views are laid out for the students to consider and make their own value calls, but it is impossible to teach history without reference to religions and the conflicts inspired by contradictory practices. There are some cases where strident religiosity is the only perspective a teenager will accept, but now and then, students pause and ask questions. Often just a bit of history's basic information can cause a child to sit up and take notice.

Some students who have been normally silent and withdrawn—outcasts to the rest of the class—brighten and confide in me later that they had been considered "different" from their classmates because they had questioned the reality of accepted religious views, and that it was rewarding to find a teacher who confirmed what they had discovered. Other students are happy to have a balanced picture and say that their parents raised them to be independent thinkers, and that it is refreshing to have a teacher who doesn't expound conventional religious beliefs. It is my impression that the teenagers of today are much more interested in truth and the validity of religious principles, and this is sometimes misunderstood by adults as defiance and lack of morals. Instead, they are asking questions their parents may have been too frightened to ask, and they are seeking their own meaning for life.

Pagan Roots

My research into the roots of mainstream and Pagan religions took me back to the Indus Valley of the Dravidians, and connected those people with the Celts of my maternal heritage. I have thus brought into my personal pantheon a mixture of deities that have moved along the waterways from India to the Mediterranean to the Atlantic coast of Iberia and onto the British Isles as well as overland through Eastern Europe to the Western expanse. My paternal heritage is English, and some is German, but these two aspects were never emphasized in my life. Instead, I have been drawn to Shiva and Uma Parvati, to Hecate and Rhea, to Hades and Herne, and to Cerridwyn and Cernunnos.

When I think of the God, the Lord, I envision Shiva in one of many forms—cosmic dancer, teacher, and paternally loving being. When I think of the Goddess, the Lady, I envision Hecate—not as a crone so much as the crone energy expressed as a beautiful, maternally loving Goddess of wisdom, magic, and the moon—the Goddess of the Witches. She is said to have originated in Thrace, as did Dionysus, who other historians (such as Danielou) have already linked to Shiva. She, too, can be traced to the people of the Indus who settled in Thrace several thousand years ago. Because Uma Parvati is the Earth Mother Goddess, I use her image as a counterpart to the Shiva image. I also like the image of Rhea as the Snake Goddess, snakes being symbolic of wisdom and rebirth. The mythologies, however, do not factor into my practice much. The storytelling aspect of Pagan tradition is something that is experienced through daily activities and the changing of the seasons.

The deities of Egypt and Olympic Greece have not captured my heart; perhaps I feel they are overexposed by Hollywood and popular fiction. The only Egyptian deity I feel closeness to is the most ancient image of the pantheon, Bastet (the later division of this Goddess into Hathor, and then Isis, caused her to be altered in modern view as more of a Goddess of cats, joy, and the fine arts than one of the power and creativity of Hathor and Isis). How Shiva managed to be in my maternal line remains a mystery to me, as I did not learn about this connection until just before my mother passed away. Somehow I had independently arrived at the same God image my mother had secretly maintained for at least sixty years without it ever being discussed. I have since determined to be much more communicative with my own children, although they will be free to choose for themselves the identity of the Lord and Lady. My daughter is drawn to Isis and Anubus; my young son is drawn to Shiva and Herne, with the Goddess being as yet unnameable (but I am sure an image of the Lady will come to him as he matures).

The Sabbat Altar

My Craft tools on a Sabbat altar are arranged as follows:

GODDESS AREA	AREA FOR BOTH	GOD AREA
	3-armed candelabra	
statue of Parvati	statue of Ardhanari	statue of Shiva
	candle snuffer	
water bowl	censer	salt bowl
wine cup	pentacle	incense
wand (and oils)	cauldron (and matches)	athame
bell	book/cakes	bolline

Keep in mind that these are the pre-Hindu deities of the Indus River region known as Sind, from which I have traced the very word "sin" as relating to "non-Judaic." I discuss the relevancy of these deities to modern religions, as well as to Paganism in general and Witchcraft in particular, in my book *Dancing Shadows*. Here it is only necessary to say that Parvati is the Mother Goddess; Ardhanari is an androgyne figure of the Divine in unity, half female and half male; and Shiva is the Great God, cosmic dancer of life and death and rebirth. The choice of deities is always up to the Witch.

The circle, at the center of which sits the altar, is marked at the quarters with a green candle in the north for the earth element, a yellow candle in the east for the air element, a red candle in the south for the fire element, and a blue candle in the west for the water element. I have special pottery dishes I use for these candles, with each dish decorated with an emblem that I relate to the element: a square for earth, wings for air, a Solar Cross for fire, and a Lunar Spiral for water.

Decorations for the altar vary according to the Sabbat, but no magic is performed during these festivals. Magic spells and divination are normally left for Esbats, the celebrations of the new and full moons, although divinations at Samhain are also a tradition. As in the Green level, the altar faces north, and the casting of the circle is done from right to left (*deosil*), from north to east to south to west and back to north. There are many Wiccan traditions that have the altar facing east relating to the rising sun, but I am drawn to the north for the polarity of north and south and for the fairy reference. The north is the realm of Black Annis, of the Snow Queen, and the Goddess as crone. There lies wisdom, and in all Pagan systems the Goddess is identified with wisdom, be it with snakes or with the tree of life and knowledge.

The components of the Sabbat ritual begin with a purifying bath scented with herbs such as vervain, rosemary, thyme, lavender, basil, and fennel. Next the space where the circle will be created is purified and swept with the Witch's broom (*besom*). The sacred space may be delineated with a cord, although I usually do it with visualization aided by the candles situated on the floor at the quarters. I give myself sufficient space to move around in without contacting the candles, and do not use a measurement of feet or yards. Rocks can also be used, or other natural objects signifying the elementals.

The tools to be used are laid out on the altar, and the incense and altar candles are lit. In casting the circle the quarters are illuminated, lighting the candles with the center candle of the three altar candles, and the circle boundary is created with the athame or the power hand, purified, sealed with blessed water, and incensed by carrying the censer around it. Then there is the invocation in which the elementals are called, followed by the welcoming of the Lady and the Lord to the temple. The Sabbat observances come next (each one being different) where the energy is raised, and the residual power is earthed. The Goddess and the God are acknowledged and the elementals are blessed and released as the circle is then opened with the athame or the power hand. The term "released" should be seen here in the same usage as when you and a friend hold hands, and then release each other's hand. This is not the same as forcibly summoning and then banishing an elemental—it is calling upon a friend and holding hands for a time, then saying farewell for now.

Esbat Celebrations

For the celebration of an Esbat (moon observances) the components are basically the same, but with variations depending upon the type of moon involved and any spell work, divination, consecrations of tools, or craft work being accomplished. If there is a full or new moon the day of the Sabbat, the two observances may be combined if there is no spell work being done, or the one may follow the other. Although either can be first, I prefer the Esbat. But it is not necessary to leave spell work for an Esbat. In fact, it might be preferable to do spell work on an as-needed basis, and you can make whatever correspondence between days and hours you require to aid the work. I rarely consider days and hours for spell work, only need. It would not be very helpful to put off doing something simply because of the day or hour. Scott Cunningham writes that you could work in the day and hour at any time; if the time was not right for an increase spell, change it to be a banishing of decrease. For my own part, the main determination is the phase of the moon—waxing for increase, waning for decrease, full for accomplishment, new for endings and new beginnings.

Alternative Rituals

There is no need to always have a stylized ritual with an altar, tools laid out, statues, and bowls of things. There is another way to celebrate the Sabbats, and that is simply with the forked staff (*stang*) as your altar. The stang is stuck into the ground, a circle is delineated about it, and it is decorated with a wreath of natural flowers or greenery pertinent to the season. With a candle at the base of the stang and a cup for your wine, all is ready. It is easy to carry your materials in a belt with pouches for herbs, salt, and cakes, a flask of wine on a thong, and another thong to hang a wooden cup. This can be draped over the prongs of the stang if belts with pouches are not desired. The wreath can be left behind on a tree branch or on the ground as food for animals if it is composed of seeds and berries.

I have found that there are times when I want an elaborate ritual, others when I want things relatively simple, and some when I skip the matter altogether. The conversation between the practitioner of the Craft and the Deities is ongoing and the rituals are for our benefit, not theirs—they do not need nor require them. These rites serve as a point of focus for raising energy and recharging our psychic batteries. Among Shiva worshippers in India, it is ideal to come to the recognition that rituals and ceremonies are totally unnecessary, which is how I feel occasionally. Just being out-of-doors, at the beach, or in the yard during a Sabbat time puts me into communion with the Lady and the Lord.

The Significance of Names

For someone starting into a new view of unity with the cycles of the earth, the stars, and the energies of the universe, the whole prospect of doing something different—such as choosing a Craft name—may feel strange or arouse feelings of uncertainty. There is nothing wrong or unusual about this. For centuries the Christian churches have tortured and murdered suspected Witches, filled society with a doctrine of damnation and hellfire for any non-conformity, and threatened anyone who dared to defy the standard with social and eternal separation. It is a very big and important decision for people to turn their backs on the terror that has been heaped onto their psyches over the years.

I spent many years practicing the Craft with a different Craft name. When I felt that one had become compromised, I simply made a new one and performed another initiation rite. The Craft name is the one by which you introduce yourself to the Ancient Ones when you first begin to practice, and this is done in a self-initiation ceremony. The term initiation (especially self-initiation) is one of those expressions that can have a very traditional or ceremonial connotation. Although some Pagans would not use it except in a coven setting, the expression of "self-initiation" is one that has been used by Scott Cunningham, D. J. Conway, Marion Green and other noted Craft writers. There is a distinct difference between an initiation and a dedication, and these terms have different meanings depending upon the focus of the people using them. In Chapter 5 of his book *Living Wicca*, Mr. Cunningham defended his use of this expression, and to be honest, I would never have thought such a simple matter would need defending. He did an excellent job of it, though, and I refer any criticism of the use of these terms to his work.

To perform this rite you prepare as for a Sabbat, but for the observance portion, the initiation is done instead. The wording and gestures are best planned out in advance to keep your focus on all facets of the initiation. There is a sample ritual in Chapter 7 that works not only for the basic Green level, but for nearly any other Wiccan path. The name you choose for yourself is one you should reveal only to people you can trust, but for the most part (particularly for the solitary) it is kept secret. The problem with letting others know your name is that sometimes situations change, and then you may feel compelled to create a new name to avoid bringing negativity through association into your circle.

The use of a Craft name is fairly common in Witchcraft, and there are actually two kinds of names used (a Green element books rarely illuminate upon): the Craft name, which is one the practitioner chooses, and the working name, which is one bestowed upon the Witch by the Lady and the Lord. There can also be a third, coven name if the Witch joins a group. Amber K in *True Magick* writes of having a number of names that fit her at different times. I have a Craft name, a working name, and a coven name (although the coven functions through correspondence and is eclectic), and have not found the use of a deity name desirable, but that is a matter of personal preference.

The Craft name is usually significant only to the person who creates it. It can be a flower, tree, gem, rock, or anything else of nature, or it can be more symbolic. Marion Green does not approve the use of deity names (such as Rhiannon, Cerridwyn, Isis, Herne, Horus, etc.) as Craft names. In my case, Aoumiel (Awm'mee-el) was constructed to express my feelings about the unity of the Goddess and the God, because I view the deities as equals and in balance with one another (Aum [Om] and Uma are the united "God" [El]). Even when friends pronounce my name "A-oh' me-el," I feel the essence remains, as Ao is the ancient name of the God, Uma (or *Oma*) is the ancient name of the Goddess, and El is the term for Divine Being. More than one Craft name can be used at a time.

The other type of name in the Green level is called a working name. Often the Craft name will be used in the association of other people interested in the Old Religion, but the working name is a special gift that comes after the Craft name has been used for awhile. Until a dedication the Craft name may double as the working name, but after a dedication, the Witch is given a new name that is always kept secret (until the working name is given by the Lady and the Lord, the Craft name may serve in magical functions). This working name is literally bestowed by the Lady and the Lord, and is their personal link to you and yours to them. The Craft name then becomes available for more public use. The significance of the working name is that the Lord and the Lady are telling you who you are. That is why it is kept secret—the name defines you.

I have read of the Craft name and study coming first and then followed by initiation, making one a full-fledged member of Wicca or a coven tradition, but I see the initiation as the beginning rather than the end product of study. This is the stage of learning the basics of the Craft, and it is not the same as making a commitment to the Lady and the Lord founded upon that learning. A dedication is a conscious decision to do something meaningful with the knowledge gained after your initiation. I know there are others who have this same point of view as there are other Witches who tell me that yes, they have a Craft name, but also a working name that no one else knows. The Craft name is used in an initiation, but the working name comes from the dedication.

The Dedication Ritual

The dedication ceremony can take place as early as a year and a day after your initiation, or many years later. I worked with two different Craft names in succession for over twenty years before taking the final plunge, as it were, into dedication. Afterwards, I wondered that I had waited so long—the practice of Witchcraft is definitely enhanced through dedication. The timing will vary with the practitioner, because only the individual knows when he or she is ready for this commitment. You have spent your time learning, practicing, and formulating your Sabbat and Esbat rituals, and becoming familiar with magic, the deities, and the elementals. When the time for a dedication is decided, it is a solitary ritual, for it is a very personal experience.

No one else can give you an initiation or a degree that places you in contact with the Ancient Ones, and it is in the self-dedication that you will come face to face with the Lady and the Lord of the Old Religion. Without a sincere desire to serve the Lady and the Lord, this step should not be taken. In this ceremony you put into practice the Wiccan adage of "perfect love and perfect trust" relating not to other practitioners, but to your relationship with the Lady and the Lord. You must trust them. This ritual should not be commenced until you have made a vigil and considered your reasons and what you want to achieve in making this connection. The vigil is your chance to question your motives, address your fears and hopes, and answer your doubts. You are moving from a worker of magic with the grace and love of the Lady and the Lord to a commitment to them. Until now, you have taken from them, and they have made no demands upon you, nor will they ever. But with the dedication, you are freely giving something back to them—your pledge and your unconditional love. My own dedication ritual is described in Chapter 7.

After dedication, whenever you call upon the Lady and the Lord you should do so in the working name they have bestowed upon you. The Craft name becomes the name by which you can associate with others of like mind and in your public work. But for your private rituals, you call upon them as "Your child, whom you have named (*name*)."

Travel Aids

The thing to remember in doing a dedication is that now the connection is like a continuous conversation. Your needs and desires are filled almost before you can speak them or are even aware you have them. Divination becomes almost second nature, as this is their way of talking to you. When the need arises for them to tell you something, they will use whatever means are available. You may spontaneously see visions in clouds, smoke, fire, cards, water, the wind, crystals, and so forth. If you hear your working name, you will know they are contacting you. And they will respond whenever you call upon them. Elaborate rituals are not needed, although some kind of meditation will help you learn to focus your attention. A simple mental call will elicit a response. Most importantly, they will be your loving Mother and Father. Listen to what they say.

For some practitioners the use of a power animal, a magical animal who aids you in your travels to the Otherworld, is involved. By meditating upon your desire for such an animal and asking for a power animal, or simply by thinking about having one, you connect with the deities. They will respond when perhaps you least expect it. I tried to choose the sort of animal I felt drawn to but could not come to any decision, so I put the matter out of my mind. A few months later, I had a very rich and musical dream in which I called upon the Goddess and called for the animal I wanted. A great number arrived all at once and I chose one, or perhaps we chose each other, and the animal's name dwelled in the back of my mind until I realized what it was. The dream was filled with song, which I crafted into a poem the next morning. Now, I can call upon my companion for aid in divination and travel to the Otherworld at any time. But not everyone has or wants a power animal—the choice is always yours.

The elementals, too, are close to you and are your kindred. They will aid you and be there for you when you need them. Do not feel that everything must be serious, however. I have heard the laughter of the Lady and the Lord, and I have teased and been teased back by the elementals. Yet always, there is respect. With the elementals, you are dealing with great powers—the forces of nature as wild winds, thunderous rains, lightning or consuming fires, and rugged, tumultuous earth. Do not perceive of these great powers as little creatures, for that is to understate who they are. The elementals are Forces, and they do not take well to being diminished. Remember who and what you are working with: that is why one should not "summon" or "banish" the elemental powers at a circle. They are called upon to guard and witness the rite, and when the ceremony is over, they are blessed and released in peace.

Giving Proper Thanks

Another practice I have always followed that varies with a number of Wiccan traditions is that neither the Lady and the Lord nor the elementals are thanked. My mother used to be very annoyed whenever someone used an expression like "Thanks be to God." If required to copy this form in a Mass, her tone was always distanced, as if she were verbally having an inoculation and was looking away with a grimace. This prohibition of saying the word "thanks" or "thank you" is not a lack of courtesy or gratitude, but can be found in ancient fairy motifs, foremost among them being that it is insulting to thank the Other People. This sensitivity is easily carried over to the elementals because, like the Other People, they are also aspects of the Lady and the Lord who are the source of all life and all form.

The reasoning for not saying "thank you" lies in the fine nuances of relationships. By thanking, you put yourself apart (rather than being connected in oneness) and turn a gift into a finalized mundane transaction. It is as though you have dismissed them. However, this is a viewpoint that some (or even many) people will not accept, so you must make your own decision intuitively. For myself, it is the heritage of my mother and her mother that I have passed along to my own family. Curiously, when I discussed this with my husband and my daughter, they told me that they too felt thanks were awkward and counter-productive, so perhaps there is indeed more to instinct than formats.

It is significant to make a distinction here. I am not saying that you should not feel gratitude for the presence and assistance of the Divine, no matter what form is involved. I am saying that reams of "thank yous" are not the same as feeling gratitude. With gratitude there is an inner warmth that they can feel emanating from you, but with verbal "thanks" mere form can be served, whether felt or not. I have read Sabbat rituals as presented in a number of Wiccan books that are rife with the words "thank you" and after awhile, it becomes rote and unfeeling. Doing these rituals Sabbat after Sabbat can blunt the intended effect and make the words meaningless. You can use these popular words if you feel comfortable doing so, but try coming up with alternatives that help you express your emotional ties and inner sensations. By eliminating "thank you," you will be forced to describe what it is that you are grateful about. The Other People in legend appreciate being appreciated, but dislike a dismissive thanking.

3

Witches and Herbs

Witches have a history of being feared and persecuted for their special relationships with nature, being seen as people with "scary" powers that few others possess. This was not always the case; *The Witches' Almanac* quotes Robert Graves as saying that natural occult power exists in one out of twenty people, and Colin Wilson, a British author, was quoted in the *New York Times* as saying five out of every one hundred people were natural Witches. Wilson went on to say that this was so normal no one seemed to be concerned about it until the Church began its persecutions in the thirteenth century.

There is an excellent video (broadcast on The Learning Channel) called *The Burning Times*, in which the history and possible causes for the Witch burnings in Europe are covered. It convincingly suggests that the so-called religious cases were a mockery of human intelligence and a thinly disguised cover-up for the real cause. The cases were political events designed to wrest power from independent women who had wealth or property, prevent women from being educated, and place women under the domination of a legal male guardian. For example, the use of midwives was curbed so that only male doctors, whose education was actually inferior to that of the country herbalist Green Witch, would dominate in the field of medicine. Religion of this persecutory sort served to elevate an elite ruling class, and had little to do with the Divine.

Today, churches decry a woman's right to abortion as the murder of infants, but for four centuries, churches both Catholic and Protestant tortured, hung, and burned to death millions of women and children, including infants, as Witches. The figure of nine million killed is frequently seen in Craft writings, but cannot be substantiated. Nevertheless, this terror devastated the population of Europe, and in some cases is known to have wiped out entire villages with the cry of "Kill them all and let God sort out the righteous!"

As then, the matter today is not one of faith, but of domination and authority. For people who believe that abortion is the only cause of the Fundamentalists, a quick look at some Fundamentalist literature makes their agenda clear. It includes far-reaching controls on society, including the banning of contraceptives, enforced Christian faith in public schools, outlawing of Wicca and Paganism, restrictions on the Constitutional freedoms of the Bill of Rights, and inclusion of religious tests for the holding of public office (which is specifically prohibited in Article 6 of the Constitution). For Fundamentalists, the idea of creating God's heaven on earth—a concept that denies God's ability to do anything on his own—would require the destruction of the Constitution and the establishment of a dictatorship.

The Importance of Herbal Knowledge

In modern times, what has remained of the herbal lore of the Witch is being painstakingly rediscovered and compiled by numerous herbalists. The medical profession is once again opposed to people having the right to approach their health needs through the use of herbs, and severe restrictions on the sale of herbs have been imposed around the United States. For the most part, herbs can be acquired in health food stores, but for the past fifteen or so years, the employees have been forbidden by law to aid the buyer with any information about the benefits or uses of herbs. While something like bulk senna tea is available, the information that too much tea will cause severe diarrhea (it is used as a laxative) is withheld. Likewise, the information about what combinations of teas will promote menstrual flow and which ones can induce abortion is also withheld. By doing so, herbs can then be portrayed as dangerous, and articles can be written about people developing ailments because they misused or overused an herb.

Case Study: Herbs as Contraceptives

It would undermine the power of the predominantly male-dominated medical profession for ordinary people to have an understanding of herbs and their uses. Yet, if a pregnant woman reads in one book that tansy tea is good for morning sickness, she needs to know that it is described in another book as good for inducing menses—hence, a possible spontaneous abortion could result depending on the strength of her tea and the amount consumed. Some books discuss dangerous herbs, and the reader must use caution as serious injury might ensue since a strong dosage could result in anything from no effect to menses to abortion to death. A number of common herbal contraceptives were covered in the March/April 1994 issue of a *Newsweek* article on ancient contraceptives and abortion techniques, "Ever Since Eve...Birth Control in the Ancient World." Here it was stated that in rural America, ingesting a teaspoonful of seeds from Queen Ann's Lace (a common weed with lacy white flowers) stirred into a glass of water after sexual relations is still a country practice. Contraception was not officially illegal in the Catholic Church until 1869, but as early as the first century C.E., the approach of male physicians was inclined against abortion. Nevertheless, population control was being discussed in the ancient world as beneficial to society.

The natives of an isolated Amazonian Jungle tribe only have children every three years because that is all they can feed and support, so they end unwanted pregnancies with herbs. But modern Americans are forbidden this knowledge because of the imposition of Judeo-Christian religious codes, despite the alleged freedom of religion. The insidious undermining of freedoms due to laws based on religious beliefs has resulted in Americans being denied access to the simple French drug that terminates pregnancies with only a pill, taken in the privacy of the home. There would be no need for abortion clinics with the availability of this pill, and private decisions affecting their bodies and their lives would again be in the hands of women. There is a promise of releasing this pill in America in a few years, but already the price being projected is exorbitant. In Europe, it is affordable.

Educating Yourself about Herbs

For those who want herbal information as part of their personal education, there are books available on the subject and courses through correspondence at some local colleges. But for that same person to then tell others about the herbs is to risk a charge of practicing medicine without a license. So the Witches of today may suggest acetaminophen to a friend with a headache and no one complains, but recommend an herbal remedy to someone, and you are culpable under the law. The ramifications of all this have caused public schools to forbid students bringing any medication at all to school—including any kind of over-the-counter headache or menstrual symptom remedy—to avoid the possibility of lawsuit should any adverse reaction take place on school grounds. Self-medication has been presented by the medical profession as highly dangerous and reckless, yet people have a history of self-medication that spans the millennia.

For further study about the medical uses of herbs, I recommend *Rodale's Illustrated Encyclopedia of Herbs*, *Jude's Herbal Home Remedies* (by Jude C. Williams, M.H.), and *The New Age Herbalist*. For a wealth of magical information about herbs, I recommend Scott Cunningham's *Encyclopedia of Magical Herbs*. The Green element of the Craft is basically an herbal one, and herbs are used both for medicinal and magical purposes. Almost any spell or charm is improved if herbs are worked into it. For practicing the Craft, a basic garden of favorite herbs is a must, even if this means potted plants. The very contact with Mother Earth and green growing things is a source of renewal of energy and power for any Witch.

Most herbs prefer sandy, well-drained soil, but there are some that thrive in damp, water-retaining soil. If you do not have both types in your yard, as is most likely the case, you can get around this problem by planting your herbs in raised herb beds filled with the appropriate soil. Planting and harvesting tips along with sun and water needs (and even some arts and crafts suggestions) are in many herb gardening books. Starting seeds in cups with bottom drainage holes is easiest, and then transplanting the seedlings into the garden.

A Witch's Herb Garden

Since there are reliably good books on herbs, how to grow them, how to use them, and what crafts can be made of them, I shall not focus on these matters. Instead, I want to consider the magical use of herbs. Many herbs can be purchased by mail order and at occult supply stores, and Appendix B lists stores I have found good for ordering herbs, oils, and various other supplies. There is nothing wrong with being a busy Witch and ordering supplies from a reputable source, but of course it is always more rewarding to make your own oils and grow, collect, and store your own herbs. I have done it both ways, and, as in all practice of the Craft, the magic comes from within the practitioner—the supplies are an aid in focusing that magic.

The Witch's garden should contain certain basic herbs. The individual knows what use the herbs will be put to and should plant with this in mind. Depending on how much you feel you will need, the plots may be small or large. Some Witches create herbal crafts for others or grow herbs for distribution at shops, requiring large gardens, while others have more simple needs, and maintain smaller gardens. The following lists give examples of herbs found in an all-around versatile Witch's garden:

agrimony	angelica	avens
basil	bay	betony
birch	broom	burdock
catnip	chamomile	chives
cinquefoil	coltsfoot	comfrey
coriander	dandelion	dianthus
dill	elecampane	fennel
feverfew	garlic	gentian
heather	hops	hyssop
lavender	lemon balm	lemon verbena
lovage	marigold	marjoram
mint	mugwort	mullein
nasturtium	oregano	parsley
rose	rosemary	rue
sage	St. John's Wort	savory
tansy	tarragon	thyme
trefoil	vervain	valerian
woodruff	wormwood	yarrow

The Green element of the Craft is basically an herbal one, and herbs are used both for medicinal and magical purposes. . . The very contact with Mother Earth and green growing things is a source of renewal of energy and power for any Witch.

Trees, shrubs, and flowers useful for their particular properties and as ornamental accents may include:

alder	elder	foxglove
hawthorn	hazel	heather
oak	rowan	willow

Herbs and their Qualities

Some common cooking spices do double duty as herbs that can be utilized in the Craft. Using these herbs fresh in food preparation adds magic to a meal, and can make it part of a ritual. By learning what uses you can make of herbs in magical practice, the creating of spells begins to follow a pattern that works for the individual, yet is based upon accepted attributes. Scott Cunningham's *Encyclopedia of Magical Herbs* is a very useful tool, particularly if you desire to match the spell you want to create with an herb by its characteristics, planetary and elemental associations, and so forth. I rarely give very much attention to astrological relationships as regards the herbs themselves, but many people do. My listing of herbs and their uses tends to be more succinct. The following is an herbal listing I keep in my spellbook. **Caution:** *Be careful with poisonous plants since even inhaling the smoke may be dangerous.*

HERB	QUALITY
acacia	burn for altar offering, aids psychic powers, meditation
agrimony	protection, returns spells to their sender, promotes sleep
alder	whistles entice the Elemental Air
allspice	burn for prosperity
angelica	sprinkle about the house to ward negativity, protection, divination
anise	purification, protection, entices spirits to aid in spells
apple	bury in the garden on Samhain as food for the departing spirits, love (share an apple with the one you love), health, attracts unicorns

ash	wands, protection, leaves for prophetic dreams, prosperity
avens	purification, love
banana	fertility, prosperity (I mention this for those in tropical climates because the flowers are hermaphroditic and can be used as altar offerings for the Goddess and God as One—I use the image of Shiva Ardhanari for this aspect of the Divine)
basil	protection, wealth, love, repels negativity
bay	burn for psychic powers, purification, wish magic
benzoin	burn for purification, prosperity
bergamot	success
betony	burn at Litha for purification, protection, to be rid of nightmares (put in a pillow under your own pillow), to send away despair (sprinkle around doors and windows), psychic awareness
birch	protection, purification, wards negativity
blackberry	protection, health, prosperity, pies for Lughnassadh
blackthorn	returns evil to the sender
borage	tea aids psychic powers, carry leaves for protection
briar	add to tea for clairvoyant dreams
broom	purification (sweep the circle), hang indoors for protection (fairies do not like this plant, and by working with the devas you may also come to loathe the musty scent of broom)
burdock	wards negativity, purifies, protects (can be used in washing floors or wear the dried root strung on red thread)
cardamon	burn for love spells, use in love sachets
carnation (*Dianthus*)	protection, altar offering for the Goddess, strength
cassia augustifolias (*Indian Senna Leaf*)	**Caution:** *Tea not to be taken during menstruation or pregnancy* (this tea will induce both menses and diarrhea, and if used to bring on menses or to overcome constipation, may be followed up after the

	desired effect with a tea of China Black, chamomile, and rose hips)
catnip	love and cat magic
chamomile	meditation, rest (drink in tea), purification, calmness, prosperity, incense for the God
cherry	chips burnt at Sabbats, creativity
cinnamon	burn for spiritual and psychic powers, protection, success
cinquefoil	prosperity, protection, purification, divination dreams
citron	eat to increase psychic ability (the traditional Yule fruitcake usually includes citron in the ingredients)
clove	burn for wealth, purification, and to ward negativity
comfrey	root or leaves for healing, carry for safe travel
coriander	health
cumin	prevents theft, burn for protection
dill	seeds draw money, leaves for protection, flowers for love
elder	**Caution:** *Seeds are poisonous.* Wards negative thoughts when used as wind chimes, blessings, wood **not** to be burned as it is sacred to Hecate, see fairies in these trees at Litha, flowers may be used as an altar offering, berries may be made into Esbat wine, the flowers may be added to a candle spell addressed to Hecate during the new moon
elm	attracts elves, love
eyebright	tea for aiding mental powers
fennel	protection, sacred to the God, hung over doors at Litha
ferns	burn indoors for protection, outside for rain
feverfew	wards sickness, wards accidents in travel
foxglove	**Caution:** *Poisonous, although digitalis comes from it.* Grow in the garden for protection of house and yard
frankincense	protection, blessing, spirituality, meditation, power

furze/gorse	burn at Ostara for protection and as preparation for any conflict
garlic	sacred to Hecate, flowers for altar offering, cloves for protection
ginger	love, success
hawthorn	powerful wands, fertility magic, protection
hazel	string the nuts on a cord and hang it in the house or ritual room to invite the help of plant fairies, used for wands, healing, protection, luck
heather	red to start or end an affair, white for protection, purple for spiritual development, use at Samhain to invite spirits to visit
hops	health, aids sleep
hyssop	purification, wards negativity
kelp	wind spells, protection, psychic powers
lavender	attracts elves, burn for purification, peace, use in bath for purification, burn at Litha as offering, love, psychic awareness
lemon balm	success, health, love (soak in wine for three hours, remove and serve wine)
linden (*lime tree*)	bark used for protection, leaves and flowers for immortality, good fortune, sleep, and love
loosestrife	purple restores harmony and brings peace (can be sprinkled in the corners of rooms or given as a gift to bring about an accord)
mace	burn for psychic power
marigold	marriage spells, clairvoyant dreams (in a pillow), mixed with water and rubbed over the eyelids to see fairies, protection, enhanced psychic powers, pick in full sun
marjoram	love, protection, wealth
mint	protection, prosperity, altar offering for helpful spirits
moonwort	divination, love, prosperity

mugwort	divination, rub fresh herb on crystal balls and magic mirrors to increase their strength, pick on full moon night
mullein	protection, divination, health, courage
mustard	health, protection, and fertility
myrrh	protection, wards negativity, burn for purification and consecrations (usually combined with frankincense)
nutmeg	burn for prosperity
nuts and cones	use to tip wands for fertility magic
oak	the God, wands, burn leaves to purify the atmosphere, use galls in charms, acorns draw money, burn wood for good health
oats	wealth, offering for the God
orange	peels for love, incense for good fortune, divination
parsley	purification, protection
patchouli	incense for drawing money, fertility, earth, Underworld
pecan	prosperity
pepper	use in amulets or grow for protection, wards negativity
pine	brush outdoor ritual area with a branch to purify and sanctify, burn for cleansing, pine needles used in money spells
rosemary	burn for purification, wards negativity, protection, love, health, grown to attract elves, blessing, consecration
rowan	wands and amulets for knowledge, incense of leaves and berries for divination, fires to call upon spirits for help, grow for protection of the home, inspiration
rue	blessing, consecration, protection, use in altar oil, health
sage	protection, wisdom, health
St. John's Wort	burn at Litha to send away negativity, wear for invincibility, health, willpower, gathered at Litha
sandalwood	burn for protection, full moon Esbats, wards negativity, spirit offering

Solomon's Seal (*dropberry, sealroot*)	an offering to the elementals for their aid, protection
star anise	burn for psychic power, good fortune
straw	attracts fairies, do not burn magic-infused straw as that will bring ill fortune, can be used as an image to protect an area (when no longer needed, release and toss to the wind)
tansy	health
thyme	wards negativity, burn for purification and healing spells
trefoil	decorate altar, protection, luck, when taking one, leave a bit of ginger or milk poured into the ground as payment to the fairies
vervain (*verbena*)	gather/burn at Litha, altar offering, love, purification, draws riches, creativity, wards psychic attack
vetivert	love, money, wards negativity
wheat	fertility, wealth
willow	burn bark with sandalwood for divination, love, protection
woodruff	add to Beltane wine to clear away barriers, protection, success, changes, psychic awareness
wormwood (*absinthe*)	**Caution:** *Poisonous.* If burned, use in well-ventilated area, preferably outdoors, evocation, divination, and scrying (stronger when combined with mugwort) at Samhain, protection, sacred to the moon
yarrow	divination, love, happy marriage (a wedding bouquet), wards negativity, defense, protection, gather at Litha
yew	**Caution:** *Poisonous.* Yule symbol of death and rebirth, used for dagger handles

Herbs and the Moon's Cycles

In planting and harvesting herbs for magical use, the phases of the moon play an important part in your schedule. For planning purposes, most calendars designate the days of the new moon, first quarter, full moon, and last quarter (an almanac will also have this information).

Plant flowering annuals and above-ground crops with exterior seeds (such as wheat) when the moon is waxing between the new moon and the first quarter. Between the first quarter and the waxing full moon, plant above-ground crops with interior seeds (such as peas). Root crops, bulbs, biennials, and perennials (such as most herbs) should be planted between the waning full moon and the last quarter. Nothing is planted between the last quarter and the new moon.

Many people not only plant during the right phase of the moon, but under the proper astrological sign as well. Using the moon in relation to astrological signs is often featured in almanacs. Since the information is a common feature of Wicca, you should know that the moon remains in an astrological sign about two and one-half days, and again an almanac is your best source for this information. Fruitful signs, used for planting and pruning for growth, are Cancer, Scorpio, Pisces, Taurus, Capricorn, and Libra. The barren signs, used for weeding, cultivating, and harvesting herbs, are Leo, Virgo, and Sagittarius, with Aries, Gemini, and Aquarius for harvesting herbs and roots in particular.

I have found from experience that conditions vary according to what region you are in, so I have gone by the phase of the moon and how nature prompts me for my planting and harvesting. The order of harvests is determined by the plant's natural growth cycle, and weeding and pruning come as required. This is based on the natural interaction of the earth, moon, and sun for the signals of seasonal changes. The generic nature of the Green level of the Craft allows for the incorporation of astrology for people who like more ritual in their lives.

Herbs for Incense and Candle Magic

Herbs are often burned for incense during a spell or ritual. Charcoal blocks are available for this purpose in gift and candle shops as well as occult supply stores, but there are times when the herbs are burned in candles that are consecrated to a particular work. This herbal listing shows uses for incense or candle magic. **Caution:** *Remember, wormwood is poisonous if burned, so use good ventilation.*

QUALITY	HERB
balance	basil, chamomile, comfrey, mullein, woodruff
blessing/ consecration	chamomile, dianthus, elder flowers, fennel, mint, oats, rosemary, rue, vervain

cleansing/ purification	avens, betony, benzoin, burdock, clove, hyssop, lavender, mullein, parsley, rosemary, thyme, vervain, wormwood, yarrow
creativity	vervain
courage	mullein, rosemary
divination	bay, cinquefoil, marigold, moonwort, mugwort, mullein, orange peel, thyme, woodruff, wormwood, yarrow
encourage changes	linden, purple heather, woodruff
energy/power/ strength	cinquefoil, elder flower, fennel, St. John's Wort, vervain
fortune/justice	bay, bergamot, cinquefoil, lemon balm, orange peel, star anise, vervain, violet, woodruff
happiness/ peace	jasmine, lavender, rosemary, vervain
healing	cinquefoil, comfrey, coriander, hops, lavender, lemon balm, mullein, mustard, rosemary, rue, sage, St. John's Wort, tansy, thyme
love	avens, cardamon, dill flowers, ginger, lavender, linden leaves, marigold, marjoram, moonwort, mustard seed, orange peel, vervain, vetivert, wormwood, yarrow
meditation	acacia, chamomile
money	basil, bergamot, chamomile, clove, dill seeds, mint, moonwort, nutmeg, oats, vetivert
protection/ defense	betony, birch, burdock, cumin, dianthus, dill leaves, fennel, fern, marjoram, mint, mugwort, mullein, mustard, parsley, rosemary, rue, sage, vervain, white heather, woodruff, wormwood, yarrow
psychic awareness	bay, betony, burdock, cinnamon, elder flower, lavender, mace, marigold, star anise, woodruff
releasing negativity	betony, clove, hyssop, mugwort, rosemary, St. John's Wort, thyme, vervain, vetivert, yarrow

sealing/ sending positive energy	Wormwood. **Caution:** *Poisonous if burned.*
spirit contact/ blessings	lilac, purple heather, mint, Solomon's Seal
strength/ willpower	rosemary, St. John's Wort
wisdom	sage

Witches and Trees

Besides herbs, trees are also used in the Green practice. They are grown for a variety of purposes: wands, staffs, and stangs (the forked staff) are made from them, and the bark, wood, leaves, flowers, and fruit are used in spell work. The following is a list of trees and the properties for which they may be utilized:

TREE	QUALITY
alder	water magic, strength
apple	love, spirit food
ash	study, health, enhances magic, besom, stang
birch	purification, blessing, health, beginnings, besom
elder	cleansing, offering
fir/pine	prosperity, birth and rebirth, stang
hawthorn	purity, protection, wand, attracts fairies
hazel	wisdom, all-around Witch's wand
holly	enhances magic
ivy	fertility, love
mountain ash (*rowan*)	protection, enhances magic, stang
oak	fertility, power, balance, protection, success, stang
poplar	success
vine (*grape*)	happiness

willow   moon magic, wishing, spirits, death passage, besom

yew   psychic awareness, spirits, death passage

Days of the Week and Trees

Trees also have traditional associations with days of the week, certain deities, and other aspects of Craft and spell work.

DAY	TREE; DEITY; ASSOCIATIONS
Monday	willow; Hecate (crone); elder, willow
Tuesday	holly, cedar; elves; elm
Wednesday	hazel; Lady & Lord; rowan (mountain ash)
Thursday	oak, pine; Lord; oak
Friday	apple, myrtle; Lady; birch
Saturday	alder; fairies; hawthorn
Sunday	birch, laurel; Witch's tree; hawthorn

Ash, oak, and hawthorn grown or found together form what is called a Fairy Triad, where the fair folk may visit and may be seen.

Herb Collection and Storage

Herbs should be collected on a dry day, preferably cut with your bolline. Tell the plant why you are taking a piece and ask for permission. You should either leave something in return or give the plant your blessing, however your herb garden plants are likely to be more generous and less interested in receiving a "gift" because they know you tend them. Nevertheless, it never hurts to be polite to the energies (*devas*) that inhabit and empower the plants. To retain the magic properties, do not set the cutting on the ground. A garden basket over one arm is very useful. Tie the herbs in small bundles and hang by a string in an airy, dark place to dry (I use red thread or embroidery floss to enhance the power of the herb). Leaves and flowers without stems can be dried in a muslin bag, although I have used paper sacks with equal success. After a week, the herbs should be ready to be crumbled, minced or ground, then stored in the dark in tins or in bottles with screw-top lids. I save larger sized bottles from ready-made sauces and jams for re-use in storing my herbs and teas in a cupboard away from light.

Herbal Treatments

The spellbook you create for yourself should contain a listing of herbal treatments and characteristics. Some may be used internally, others are only for external treatments. There are herbs to stimulate appetite and digestion, others that are tranquilizers or calmatives. Herbs can be used as astringents, laxatives, expectorants, and mild sedatives. The best place to look for information on how to use herbs for medicinal purposes is in a book on herbal remedies. *Buckland's Complete Book of Witchcraft* has a listing of properties and equipment, and while my focus here is on magical herbal use, my spellbook also contains references to medicinal uses. Witches normally study all aspects of herbs to be able to apply that knowledge. *New Age Herbalist* also works well as a reference.

Medicinal Terms

TERM	MEANING
decoction	add boiling water to the herb for extraction (teas)
infusion	pour hot or cold water over herbs for extraction
maceration	steep in alcohol or oil (olive is best) and shake at intervals for extraction
percolation	like coffee percolators, only with herbs (or use special equipment)
filtration	like coffee filters, only with herbs (or use special equipment)
clarification	melt and skim or filter
poultices	mix crushed herbs with water and cornmeal into a paste and place on affected area (used for swellings, boils, sores)
salves	mince herbs with vegetable fat (or lard) and beeswax, cover and place in sun or low oven for four hours, strain through cheesecloth and let set in a clean container (do not re-melt)
composition powders	mix dry herbs as medicine for flu and fever
syrups	dissolve brown sugar and add to herbs until sappy, then strain through cheesecloth into a clean bottle and store

simples   steep herb in hot water for twenty minutes (do not use aluminum)

Herbal Baths

To make an herbal bath, combine the minced leaves/flowers in a jar, then place two or three tablespoons inside a cotton or muslin bag (sufficiently porous for the herbal essence to pass through but still prevent the leaves from scattering into the bath water) with a drawstring. Tie it off and place inside the tub as you fill it with water. You may want to add salt for purification baths. Herbal baths may consist of combinations of chamomile, clove, heather, hops, lavender, lemon balm, marigold, mint, pansy, rose, rosemary, and savory. Think of the benefits of the herbs you are using and call upon the energies of the plants to cleanse, energize and revive you as you bathe.

Dream Pillows

One of the popular magics for herbs is fashioning Dream Pillows. These are little pillows stuffed with herbs to affect a desired result and placed under the pillow of the person to be affected. I have made pillows for everyone in the family and vary them according to need or special request. They make lovely gifts for Imbolc. The color of the pillow varies as do the herbs depending on the purpose for which it is made. Combinations of colors can also be used. For Imbolc, the typical herb mixes stuffed into the pillow are mugwort, rosemary, and hops, or lavender, mugwort, and rose. Herbs for dreaming should be collected during the waxing or full moon.

The colors for the pillow material (cotton is best for herbal containers as it is a natural plant fiber) are white for meditation; lavender for psychic growth and divination; green for balance; pink for emotional love; purple for intuition and spiritual development; light blue for meditation and understanding; and yellow for clairvoyance and divination. I like to make each side of the pillow a different color: yellow/purple for divination and spiritual development; green/white for protection and peace; blue/white for understanding and peace; yellow/blue for divination and understanding; yellow/green for divination and balance; and pink/green for emotional love and balance.

Color Relationships

COLOR	ASSOCIATION
amber	develop Witchery skills
black	ward negativity, remove hexes, protection, spirit contact, the universe, night, truth, remove discord or confusion
blue (dark)	the Goddess (representative ritual candle), Water Elemental, truth, dreams, protection, change, meditation, impulse
blue (light)	psychic awareness, intuition, opportunity, understanding, quests, safe journey, patience, tranquility, ward depression
blue (any shade)	health
brown	Earth Elemental, endurance, animal health, steadiness, houses and homes, physical objects, uncertainties
gold	the God, solar energy, power, physical strength, success, achievement, mental growth, skill sought, healing energy, intuition, divination, fortune
gray	non-nature-type fairy magic such as communication with the fairy realms, travel to the Otherworld, vision quests, veiling, cancellation, hesitation, neutrality
green	Lord and Lady of Greenwood, Earth Elemental, herb magics, nature-type fairy magic (such as blessing a garden), luck, fertility, healing, balance, employment, prosperity, courage, agriculture, changing direction or attitudes
greenish-yellow	to negate discord, sickness, anger, jealousy
indigo	meditation, spirit communication, karma workings, learn the ancient wisdom, neutralize another's magic, ward slander
lavender	spiritual development, psychic growth, divination, sensitivity to the Otherworld, blessings

orange	the God (representative ritual candle), strength, healing, pulling things to you, adaptability, luck, vitality, encouragement, clearing the mind, dominance
pink	honor, morality, friendships, emotional love
purple	power, spiritual development, intuition, ambition, healing, progress, business, spiritual communication, protection, occult wisdom
red	Fire Elemental, strength, power, energy, health, vigor, enthusiasm, courage, passion, sexuality
silver	the Goddess, lunar magic, meditation, psychic development, success, balance, wards negativity
variegated	inner development through relaxation and introspection
violet	self-improvement, intuition, success in searches
white	the Lady and the Lord together, full moon magic, purity, protection, truth, meditation, peace, sincerity, justice, warding of doubts and fears
yellow	Air Elemental, divination, clairvoyance, mental alertness, intellectual growth, prosperity, learning, changes, harmony, creativity

Herb Significance

Besides Dream Pillows, there are other types of dream charms using herbs. Various herbs are conducive to producing specific results:

HERB	USAGE; RESULTS
agrimony	sprinkled under the pillow (hereafter abbreviated as U/P); calms and brings healing sleep
anise seeds	(U/P); spiritual protection
ash leaves	(U/P); insightful and prophetic dreams
bay leaves	(U/P); dreaming of the future
bracken fern root	(U/P); dream solutions to problems
buchu leaves	burn at bedtime with frankincense for guidance dream
catnip	drink as warm tea for restful sleep and healing dreams
cedar	burn at bedtime for spiritual healing, cleansing, and protection

cinquefoil	(U/P); guidance in love and insights to the future
frankincense	burn at bedtime to dream spiritual growth and insight to the future
heliotrope	(U/P); divination

Herbs in Rituals

As Offerings

Herbs may be used as tokens of esteem and respect for the deities and energies of the Craft. The Goddess may be honored by herbal offerings at those phases of the moon in which her identity is that of maiden, mother, or crone. I do this to relate to a particular aspect of the Lady through the visual appearance, texture, and scent of the appropriate herb. The act of dropping the herbs into the flame brings the focus of the ritual to the altar and stimulates the intimate bond between the Witch and the greater deity aspect. It is a gift rather like saying, "All things, including myself, come from the Lady and Lord, and I offer back to you a portion of what I have gathered from you." In the Bible, the gift of Cain was rejected by the Judaic god because at the time the Bible was written (625 B.C.E.) it was a gift recognized as being suited to the Goddess. As plants of various kinds have customarily been offered to the Lady, herbal offerings can be especially meaningful for their particular significance and properties.

In Sabbat Rituals

During the eight Sabbats, some herbs are burned and others are used as altar offerings and decorations or hung about the ritual area.

SABBAT	RELATED HERBS
Samhain	heather, mullein, patchouli, and sage may be burned; acorns, apples, pumpkins, oak leaves, straw, broom, dittany, ferns, and flax may be decorations
Yule	bay, bayberry, chamomile, frankincense, rosemary, and sage may be burned; holly, juniper, mistletoe, moss, oak, pine cones, cedar, evergreen, and blessed thistle may be decorations
Imbolc	basil, bay, benzoin, and celandine may be burned; angelica, myrrh, yellow flowers, and white flowers may be decorations

Ostara	celandine, cinquefoil, jasmine, rose, tansy, and violets may be burned; acorn, crocus, daffodil, dogwood, honeysuckle, iris, lily, and strawberry may be decorations
Beltane	almond, ash, cinquefoil, frankincense, marigold, meadowsweet, and woodruff may be burned; angelica, bluebells, daisy, hawthorn, ivy, lilac, primrose, and rose may be decorations
Litha	chamomile, cinquefoil, elder flower, fennel, lavender, mugwort, thyme, and vervain may be burned; hemp, larkspur, pine, rose, St. John's Wort, and wisteria may be decorations
Lughnassadh	cornstalks, heather, frankincense, and wheat may be burned; acacia flowers, corn ears, hollyhock, myrtle, oak leaves, and wheat may be decorations
Mabon	benzoin, marigold, myrrh, sage, and thistles may be burned; acorns, asters, ferns, honeysuckle, milkweed, mums, oak leaves, pine, and rose may be decorations

In Moon Rituals

The new or crescent moon represents the maiden aspect and is a time for personal rituals and meditations, setting new goals, and doing wish magic. The herbs that may be used at the start of these rituals are jasmine, myrrh, rosemary, or vanilla, burned in a white or silver candle. During the full moon, the mother aspect may be honored with ash, gardenia, lotus, oak, palm, or rose, burned in a red or green candle during a ritual for acknowledging successful workings, completions, and honoring the energies or spirit guides. The waning or dark moon represents the crone aspect and is a time for banishings, purgings, letting go of bad habits, removing obstacles, divination, and purification. The herbs that may be used at the start of these rituals include frankincense, elder flowers, or willow, burned in a black candle.

During a particular moon ritual, the altar may be prepared with the above suggested herbs in the color of candle listed, but if you are performing a specific spell or other magic for a particular purpose at an Esbat, you may want to show your respect for the Lady first, then use candles and herbs appropriate for the work you have in mind afterwards. There is a great deal of flexibility in the Green level of the Craft, and the Witch is encouraged to do what feels right.

In Timing Rituals

For some people, the need to get as much positive alignment as possible leads to concerns about the proper day to do a spell, the time of day, and the planetary influence. The Green element has a moon and sun orientation rather than an astrological one, but since it is the base level of any Craft practice, it can be adapted, or overlaid, with the use of favorable days, hours, and signs. The normal reality, however, is that rituals are usually very simple, and these factors really do not enter into consideration. I have felt a need for a spell and performed it, then out of curiosity checked to see if the timing was appropriate, and I have never found that it was not. There are many ways to approach the timing of magic workings, and a listing of days and hours can be easily manipulated to suit your needs whenever they arise. Nevertheless, since this is a common feature of Craft practice, I do keep a fairly standard schedule for reference should I feel inclined to use it.

Days

DAYS	ASSOCIATIONS
Monday	*(planet)* Moon *(colors)* silver, white, gray *(herb)* moonwort *(influences)* dreams, emotions, clairvoyance, home, family, medicine, cooking, personality, merchandising, theft
Tuesday	*(planet)* Mars *(colors)* red, orange *(herb)* basil *(influences)* dynamic energy, matrimony, war, enemies, prison, hunting, surgery, courage, politics, contests
Wednesday	*(planet)* Mercury *(colors)* yellow, gray, violet *(herb)* lavender *(influences)* communication, teaching, reason, divination, skill, self-improvement, debt, fear, loss
Thursday	*(planet)* Jupiter *(colors)* blue, purple *(herb)* cinquefoil *(influences)* health, honor, luck, riches, clothing, money, legal matters, desires
Friday	*(planet)* Venus *(colors)* pink, aqua, green *(herb)* thyme *(influences)* love, friendship, social activities, strangers, pleasure, art, music, incense and perfumes
Saturday	*(planet)* Saturn *(colors)* black, indigo *(herb)* mullein *(influences)* self-discipline, life, building, doctrine, protection, freedom, elderly, destroying diseases and pests

Sunday   *(planet)* Sun *(colors)* yellow, orange, gold *(herb)* St.
                  John's Wort *(influences)* individuality, hope, fortune,
                  money, work, power, healing, promotions, strength,
                  spirituality

Hours

An almanac with a magical focus will have a schedule of the hours of
the day (after sunrise and after sunset) showing what planet rules when
for each day of the week. The sequence is Sun, Venus, Mercury, Moon,
Saturn, Jupiter, Mars, then repeat, beginning on Sunday; the same
sequence begins on Monday with the Moon, Tuesday with Mars, and
so forth so that each day, the first hour after sunrise is ruled by the
planet of that day, and you progress through twenty four hours with
the first twelve being the after sunrise hours, and the second twelve
being the after sunset hours. You can make up your own chart with the
days of the week across the top, and the hours of the day listed down
the side, then simply start in the sequence shown for each day. You can
adjust your workings according to what hour it is after sunrise or sunset, because the times are not equal but twice a year. Once you have the
chart made, the use is easy.

A Witch's Spellbook

You may have noticed that I refer to my spellbook rather than to a
Book of Shadows, as is most common in Wiccan traditions. There are
actually two distinct books that form the backbone of my approach to
the Craft—the spellbook, which contains the information gathered
over years of practice and experience from which spells, charms, and
rituals may be derived; and the Book of Rituals, recognizable as a facet
of the Wiccan Book of Shadows, which contains the rites for Sabbats
and Esbats. Rites of Passage and individual Sabbat celebrations can be
found in Chapters 7–16, but you really should not attempt to leap into
rituals without knowing the basics and basis for them. The spellbook is
a useful tool that the Witch composes, rather like a recipe book, under
different headings.

I like to use bound and lined journals with decorative covers that can
be found in almost any bookstore. I use small tabs (stationary and business supply stores carry these) to index the pages. The book will
acquire a friendly, useful feel about it as you fill it with pertinent infor-

mation. You can select the cover that appeals to you and expresses what you want to achieve in the Craft. I have never liked the solid black books often associated with Witchcraft simply because the Green elements are those of browns and greens, flowers and herbs, sun and moon, sky and earth. My spellbook is brown with a green, leafy vine around it and a red-orange rose in the center, but my Book of Rituals is green with clusters of gold leaves and red roses in the corners.

Besides these two books, I also keep a book of divinations and a journal that acts both as a dream diary and a record of impressions from other events, such as meditations and visions. Most Witches keep dream journals, divination records, and descriptions of their encounters with the Otherworld for reference, and I highly recommend the practice.

A Witch's Relationship with Nature

The Witch whose practice is centered on the Green level feels close to the growing things of the earth and frequently talks to plants, insects, rocks, and all the creations in nature. The animistic and pantheistic aspect of the Craft makes this a logical step, albeit one that has often been used by other people with varying degrees of hostility. The non-Witch will curse at weeds, for example, whereas I will scold them and remind them that they have the whole yard to play in, so stay out of the herb garden. When I pick weeds out of the garden (I never cut them, but pull them out roots and all), I simply toss them onto the ground where they quickly take root and live quite happily. To me, weeds are not pests, but more like mischievous children playing hide and seek among the herbs, waiting to see how long it will take me to notice them.

With trees, I have found that some are more receptive and predisposed to communing with people than others. Some trees need to get to know the person close by them before bothering to respond. I have encountered trees that are rather aloof, and others that are quite content to be visited and talked to. But there are a few trees that effuse love and affection for humans, and these are a joy to be near. Generally, however, once a tree recognizes that you care about it and are not exploitative, it will blend its energies with you. The devas of the plant world bond with people who care about them, and you will be changed so that wherever you go, the green growing things will recognize you are a friend and reach out to you with their energies.

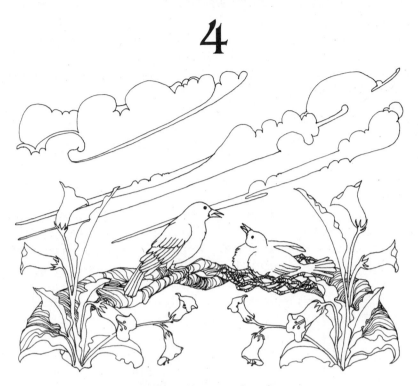

Green Living

There is a difference between practicing magic and living the Green level of the Craft. In the first case, the individual studies to master a number of rituals in order to enter a different state of awareness when attempting to manipulate external energies in the performance of magic. In the second case, the very life of the individual is an ongoing magical experience highlighted with special bursts of magical power.

Ceremonial Magic

The modern fascination with ceremony composed of strict rules and regulations for the practice of magic can be traced back to Medieval and Renaissance writers of magic books called grimoires. These were the early Ceremonialists who wrote extensive and complex rituals by which the Adept could contact the higher realms and effect magic (González-Wippler in *The Complete Book of Spells, Ceremonies & Magic* gives some examples). The rituals themselves, however, relate to angels, demons, devils and the Son of God. They reflect not an ancient tradition, but a relatively recent one dating back to the Judaic heritage of around 1000 to 600 B.C.E.

The Aryan Influence

I discuss the historical background of the invasions of various Aryan tribes from Central Asia, circa 2000 to 1200 B.C.E., and how the Aryan influence altered religious expression in the lands they conquered in Appendix A. What is important to remember here and in the practice of magic is that the angels, demons, devils and rulers of various realms are derived from the ancient gods and goddesses of conquered peoples. For myself, that knowledge makes it impossible to practice a completely ceremonial type of magic. In order to call upon an archangel, for example, the magician must subscribe to some of the beliefs of the relatively more modern religious systems. This does not mean the system cannot work, only that in order for it to work, the practitioner needs to accept and follow the basics of the Aryan methodology that emphasizes the power of deities who may be described as being of a social class (rulers, priests, and warriors) rather than of nature (the Lady and the Lord, matter and energy of the foundation level).

The politicization of religion is the heritage of the ancient Aryans. It has left its mark in modern faiths through a subsequent pattern of clerical elitism and dominance, with the subservience of the community of believers enforced through ritualized dogmas and doctrines. The word "Aryan" should not be interpreted as a negative term despite its misuse in modern contexts of racial prejudice and ethnic bigotry, since all modern mainstream religions are Aryan-based. The conflicts that occur between these faiths are mainly the result of the degree of emphasis given to Green-level concepts in the different sects. The original purpose for changing the religious practices of a region was to ensure control by a ruling invader over the conquered people.

The persecutions and wars of religion that have been, and still are, the hallmark of Western history were unknown prior to the migrations of the Aryans. This aggressive advance of people was possibly due to overpopulation and a successful change in societal organization meant to deal with the problem. Beginning around 2000 B.C.E., the arrival of these people into the southern reaches of the Indian subcontinent, the Near East, and the Mediterranean gave birth to the faiths of Hinduism, the classical Greek pantheon, Buddhism, Judaism, Christianity, and

Islam—all of which then fought among themselves (for each group had, and most continue to have, numerous sects and denominations) and with each other over which doctrine was the true faith. The answer, of course, is "none of the above" and "all of the above."

The Green Influence

The Green-focused Witch turns away from artificial creation and instead embraces the primal religion that honors the natural forces active in the creation of the world. Although there are many people who feel Ceremonial magic is a valid approach to magic, anyone who studies history and understands the derivation for the rituals of Ceremonialism is unlikely to be able to continue to use the system with any degree of success because knowledge, which is the gift of the Goddess, alters the perception. Joseph Campbell was unable to remain a Catholic after his study of world mythological patterns, and numerous historians set aside religion after discovering the origins of various faiths, so it should not be considered unusual for a person who rejects mainstream religions to also reject a magical system that has connections to those beliefs. My purpose here is to attempt to locate the elements underlying even the magical systems based in the modern faiths and bring these to the foreground.

Craft History

The beauty of the Green practice is that laughter and exploration are not destructive to the atmosphere created for magical work. Indeed, the Lady and the Lord thrive on laughter and want their children to be happy. Yet even in Witchcraft there is a different sort of problem, similar to the ritualistic approach of Ceremonialism, that needs to be addressed for a balanced view of the Craft today and how it connects to the Green elements of the ancient past. Numerous articles and a few books on the subject of the origins of Wicca have been, and will undoubtedly continue to be, written over the years. The real question brought forward by these writings is not how the Craft developed or what its origins are, but how well it can stand up to analysis and historical research. If people fall away from mainstream faiths because those religions could not stand up under critical review, why should people approach magic and the Craft and not give these the same degree of scrutiny? How a person responds to the development of the modern Craft will affect how (or if) a person practices Witchcraft and magic.

The Green-focused Witch turns away from artificial creation and instead embraces the primal religion that honors the natural forces active in the creation of the world.

Each individual needs to find a personal satisfaction in what is done for spiritual, physical, emotional, and intellectual development, and in doing so, to paraphrase Joseph Campbell, each person will come to know what bliss is being followed.

Many people who were members of the fashionable secret societies of the Victorian Age became influential in the area of Witchcraft. By the early part of the twentieth century, they had taken Ceremonial aspects and applied them to the Craft, and adapted or created dogmas like the Charge of the Goddess (I envision Athena on horseback racing down a hillside in battle gear with her spear pointed at a startled suppliant, but I tend to have a droll sense of humor), a poetic Witch's Rede (which has been criticized for its artificially quaint language) containing the Law of Threefold Return (in contrast to a karmic view of one-for-one), the Witches' Rune, and the Fivefold (or Sevenfold) Blessing.

Early people involved in the Witchcraft revival wrote books, lectured, created traditions, and some even authorized covens based on a system of initiations by degrees. In this system, the highest degree was obtained through sexual union with a Priest (or sometimes a Priestess) of the organized coven tradition. They pronounced themselves to be Kings and Queens of Witches, wrote "Witch's Bibles," and became so well recognized in the media that it became accepted that there were only certain kinds of Witchcraft—Gardnerian, Alexandrian, and the creations of several other individuals. These were complete with ceremonies that might include nudity and sexual relations among the coven members, which now looks rather dated. Meanwhile, Witches all over the world had been quietly going about their business, privately practicing the Craft. Suddenly, they and their children were not considered "legitimate" although they had not even sought recognition. A few writers of Witchcraft books made this distinction, and for a long time, there were people who actually believed that either there were no solitaries or family practices, or that if there were any, they were not "real" Witches because they had not been initiated by the leader of a recognized coven tradition. It has only been in recent years that the solitary Witch has regained recognition and acceptance within the established Wiccan community.

The village witch, hedge witch, cottage witch, and even the kitchen witch are all direct descendants of the Green practice of Witchcraft— the Old Religion. It can be considered irrelevant when some twentieth century coven traditions boast of a chain of initiations back to Gardner if you consider that there have been and still are practicing Witches all over the world who have never heard of Gardner, much less care about any initiation he might have wanted to bestow. I have heard from family tradition Witches who find the coven requirement of a chain of initiations for "legitimacy" as anything from amusing to rather insulting, but I have also heard from newcomers to the Craft who are confused about whether or not they must subordinate themselves to a coven leader in order to be a "real" Witch.

The notion of "real" and "unreal" Witches should not be a factor for the practice of the Craft, and it certainly does not relate to the Green elements of the Craft. The Witch is one who is united with the Goddess and the God, and that is a personal matter. This is rather like Christians differentiating among themselves between who is merely Christian and who is born-again Christian. Different, individualized approaches to the Craft are not encouraged when there is an attitude of exclusivity, and recent proposals of creating a Wiccan orthodoxy have resulted in a need for further introspection on the meaning and purpose of Witchcraft as a religious expression.

Core Traditions

The coven traditions of this century have certainly made a significant contribution to modern Wicca, particularly in the way of literature and ritual content, so that almost all Witches in westernized societies are familiar with such standards as the Charge of the Goddess and the Witch's Rede. How these coven formats affect the Green level is a matter worthy of consideration. The main items I have examined, which form the core of most modern Wiccan traditions, are the Wiccan Rede, the Charge of the Goddess, the Witches' Rune, and the Fivefold (and Sevenfold) Blessing.

The Wiccan Rede

> Bide the Witch's law ye must,
> In perfect love, in perfect trust.
> Eight words the Wiccan Rede fulfill:
> An ye harm none, do what ye will.
> What ye send forth comes back to thee,
> So ever mind the Rule of Three.
> Follow this with mind and heart,
> And merry ye meet, and merry ye part.

This has its origins with Gardner, but perhaps only in the rhyming of the ideas. The criticisms leveled at the pseudo-archaic language is one of those little things that annoy people about the Craft of today—it seems to be built upon a false foundation that was first presented as literally true, then re-defined as based on a real code, but finally accepted as the start of a new religious application that is just as valid as any other new creed. Yet, from my point of view as a historian and as one having a family heritage of Craft usage, I find it offensive that because the truth was not stated at the outset, it may now be completely lost.

The original implication that the Rede as written above was a secret passed down through the ages (and therefore "legitimate") and that Gardner was sharing this ancient secret with people has sullied the genuine underlying truths. Because my Brazilian mother and grandmother used the same ideas contained in the Rede, I am inclined to believe that Gardner based his writings and teachings on a genuine Craft guideline. Therefore, his innovation of creating a litany for the benefit of others who sought directions for experiencing the Craft themselves has been erroneously labeled as a new creed. From the Witch's perspective, it is much better for such articles of faith as the Rede and the Charge to be accepted as literary creations for a larger revival of the Old Religion than to pretend that these are the original ancient litanies. The Gardnerian tradition, as an example, then takes on no different an aspect than that of a contemporary Christian denomination like the Christian Scientists or the Universalist Unitarians. Accepting this as the case, only the stilted language employed may be an annoyance. Today, there are other versions of these litanies in wide use which are re-phrased in modern language forms, some better than others.

The deities of the Craft are not stuck in the seventeenth century, but I believe that the use of old language forms comes, for the most part, from a desire to emulate the style of the King James Bible (which is criticized as flawed by translators). The reason for doing so is the same reason the King James version has remained popular despite the newer, more accurate translations: the air of "legitimacy" wrought by time, not because it is right, but because it is old from a modern perspective.

My mother and grandmother were very practical people who considered themselves Catholics, yet they also held onto spiritist traditions. I learned the rules of magic in plain terms, but the Green elements may be expressed through the Rede without difficulty because the essence is drawn from the same source (except for the Threefold Return). In examining the Rede, I will compare it line by line with what I call the

Rules of Conduct, although my mother did not give these any title—she merely told me the rules repeatedly over the years. I can still hear her low voice patiently repeating the rules to me:

For "Bide the Witch's law ye must," she said, "Be careful what you do." For "In perfect love, in perfect trust," she said, "Be careful who you trust." For "An ye harm none, do what ye will," she said, "Don't use the power to hurt someone because—" for "What ye send forth comes back to thee," she concluded with, "what is sent comes back." ("Eight words the Wiccan Rede fulfill" and "So ever mind the Rule of Three" were not used.) For "Follow this with mind and heart" (which reflects the Green level use of magic), my mother stated simply, "To use the power, you must feel it in your heart and know it in your mind." For "And merry ye meet, and merry ye part," my mother told me that Grandmother admonished her, "Never use the power against someone else who has the power."

The "merry meet" line appears to be a poetic version (based on older language forms) of the code among pre- and non-Gardnerian Witches to respect one another. This implies to me that Gardner did have genuine Craft information to work with and had made an effort to compose it for general use. This is an element of relationships—if a person has the power (is a Witch) then that person is actively connected to the Divine, so another person so connected would be damaging their own power by working it against one so connected. Since my mother's background is different from Gardner's, it could be that the Threefold Return was a verbalization of this connection between the Witch and the Divine. By working against someone, the Witch could incur a return not only from the individual but also from the Lady and the Lord. The bottom line is that Witches do not perform magic against other Witches because the repercussions would be on the sender.

Should a student try to set one Witch against another (I know of such a case), the Witch will contact the other. Together they will share information and both will disconnect from the student. Usually this situation only arises if the seeker turns out to be not ready for instruction, perhaps because of immaturity or emotional instability. By withdrawing from the seeker, the Witch gives the individual time to mature or to get personal problems under control. There is not any real danger from discontented people throwing magic around in a fit of temper because the negative power always returns to the sender. The two Witches in the above scenario were not afraid for their own safety but rather for the welfare of the student, who was in danger of self-harm through a desire to have power over other people.

Because the Gardnerian version of the Rede is widely accepted in the Craft, it is an acceptable expression of a basic element of Pagan systems. Although I feel that the threefold aspect is reminiscent of an Aryan threat—severe retribution from the unapproachable God should the faithful deviate from the laws of the clergy—the fact that Gardner may have been a member of the Ceremonial magic order called the Golden Dawn might explain why he has this element in his Rede. The other possible interpretation of the Witch incurring a return from the Craft-connected recipient as well as from the Lady and the Lord makes this usage understandable on a more natural level.

The Charge of the Goddess

This first appeared in Charles Leland's 1897 book *Aradia, Gospel of the Witches*, and was lifted for part of the more familiar version found in Gerald Gardner's *Book of Shadows* and used throughout modern Wicca. Leland's "Charge" was later given a poetic ending by Gardner. The first section is written in the first person as from the Goddess herself, and tells Witches to meet in secret monthly, preferably during the full moon, to adore the spirit of the Queen of all Witches and there learn to work magic. To show they are really free from slavery, the Witches are exhorted to be naked, to "dance, sing, feast, make music and love" in her praise. This is a reference, then, to full moon Esbats rather than to Sabbats.

The problem with this doctrine is the time period in which it was written—the era of Victorian moral and societal strictness when secret societies flourished primarily as an escape from the oppressive social atmosphere. While the Charge is an instruction for freedom in life, it is also male-oriented, referring (as an example) to joy in the heart of man. Even with a Goddess voicing the Charge, the focus is on males, not females, and not both as equals.

Because the Charge is a product of its times, only the bits of generally accepted aspects of the Goddess (such as her giving knowledge of immortality, not demanding sacrifice, and being the mother of All) are relevant, and the rest, in stilted language, is already outdated. The second part of the Charge, which demonstrates Gardner's Craft connections, is more reasonable as it reminds the seeker that those who look for her outside themselves must first find her within, "For behold, I have been with thee from the beginning; and I am that which is attained at the end of desire." From the perspective of the Green level of the Craft, this is the only part of the Charge that is especially meaningful and indicates again that Gardner was incorporating an authentic Witch tradition.

The Witches' Rune

Used to raise power at a coven meeting by some traditions, and relating to Christian concepts of heaven and hell, the Witches' Rune does not appear to be a Green element. The references to the use of a sword and scourging also reveal this Rune to be Ceremonial in nature. Witches of the Old Religion did not have swords, and it is unlikely they practiced scourging. However, the latter inclusion could be related to nineteenth-century British tourism discovering the fresco scene at the Villa of Mysteries in Pompeii depicting as yet unidentified rites (although some Wiccans tend to attribute them to Dionysus and Arianna—Leland's Aradia, perhaps?). Having seen these particular wall paintings myself, I am more inclined to consider them related to the resurrection cult of Cybele and Attis. The entire Villa of Mysteries contains depictions indicating a cross-section of a number of diverse resurrection sects, from Isis to Dionysus to Cybele. This last one was very big in the Roman Empire from circa 150 B.C.E. until it was outlawed by Christian lawmakers in the time of Constantine. Scourging was also a historical aspect of convent life in some of the stricter Catholic traditions (there are paintings in Mexico of nuns praying as they walk in a circle with each nun whipping the nun in front of her).

The call of "Eko, Eko" is reminiscent of the call of the Bacchantes of Dionysus, "Evoa!" (from which may come the Latin word *evocare*, meaning to summon or evoke). The names added to the Rune are not Wiccan but are based on Ceremonial demons and archdemons (fallen angels who rebelled against God). To use the name of Lucifer as the brother of Diana (they were supposed to be Aradia's parents) and then say he was kicked out of paradise for his arrogance shows the unfortunate extent of this infiltration of Christian ideas into the Craft. Lucifer was actually quite simply the Roman God of the Morning Star, Venus. Here again is the androgyne quality that the early Christian Church hated, with Venus seen as both female and male depending upon whether it is the Morning Star or the Evening Star. Because the Morning Star equates to Lucifer, González-Wippler equates Lucifer to

Apollo, which is not far off as the typical parallel between the God and Goddess with the sun and the moon or Apollo and Diana.

The Fivefold and Sevenfold Blessing

I have already mentioned the Fivefold (and Sevenfold) Blessing in the sense of Victorian escapism, but there are some later variations to this Blessing which make it more balanced than the original. From this blessing comes the familiar expression among Witches, "Blessed be." This is often used as a greeting or as a farewell. The blessing can be accompanied with a hug and kiss, and/or anointing with oil. This is the Fivefold Blessing:

> Blessed be thy feet, that bring thee on this path.
> Blessed be thy knees, that kneel to the Lord and Lady.
> Blessed be thy womb, without which we would not be.
> Blessed be thy breasts, formed in beauty and in strength
> Blessed be thy lips, that speak (utter) the sacred names.

The Sevenfold Blessing begins by asking for a blessing from the Goddess, and adds a blessing for the eyes to see her path and for the nose to breathe in her essence. It drops the blessing for the knees, and changes the womb to the loins. Depending on the tradition, the blessings move from feet to lips or lips to feet.

The obvious problem with these blessings is that unless a generic form is used, only females are being blessed—presumably by a male priest. Again, this demonstrates the age in which these litanies were created, but that does not mean the Blessings should be discarded. The Blessings today vary between Craft traditions and practitioners. The central theme of blessing is found throughout ancient religions, and can be considered an appropriate expression of a Green element underlying the various systems.

One main difference in my approach to the Divine as learned from my mother is that there is no ritual kneeling before the Lady and the Lord—they made us to stand upright in their presence, and the Green altar of ancient heritage was apparently not a low one, but at a comfortable height to stand before. To determine what place any altar has in the basic level of the Craft, you only need to consider that even if it is an Aryan invention, it had to have come from a time when the Green elements were in use because high altars were used prior to the advent of those later Aryan faiths that tried to eliminate the natural (Green) level.

The Witch who focuses on the Green element may sit to meditate or to enjoy cakes and wine after a ritual, or kneel before a shrine in meditation if so inclined, but the knees ought not to be perceived as bending before the Divine if we accept that we are the Divine and the Divine are us. That is the key to being one with the All. The kneeling aspect is a holdover from Ceremonialism and the ritual Aryan distancing of God (as seen in the Catholic Mass, as an example). With my own practice, the body is being blessed (without the kisses) for while it has many independent functions (breathing, heart beat, nervous system, and so forth) it works with and contains the spirit of the Witch:

> Blessed be my feet, that take me on my path.
> Blessed be my knees, that support me before the Divine.
> Blessed be my abdomen, that gives me inner strength.
> Blessed be my breast, that holds my heart true to them.
> Blessed be my lips, that speak the secret names.

To this can be added:

> Blessed be my eyes, that see the beauty of their love.
> Blessed be my mind, that seeks their knowledge and wisdom.

The traditional greeting of "Merry meet, merry part, and merry meet again" came from the expectation that Witches were secure in each other's company ("perfect love and perfect trust" also reflects this certainty). They could not always say the same about other people. Since this Gardnerian form is a commonly used expression of a Green element of the Craft, I feel free to use it also.

Other Green Codes

It is unfortunate that so much fantasy writing depicts the practice of the Old Religion in terms of evil and good Witches attacking each other. This continuation in popular reading materials of presenting magic as something that leads to abuse and brings danger to innocent victims only serves to raise the level of paranoia and hysteria directed at the Craft and its devotees. There are many people who have no idea what the Craft is all about, and there is the danger of such tales being accepted as literal truth in substance rather than as simple entertainment.

Besides the commonly recognized rules of Witchcraft, my mother instilled in me other codes that can be found in the Green level of the Craft worldwide and even in the Pagan-based "superstitions" of Catholicism. The most important thing for a seeker to remember is that in Witchcraft, the practitioner is one with the All, so the rule most strongly emphasized is that the connection is there for positive or negative energy.

I remember my mother drilling into my consciousness that "If you say negative things, you will draw them." In our household we never were allowed to invoke "bad things," even when these were simply figures of speech. Any slip of the tongue was met with a sharp rebuke. But the lessons of childhood are well-learned, and this is one that will be most useful to the seeker in later years, for it is an exercise in self-control.

The other matter my mother was cautious about involves the negative drawing power of others who are not connected, but are careless. My mother referred to this as "bad eyes" and meant that someone was looking at another person with jealousy, envy, or simple spitefulness, and spoke things that were perhaps not intentionally mean, but had that effect. Other people have told me of similar warnings in their own families, but usually the ethnic background was Italian. I suspect that this is another Pagan superstition prevalent in the Catholic Church, particularly among Latin peoples.

The only way to know when the bad eye was being given was by the way you felt when the person looked at you or made a comment. My brother was in Vietnam, due to return home, and my mother had told an elderly neighbor how glad she was that he was finally returning. The neighbor, being crotchety by nature, commented, "Well, if he makes it." My mother immediately saw the negative power of those words and threw her own energies into lighting candles for his protection and called me to do the same. This may well have saved my brother's life, for on his departure he stepped on a land mine that failed to explode and then the helicopter he boarded was shot down, but he nevertheless made it home safe and sound. She kept the candle vigil going until she knew he was out of danger.

Normally, a word in return can negate the power of an ill-conceived remark. If the person is obstinate and does not want to let the remark be turned away verbally, then you may send the negativity back to the sender by making the sign of the horns (for the God) and visualizing the energy sent back through the horns of your fingers (index and little finger extended, rest curled into a fist). The best way to do this is to let the miscreants think they got the last word in, then send it back when they are not looking. The other option is to do a quick candle spell, or if the offense took place in your home, burn frankincense when the person leaves to cleanse the air of negativity. You may even want to open the front door and "sweep" out the negative energy with your besom after you have let the incense do its work.

Earlier I mentioned the Bacchantes, and I feel that the possible inclusion of their call and other aspects of the Cult of Dionysus in Wicca is significant. The reason for this is that much of the Green level came into the ancient European continent from the Indus by way of Asia Minor. The path leads around the Iberian Peninsula (Spain and Portugal) and into Western Europe, but also from Asia Minor across Greece and into Eastern Europe. Thrace is located in the Balkan Peninsula (Slavic lands) north of Greece, and the ancient, pre-Olympic deity of Dionysus was honored there as a Horned God of life, death, and rebirth.

The very name of Dionysus has been traced back to Shiva by several historians, particularly Alain Danielou in his book *Gods of Love and Ecstasy, The Traditions of Shiva and Dionysus*. The significance of this lies in that my mother and grandmother, Brazilians of Celtic-Iberian descent, used a Portuguese pronunciation of the Thracian Moon Goddess Bendidia (*Benedida*) in some of their spells. The connection between Celtic-descent Witches and Thrace is hinted at in Gardner's *Book of Shadows* and makes it clear through the common usage of these ideas even in Brazil that his Wiccan litany did have a basis in Witch practices, some of which had been affected by Christianity over the centuries.

One spell involving Benedida that I learned as a child was to recover lost items. When I complained to my mother that I could not find a toy, she showed me how to get it back (she presumed that it was "borrowed"). You can imagine my delight to watch her dramatically write the name "Benedida" on a piece of paper, crease it, wave it through the air and snap it closed. As she continued to wrap up the paper she solemnly intoned: "Benedida, I have you here and I will not let you go until you return the missing toy." She held the paper tightly in her fingers and then placed the wrapped paper carefully (so as not to let Benedida escape) under the leg of a heavy chair. Then she told me to look again for the toy. Needless to say, I was ecstatic when I easily found my toy. For several weeks, I gave Benedida a run for her money as I tried the spell over and over!

The other spell involving Benedida is a traditional one for New Year's Eve. We would sit at the dining room table with a cut-up pomegranate and strip of white paper folded lengthwise in half awaiting the chiming of the clock for midnight. With each chime we would take a pomegranate seed, bite it, say: "Benedida! Bring me money!" then lay the seed in the fold of the strip of paper and fold it over. It didn't matter if the clock beat us to the twelfth chime or not, the rest of the paper was then tightly folded up and tucked inside our wallets to remain there as a money-draw for the year.

With the second spell, the use of the pomegranate shows the relationship of the Moon Goddess (Benedida, or Hecate) helping the Earth Mother find her daughter, Persephone, as well as the association of the realm of Hades with riches. The first spell shows the relationship between the Moon Goddess and the fairy folk (who like to borrow things from the people they live around). I tend to view Benedida as a crone figure—rather like a grandmother—who is wise to the location of objects in any plane and traverses the regions of the Realm of Shadows.

Family Lore

As you can see by my examples, when you are living Green the lore is passed along according to need. Sometimes I got lucky and heard a story about a spell Grandmother did when Mother was a child. My mother told me about a time when she was a child and a friend of hers came to visit Grandmother because she had a terrible case of hives on her legs. Her friend told my grandmother that she had made fun of another little girl, and the girl had taken a mouth full of cornmeal and spat it at her legs. Afterwards, the hives appeared and itched beyond endurance. Grandmother was never called a Witch, mind you, but people knew who to see for spells and charms as well as for herbal cures. She told the child to get a pan of water and sneak up behind the girl who had spat the cornmeal, then dash the water at the girl's legs. My mother's friend did this, and the hives disappeared. In this case it was not a matter of finding a salve for the hives, but of negating an energy that otherwise would have returned to harm the girl that had sent it. Thus, my grandmother worked for the benefit of both children.

My mother was a source of Green Craft wisdom gently handed down to me as folk traditions without any name given. I realized much later that things we were doing were things other people said Witches did. The two times we found a nearly full-fledged bird fallen from its nest but unable to fly, my mother put it in a shoebox and fed it minced worms and water with an eyedropper until it was ready to fly away. When she would chide me for a wrongdoing that I was sure she could not have found out, she would tell me, "A little bird told me." And I never doubted her.

Although my grandmother always maintained an herb garden, my mother did not. Instead, she relied upon the magic of flowers. For security around the house, she would plant a variety called hen and chicks at the front of the house. If she wanted to move, she would plant bonina, a green bushy shrub with small, trumpet-like white flowers in which a single large round seed would form that could easily be harvested for spreading the plant. If you did not want to move, then someone else should give you this plant as a gift and you will stay put. Although my mother enjoyed one house we were in, she loved the bonina so much she planted it anyway. Sure enough, within a year we were moving again and she said she wished that she had not planted the bonina. This time she did not take the seeds along with her, and although she never planted bonina again, she continued to move around for many more years.

Mother stayed connected to the Lady through the working of the soil and the gathering and storing of the harvest. We once had a vegetable garden in one house that yielded quite a lot for canning; this was another passion of hers. At another house there were grapes to turn into jellies, and after another move, strawberries, raspberries, blackberries and vegetables. No matter where she lived, she always had green plants around the house to tend and they thrived under her care.

My father was always interested in the local plant and animal life wherever we lived, and I felt he was a naturalist at heart. So I collected plants and leaves to identify them and tape them to shirtboards for reference, or kept track of what I saw in my natural surroundings with the aid of bird, flower, animal, and sea life guides. It was my mother who taught me to set out milk for the fairies, but she was a little wary of the Other People. I generally set out milk on days when it seems appropriate, and wine or Irish Whiskey on full moons, and sometimes these days we will use amaretto or some other liqueur.

With the Green level of the Craft, the inclusion of the fairy folk is a natural extension since you are dealing with herbs and plant devas (energies, fairies). You can tell that you have attracted the fairies to your home when things disappear for awhile then turn up unexpectedly. They are very curious and will borrow things to use or to examine, but will return them in due time. Sometimes they will even leave gifts.

When my daughter was a child, she found a perfect little "teacup" made of stone. I told her to keep it safe as it was a fairy cup, and she did for many years. One day the cup simply disappeared from her room and she was very upset about it. I told her the fairies must have wanted it back and would probably leave something else for her. Sure enough, she soon found a pretty engraved golden ring that fit her finger exactly. I like to think that she has the Blessing of the Sidhe (pronounced "Shee"), the Other People.

Another aspect of Green awareness involves looking at the moon, the rising and setting sun, and the clouds on nearly a daily basis. When you get up early in the morning, go outside and look at the clouds in the early dawn. In the evening, watch the clouds as the sun sets. Often things will appear that others may not notice or consider "real," but for the Witch, everything is "real" in one form or another. I have seen black unicorns race across the sky and I have called upon the white unicorns to herd them away from where I live. These black unicorns are portents of negative energies racing to sow discord and storms where they have been drawn, but the white unicorns will come when called upon and chase away the black ones.

This is similar to seeing the Wild Hunt, the fairy host of the Lord of Shadows, racing across the sky. Danielou and Joseph Campbell relate this Celtic figure to tales of Dionysus and his wild entourage of maenads and the equally wild group (the "bhaktas," who Danielou links with the Bacchantes of Dionysus) that follows Shiva. To read the legends of both is to again see the transference of a common element from the Indus to Thrace and into Europe. I know when I see this apparition to note the direction in which they ride and avoid that place, for that is where their destination lies, and again, you can expect to hear about discord and storms from that area. Many people have become too sophisticated in the modern world to give any notice to the warnings and signs that are offered us. Some of this is due to Biblical scoldings against knowing the signs of the sky, but those injunctions were created specifically to undermine the practices of the times in which they were written. I am not the only person who reads the clouds and sees the Wild Hunt, but I mention these things here for the benefit of those who do so and would like a little confirmation that this is a normal Witchcraft practice.

The Witch who is focused on the Green element of the Craft frequently talks to plants and animals with the expectation that they will understand and respond. Part of living Green requires that the union between the practitioner and the rest of the earth is accepted. There is no room for fearfulness, doubt, or negativity regarding what nature has to offer, and from this comes the ability to feel the presence in all things. Divination of any type—looking at the clouds, moon, sun, stars, crystals, mirrors, cards, water, and so forth—becomes a daily activity that is a communication with all of nature and the Lady and the Lord. There is no dogma as this would limit the conversation and make it a script rather than spontaneous expression. The rules, such as they are, are practical guidelines for everyday living. The Craft is not meant to be a forum for self-promotion to a community of followers, nor is it a means of feeling important. By being part of the All, egotism is subdued.

In living the Craft, the practitioner is willing to teach anyone who sincerely wants to learn, but this is not a route to power and domination or fame and fortune. It is instead a way of life that brings peace and contentment in nature. The elementals form a part of each person as body, intellect and intuition, passion and energy, and the waters of life. Our contribution to all of this is our spirit, which is part of the spirit of the Lady and the Lord. We belong to our world and to our universe, and it is within us all. Because each person relates to the Divine individually, I do not feel that there can ever be an orthodox book of rules, litany, dogma, and rituals. Even the names of the Divine will vary from person to person as each Witch subscribes to a pantheon that has meaning to the individual. No belief is needed because the individual meets and communicates directly with the Lady and the Lord.

People can limit their scope by focusing on the Lady and the Lord in relation to the earth, or widen their view to see them as the united power that stands behind the very creation of our universe. The single entity called the "One Initiator" by Dion Fortune and described as "too ephemeral to define" by Marion Green is in fact recognizable as the Divine Androgyne aspect of the Lady and the Lord united. It is the 30,000-year-old image of Shiva Ardhanari (half male and half female) which then split apart to form the energy and matter of the universe and all that is within it. This imagery has been carried into numerous ancient cultures, and can be found in the modern Bible with its confusing reference in Genesis of "Let us make man in our image." The implication is that of a Dual Deity, and the word should be "humanity" rather than "man." The translation over the centuries has changed the word "side" into "rib" (Stone) so that the true first human of mythology was in fact an androgyne fashioned after the androgyne image of the Lord and the Lady in union, then separated for the sake of companionship.

Because the Green-level Witch is attuned to the tides of the energies of the Earth Goddess and Sky God, the celebration of Sabbats or even Esbats is not necessarily according to the calendar, but according to what feels right for the individual. The point to remember is that these celebrations are not done for the Lady and the Lord, but for ourselves. They do not need or require worship and offerings. You do not need rituals when you can simply let your own energies blend and flow with those of surrounding nature to communicate with the Divine. When you read about Craft practice, by all means try out different techniques and find out how other Witches do things, but always follow your own star and find your own path.

5

Magic

Magic is a basic part of the Craft, but it does not have to be the same as the religious aspect. In other words, Wicca may be considered a religion with a Goddess and a God that uses magic in a religious framework. Witchcraft may also have a religious application through the practitioner's connection with the Goddess and the God, but the magical practice itself may be religious or it may be a form of folk magic in which personal power is used in conjunction with natural objects to effect changes. This latter type of magical practice is what allows a person of any religious background to work magic without being Wiccan.

For some people, having the best of both worlds is being able to conduct spells while still being a member of a mainstream religion or without being committed to the Lady and the Lord. I practiced the arts of Witchcraft successfully for many years before I introduced myself to them in a self-initiation ceremony, followed later by a dedication to the Lady and the Lord. In this primary level of Green Witchcraft practice, I was sometimes associated with Christianity and other times I was unattached to any religious system, but always I could use the power through natural objects to effect magic from spells to divinations.

My maternal background made magic without affiliation with the Lady and the Lord an easy matter since both my mother and her mother were nominally Catholic and practiced folk arts. For them, the Lady was Mary and the Lord was Jesus, but they were Mary-oriented and had little to say about or to do with Jesus. The difference between them and me came about when I detached myself from the trappings of Christianity and became a practicing Witch. Even then, I was not a Wiccan because I put off the religious aspect of the Craft for many years.

Witch or Wiccan?

I see the Craft as functioning in three levels. Witchcraft can work as a folk practice under the cloak of a mainstream religion; it can be a practice of natural magic without reference to the Lady and the Lord; and it can be a religion in which magic can be practiced through union with the God and the Goddess. Today I can be called either a Witch or a Wiccan, but as I belong to no particular tradition I would use Wiccan only with reluctance. In that sense, I see Wiccan as not quite what I am; Green Witch or Green-level Witch is more to the point. In the Teutonic system I might be called Seidhr and I would not object, for that is the name for the practitioner of the Green level in the Northern system.

Scott Cunningham prefers the word *Wicca* and would question anyone who claimed to be a Witch to find out if the person meant "magician" or "devotee of the Goddess and the God" by the term. To me, the word *magician* connotes a practitioner of Ceremonial magic, which is neither Witchcraft nor Wicca. The Green-level Witch who is dedicated, then, performs magic through the Goddess and the God and through the elementals and the devas. When it comes to identifying yourself or your path, you need to decide if you feel Wiccan, Witch, or Magician is the better description.

The Pagan community today makes a distinction between Witch and Wiccan, but even the term Wiccan is fairly recent. The usage came about after a number of books had already been written on Witchcraft by members of traditions. The Witch's Sabbats have become merely the

Sabbats, but I have yet to see them referred to in print as the Wiccan's Sabbats. The word *Wicca* is considered masculine by some, and the word *Wicce* is sometimes used to indicate the feminine, but for the most part, the Craft as a religion is called Wicca and its practitioners are Wiccans. They may also call themselves Witches, so the terms are sometimes interchangeable depending on the magical and religious context, so it is a matter of personal choice.

The Practice of Magic

Candle magic is the most basic form of magical practice. It can be highly complicated, with the candle anointed with an oil that is scented by herbs to draw upon the power of the herb devas and prepare the candle to a magical purpose, inscribed, dedicated, and lit with some appropriate ceremony. Or it can be very simple, with merely a prayer and the lighting of the candle before an image or in a special place. For my mother, the lighting of candles before the image of the Goddess as described by Catholicism was the primary purpose for going to church. She did many of her candle magics in the incense-heavy and solemn atmosphere of shrines, but others were done in her home, sometimes before a beautiful, slender Thai image of Buddha that looked very much like an image of Shiva Mahayogi (*Great Teacher* or *Great Ascetic*, depending on the usage). These yogic images of Buddha, based on the earlier Shiva images, are an orthodox Vedic version of the Dravidic tradition. Nevertheless, I was surprised to discover at the end of her life that she had been familiar with Shiva since her youth and was thus pleased that I was drawn to this image of the God.

I have read in some guide books of the importance of doing a purifying bath and dressing in ceremonial robes before beginning a candle spell. I like to do this for a Sabbat or an Esbat, but under ordinary circumstances I have found that in actual magical practice the intuitive sense dictates what is necessary. There have been times when I felt I wanted to do a very formal spell and so I have done a ritual bath and dressed in ritual clothing, but there are times when magic is practiced on the spot or on the go, as it were. I might come home from the grocery store and suddenly have an urge to light a candle at the permanent altar. I never question intuitive impulses, but follow them through and feel the better for doing so. This is something that develops over time from practicing the Craft so that it becomes part of your everyday life. When you are comfortable in the Craft, things will simply come to you. Being a Witch doesn't mean hanging about all day looking portentous. Jeans and a tee shirt are just as appropriate for spell work as a ritual robe. For a Sabbat or an Esbat, the robe may still have to be set aside depending on where, how, and with whom you are celebrating (the Green level of the Craft may be family oriented, after all).

One of the first things I noticed when reading about the practice of magic is the number of injunctions given to people to watch what they eat: to avoid sugar, bleached flour, and meat, and to consume plenty of fruit and vegetables. This is sound advice for good health, but it really does not affect your magic ability if you like to eat things with sugar, bleached flour, or even meat. The key to all good health programs is to observe moderation in what you do. You may be an epicurean and still be a Witch. Indeed, the namesake for this facet of good living has been sadly maligned for centuries. The first name given by Christians to the Devil was not Lucifer, but Epicurus (this was not the practice or philosophy, but the man personally). Since being so identified in early Christian history, the philosophy of this man has been distorted and denounced to this day. He was an early scapegoat for the pious ascetics. Epicurus did not say that people should be hedonistic and overindulge themselves in all manner of extravagant eating, drinking and sexual behavior. He did teach that life is meant to be enjoyed, but all things in moderation lest the enjoyment fade. The same applies to Witchcraft. If you feel you are entering a severe religious order that requires self-depravation for magic to work, you are missing the picture. Enjoy your life without feeling guilty, but be responsible and exercise a healthy moderation in your enjoyment.

When doing magic that is a communication with the Goddess and the Horned God, the elementals, and the devas, spontaneity is part of the joy. The Green practice can be an ongoing connection once the dedication is performed, so there really is little point in making too much of dietary restraints. The Green level is not the same as Shamanism, which in its true expression requires the seeker to experience near-death fasting and exposure in order to better communicate with spirits. The original purpose of Shamanism was to help the sick by entering the spirit world to fight spirits of the dead over the sick and dying. This practice exists in some forms of Buddhism, but still is not quite the same thing as Witchcraft. Although Witchcraft and Shamanism share certain elements, as with contacting a spirit guide or a power animal, overall the focus of Green Witchcraft involves union with nature.

Native American Images and Magic

As a note of interest, there are many Wiccans who like to incorporate Native American imagery into their rituals—perhaps to reach something identifiable as "New World" or "American"—but I personally do not feel this is a proper connection to make unless a person is part of this heritage. The Native American people have a different, unique, and personal culture that most Americans can only romanticize or fantasize about, and to incorporate their motifs into Witchcraft always seemed shallow to me. I recently read an article by Andy Smith, co-founder of the Women of All Red Nations, in which she called such borrowings a kind of spiritual abuse and genocide to the Native American culture (*Feminist Bookstore News*). While her position is strongly against the use of Native American spirituality, the use of drumming, for example, is also very Celtic, and indeed the large, shallow, moon-like drum of both cultures (as well as North African) hint at a link to the ancient past of humankind. Feathers are also used in a variety of cultures, but when it comes to the appropriation of Native American spiritual themes into Wiccan practices, the effectiveness of this eclecticism will depend upon the practitioner. As for how a person expresses spiritual feelings, it really is not in the province of any one person to dictate to another what can or cannot be used.

Types of Magic

The other aspect of ritual and ceremony that is widely written about involves the type of magic used. The white Witch/black Witch (and sometimes gray Witch) concept evolved from applying Ceremonial uses of magic practice to Witchcraft, but these really are not applicable. If you are a Witch you do not send out negativity because it will simply rebound upon you. Anyone who claims to be a Witch and practices black magic is actually alluding to images based on mainstream religious concepts rather than Witchcraft. The dark side of nature is in balance with the light side in order for the natural world to function. This includes the Lord of Shadows, the Wild Hunt, Kali, the Dark Mother, and the Morrigu. A Witch does not fear the Dark because it is part of the Light. But to say one does black magic infers the practice of evil. Again, this is a mainstream concept that labels black as evil and white as good (and presumably gray as something in between). The Yin and Yang of Oriental systems is much more applicable to the Witch. To attempt to draw upon Darkness to harm another is simply not good karma, and not a "Witch thing." A Witch would not want to endanger his or her personal power with negativity. The Lord of Shadows is the one who gives us rest and cares for our dear ones who have passed on. The Dark Mother is the Lady leading us from this world into the next to rest before rebirth. A certain perspective is needed when it comes to describing magic.

The Components of Ritual Magic

1. Choose the timing of the spell.

2. Outline the ritual and prepare the tools and materials.

3. Purify yourself.

4. Purify the working space.

5. Create a sacred circle.

6. Have an invocation.

7. Perform the ritual observance.

8. Raise and direct energy.

9. Earth (ground) the residual power.

10. Take some refreshment.

11. Acknowledge the Lady and the Lord.

12. Release (farewell) the elementals.

13. Open the circle.

This may sound complicated, but it only reads that way. In practice, the whole process becomes as simple as a morning routine or having a friend over for a visit.

The Significant Circle

The circle is used to keep the power you are building up from dissipating, so you can focus and send it to perform the magical task assigned. Often there is no delineation of the circle except that which is envisioned, or the quarters of north, east, south, and west may be designated by candles, stones, or whatever nature provides. I have used pine cones, but usually there are objects that can be associated with all the elementals that can be placed around the circle. Although many people insist that all magic must be done in a circle for protection, the actual purpose is to gather and focus power. The idea of protection comes from the Ceremonialist practice of summoning demons (or angels, which can be equally dangerous, according to González-Wippler) and needing to keep them at bay.

If the living area is aspersed from time to time, blessed, censed and kept part of your practice, however, a natural, larger circle is built up. Like the advantage the kitchen witch has with being in close contact with the tools of the trade on a regular basis, spell work in the normal living area permeates the atmosphere and the furnishings so that it effectively becomes the circle. Again, the Craft is approached from the perspective of conversation and so the Divine, the elementals, and the devas may be addressed without the construction of a circle. The practice of working with a circle is recommended, however, so that the groundwork is properly laid until experience is built.

Magic Preparations

If the candle magic is something prepared for (rather than a spontaneous need) the spell plan and tools should be readied. The practitioner may bathe with an herbal mixture of rosemary, lavender, and thyme placed in a muslin pouch and secured with a tie-string in the bath water. Another combination of herbs that works well adds basil, fennel, and vervain to the other herbs already listed. I also like to burn a vervain candle close to the tub, but a white candle may be used instead of a scented one. This is a time to wash off the mundane cares and to center oneself. A relaxing herbal bath allows one to invoke the devas of the herbs and draw upon their powers while focusing on the unity of the individual with the earth, the Deities, and the universe. Robed or skyclad (nude) is up to the individual, and then it is time to cleanse the ritual area.

For this, a good besom is best. There are those who feel a besom of broom is needed, but for me this is unacceptable simply because I like to encourage the presence of the fair folk, and they abhor the odor of broom (as do I). As a result, straw brooms or grass brooms are fine for indoors, while in the wilderness, any leafy twig found on the ground will work well. Many stores and craft shops carry the old-fashioned "witch" broom made of straw or grass as a home decoration. Sweep the circle area with the besom from the center to the outer edges, moving clockwise (deosil) around the circle while envisioning and chanting that negativity is being swept out and the circle is being cleansed.

The easiest way to do candle magic is at a permanent altar or shrine, but if you need to set up an altar each time you work a spell, you may

A relaxing herbal bath allows one to invoke the devas of the herbs and draw upon their powers while focusing on the unity of the individual with the earth, the Deities, and the universe. . . This is a time to wash off mundane cares and to center oneself.

find the procedure as shown in Chapter 7 time-consuming. For any immediate need, it is unnecessary to go through a lengthy ceremony. Simply gather the tools and materials you will need, including a snack and cup of something to drink, cleanse the space, light the incense and candles, and go from there. The next step is to create the circle. With the athame or your power hand, point to the ground at the north and move in a circle to east, south, west, and back to north envisioning a blue light coming from the tip of the athame or your hand delineating the circle. You may want to say something along the line of:

> *This is the boundary of the circle, around me, through walls and floors, above me and below me as a sphere is the circle cast and consecrated to the Lady and the Lord that they may manifest and bless their child, whom they have named* (working name, or Craft name if you have not yet received your name from the Goddess and the God). *This circle is charged by the powers of the Ancient Ones.*

Call upon the elementals at the quarters and ask them to attend the rite, guard the circle (you don't want interruptions), and lend their aid. Greet the Lady and the Lord and welcome them to your circle.

The candle should be dedicated and inscribed to the Lady and the Lord by saying so and by using the athame to trace into the wax the runic letters of the Goddess (ᛒ) and the God (ᛋ). Then inscribe the letters that reflect your aim in the use of this candle. If runes are unacceptable to you (I use them as a kind of shorthand), the symbols of the Goddess and the God may be used instead, along with symbols that reflect your intentions. The Goddess is represented as the phases of the Moon:)O(and the God is represented with a circle and a semi-circle at the top to look like horns: ☿. Love could be a heart; luck a cloverleaf; strength a tree; happiness a smile; wealth a stack of coins; and health a caduceus (staff with 2 snakes entwined—it symbolizes the medical profession, so you would have to envision it as meaning good health). The color of the candle is derived from the color list in Chapter 3, and the runic equivalents are listed later in this chapter.

Anoint the candle with an oil of consecration (some recipes are in Chapter 6) and set it in a holder that will not catch fire. I sometimes use a small cast iron cauldron, or a votive holder that is a fired clay pot set upon a metal tripod. Whatever you use, remember that the holder itself will get very hot, so not only should you not touch it once the spell has begun, but the surface upon which it sets must also be protected. I have used anything from a thick wooden pentacle to a trivet, so it depends upon what you have available and what feels right to you.

As you perform the spell, you must envision the actions you take as leading to the completed goal so that by the time you have said all the words and added all the herbs to the candle's flame, the process is seen as accomplished, and your final words will show it as done. To raise the energy you may simply chant the spell, which may alter your breathing and be an additional way to raise energy, or chant and dance around the circle. The chanting and/or dancing continues until you feel the energy building up to a climax. When you feel it is time, send the energy to perform its task, then ground the residual energy by stooping down and placing your palms on the floor (or ground if outside) and letting the leftovers run out.

If you do not ground the energy you may feel nervous and agitated for several days, or you may feel suddenly dissipated and listless. To perform magic, you need to take care of your needs and not drain yourself of your own vital energies. Let the candle burn and take some refreshment—the "cakes and wine" ritual is good for this as it gives you a settled feeling. Although any kind of food and drink can be used, I like a corn muffin or multigrain biscuit with a zinfandel, golden chablis, or a fruity sangria, depending on the spell being worked.

When you have finished the refreshments, it is time to acknowledge the Deities, bid the elementals farewell, and open the circle. I like the rhythm of "Love is the law and love is the bond," but I sometimes say instead, "Through love are we bonded one to another; may that bond never be severed." The use of the word "we" can mean the practitioner and anyone else joining that day (if you are doing a spell for someone, as an example), but I use "we" to mean the Divine and myself have met here. I use either in my rituals, but each Witch may create a ritual that is personally meaningful. Even so, it is good to know some of the formats used by other Witches.

Hold the athame over the altar and say:

> **Lady and Lord, I am blessed by your sharing this time with me; watching and guarding, guiding and aiding me here and in all things. I came in love and I depart in love.**

Raise the athame in salute and say:

Through love are we bond one to another; may that bond never be severed. Merry have we met, merry do we part, and merry will we meet again. Merry meet, merry part, and merry meet again! The rite is ended, the circle cleared, so mote it be!

Kiss the athame blade and set it on the altar.

The elementals are blessed and farewelled at the quarters, with arms opened and wand in hand raised, then closed, then lowered at each point, and say:

Elemental Earth (then Air, Fire, and Water), depart in peace with my blessings, for we are kindred, thee and me, and though you leave, you are always part of me and I of thee.

Take up the athame and move widdershins (counter-clockwise) around the circle (north, to west, to south, to east, back to north) to open it. As you open the circle and say the following, envision the blue light being drawn back into the blade of the knife and into yourself (I like to conclude with the knife blade flat against my forehead to "seal" the energy within me) and say:

The circle is open yet the circle remains as its magical power is drawn back into me.

Let the candle burn for an hour, then put it out with a snuffer (rather than blowing it out) and watch to see how the flames go out. With herbs in a candle, there will often be sufficient flames that pinching out the wick is not recommended. Look at the melted wax and herbal residue to see what message is left from the spell. I have seen the flames turn into a blue, lightning-fast swirl that spun around the cauldron and zipped off into the direction the spell was sent before going out, and I have seen the results of the workings indicated in the remains of the candle. From this you can determine such things as when or how the spell will take effect. There are any number of possibilities, and while certain designs can be regularly interpreted in a particular way, the intuition of the practitioner is what counts the most in this (and any) form of divination.

Runic Tables

RUNE	MEANING	PURPOSE
ᚠ	wealth/good fortune/	prosperity/power/creative energy
ᚾ	physical health/vitality	strength/courage/health
ᚦ	protection/overcome resistance	protection/willpower
ᚨ	ancestor/the God	wisdom/healing power/ occult power
ᚱ	journey/quest/defense	decisions/taking control
ᚲ	purging fire/energy controlled	gift for skill/knowledge
ᚷ	union/power given & received	partnership/agreement
ᚹ	joy/comfort/blessing	happiness/success/peace
ᚻ	the unanticipated	protection thwarted
ᛁ	a need/constraint	defense/self-control/restriction
ᛁ	standstill	delaying defense/rest period/ stop slander
ᛃ	harvest/year's cycle	gestation/cyclical change/time
ᛇ	channeling	Otherworld communication/ dynamic & outgoing
ᛈ	evolving karma/hidden forces	sudden luck/discover secrets
ᛉ	protection	protection/shielding
ᛋ	sun wheel/wholeness	vital energies/centering
ᛏ	order/victory/success	justice/legal matters/success
ᛒ	Goddess/fertility	invoking/emotional stability/ new starts
ᛗ	trust/motion	safe journey/adjustments/ astral travel
ᛗ	self perfected	self-improvement/communi- cation/meditate

ᛚ	life energy/flow/water	aid intuition/influence/growth
ᛝ	God/fertility	invoking/completion/grounding/progression
ᛞ	breakthrough/twilight	between two worlds/invisibility
ᛟ	possession/ancestral power	status/invoking ancestors
ᚠ	good fortune	favorable outcome
ᚹ	love	to attract/express
ᛋ	Sun God	invocation/energy
	travel	productive journey

The following symbols are sometimes used along with the runes, and you may create your own symbols as you see fit.

	Divine in Union/wealth	invoke the Divine/attract gains
	orderliness	bring calm/order out of chaos
	healing	spiritual/physical health
	protection	protection of possessions by the elementals
	protection	protection of possessions by the Triple Goddess

It must be noted that the element of karma is very much in play with "the unanticipated" rune (), meaning that protection is thwarted. This rune is usually found in other books with the caution that it is not really to be used, but in the interests of knowledge and understanding, it is presented here. The idea behind it is to deprive an opponent of self-protections against your own magic, but this is a Ceremonial magic application and has no place in a Witchcraft whose power comes from the Lady and the Lord. Use it and your own protections would be blasted, so the net result by either a magician or a Witch would be the same: a dropping of your own magical defenses. To use this rune in this manner would be a violation of the Rule of Conduct, "Never use the power against someone else who has the power." Witches don't do magic against other Witches and again, the reason is based upon Karmic retribution.

For those who follow a Northern Path, the "ancestor" rune (ᚠ) is also the rune for Odin. But since Odin is not part of the Green level of Witchcraft, this meaning is irrelevant and is not used here. Instead, it is seen as reflecting the ancient wisdom of the Goddess and the God which is generally taught to their children intuitively. The rune is therefore useful in spell work for guidance in learning the Craft. The "/" in the meaning and purpose columns means that either meaning may be applied. There are individual runic colors, but I use the color relationships listed in Chapter 3. The purpose for using the runes is the key guide to choosing the appropriate color for the item on which the runes will be inscribed. The Celtic Ogham or other symbols drawn from a magical alphabet (Buckland offers several examples) may be used in place of runes.

Candle Magic

Candles may be used for offerings, meditations, communion with the Lady and the Lord, spells, divinations, or several of these uses combined. When herbs are added to the candles, they empower the use even more and aid in focusing and directing the energy sent by the practitioner.

Although a ritual format for candle magic has been given in this chapter, candles may be lit as a simple reverence: a kind of reminder to yourself that the Goddess and the God are in your thoughts, and you are in theirs. Sometimes we may become so wrapped up in the activities of daily existence that we forget to pause and remember the Divine around us and within ourselves. When this happens, I find that I have a sudden desire to "re-connect" and I light a candle at the altar. This sensation of wanting to re-connect comes from the need to refresh the bonds between ourselves and the Divine from time to time. The act of lighting a candle and saying a word or two such as, "I honor thee, Lady and Lord, and ask thy blessings upon me and mine," brings the body's energies back into focus. That is why I never question the desire to light a candle when I feel it because I understand intuitively that I have been too caught up in the mundaneness of life and need to remind myself of my connection with the Ancient Ones. It is a moment of physical pause and spiritual reflection, resulting in a feeling of well-being.

Once a candle spell is conducted, divination is the completion of the process by which the practitioner can determine when the spell will produce results or any other message pertinent to the spell work. The following list is an example of the kind of interpretations generally accepted for various images. These may be applied not only to candle magic, but any other workings that involve divination, such as tea leaves, clouds, and dreams. Again the intuitive perception of the individual is the most reliable and has precedence. As you gain experience, you will be adding to your own list of interpretations, but this list is meant as a starting point.

Symbolism for Divination

SYMBOL	MEANINGS
acorn	youth, strength, man, small start for large accomplishment
airplane	travel, new projects
anchor	voyage, rest, problem solved, security
arrow	news, disagreements, direct action
basket	gift, security, comfort
baby	new interests, security, new beginnings
bees (*hive*, *comb*)	fertility, industry, community, self-sacrifice
bell	celebrations, news (good or bad depending on other indicators)
bird	psychic power, flight, luck, friendship end, communication
boat	discoveries, travel, companionship
book	wisdom, learning
bottle	celebration, success
broom	Goddess, purification, healing, end of a problem, changes
bridge	crossing to new endeavors, transition, partnership, travel
butterfly	the soul, spiritual contact, frivolity, insincerity

castle	financial gain, security, inheritance, life of bounty
cage	isolation, restriction, imprisonment, containment
camel	long journey, need to conserve energy or goods, relocation
cat	wisdom, spiritual access, female friend, domestic strife
car	local travel, movement in business affairs
cauldron	Goddess, transformation, endings/new beginnings, vitality
candle	illumination, innovation, inspiration
clock	time indicated for a spell's completion, change
chair	relaxation, pause, comfort, entertainment
clouds	mental activity, thoughtfulness, problems, hidden obstacles
coffin	end of a matter, lengthy but not serious illness
clover	good fortune, success, rural location
cow	money, property, comfort, tranquility
cradle	newcomers, beginning of a new idea or project
crescent	Goddess, wish granted, newness, freshness
cornucopia	Goddess, abundance, fertility, prosperity, protection
cross	(Solar— +) God, nature works with power; (Roman—†) suffering, conflict
cup	love, harmony, close friendship, gift
dagger	complications, dangers, power, skill
distaff	creativity, changes, sexuality
dog	fidelity, friendship, companionship, faithfulness
duck	plenty, wealth, success
elephant	advice needed, obstacles overcome, good luck
egg	increase, fertility, luck, creativity, new start, hoarding
eye	introspection, awareness, evaluation, spirit
fan	indiscretion, disloyalty, things hidden, inflammations
fence	retention of possessions, defense, isolation
fish	riches, luck, sexuality, productivity

flag	warning, defensiveness, identification with group/ideals
flame, fire	purification, change, domination of the will
flower	marriage, unhappy love affair, passing joy
glove	protection, luck, aloofness, nobility, challenge
gate	opportunity, advancement, change, new directions
gun (*any type*)	power to gain goals, discord, slander, infidelity
hammer	hard work rewarded, building, creativity, fortitude
hat	honors, rivalry, independence, self-assertion
hound	advice, help given, companionship, trust
heart	love, pleasure, confidence, strength of will
harp	contentment, spirituality
horns	God, fertility, spirituality, forces of nature
horse	travel, strength, work, grace, power
horseshoe	protection, luck, start of a new enterprise
hourglass	caution, passage of time
house	security, authority, success, comfort
key	understanding, mysteries, opportunity, gain, security
kite	warning for caution, new ideas
knot	restrictions, marriage, bindings
knife	duplicity, misunderstanding, direct action
ladder	initiation, rise or fall in status, connections
lion	power, strength, influence, ferocity, pride, domination
lock	protection, concealment, security, obstacles, sealed
man	visitor, helpful stranger
mirror	reversal, knowledge, karma
moon	the Goddess, intuitive wisdom, guidance
mountain	hindrance, challenge, obstacle, journey, steadfastness
mouse	poverty, theft, frugality, inconspicuousness
mushroom	shelter, food, business complications, fairy contact
nail	labor, construction, unity
owl	wisdom, spiritual communication

palm tree	respite, relief, security, protection, blessings
parrot	gossip, flamboyance
peacock	luxury, vanity, baseless pride
pineapple	hospitality, good things hidden by harsh exterior
pipe	truth obscured, concentration, comfort, ease
purse	monetary gain, possessions kept close
ring	eternity, containment, wheel of life/year, wedding
rose	love, lost or past love, fullness of life, healing, caring
salt	purity, stability, cleansing, grounding
scales	balance, justice, careful evaluation
scissors	duplicity, arguments, separation, division, strife
shell	Goddess, emotional stability, luck, artistic ability
ship	travel, news, material gains, romance
skull	consolation, comfort, personal hurts, endings and a new life
snake	God and Goddess, wisdom, immortality, knowledge, prophecy
spider	good luck, industry, entrapments, secrecy, cunning
spoon	luck, sustenance, the basic needs of life secured
sun	the God, success, energy, power
star	good luck, divine protection, opportunity, success, destiny
swan	good luck, love, evolving beauty, noble spirit
sword	power, strife, conflict, overcoming adversity
tree	blessings of nature, good fortune, stability, power, security
turtle	fertility, security, defense against obstacles, slow gains
umbrella	temporary shelter, limited protection
unicorn	purity, nature, fairy blessings, Otherworld intervention
well	blessing from the Goddess, inspiration, spirituality, health
wheel	completion, eternity, season/life cycles, rebirth, gains
windmill	business dealings, factors working together for one goal

6

Magical Practices

A number of different magical practices involve herbs in the Green level of Witchcraft. Herbs can be used for health, comfort, treatments, and divinations. They are added to spells in charms, candle magic, oils, and incenses, and they are used in bulk for sprinklings, aspersions, and magic packets. In oils, herbs are used for consecrations, anointings, blessings, altars, and cleansings. All these uses may seem familiar to the practitioner of the Craft as they are Green elements that have been in the foundation of a number of Wiccan and Pagan traditions.

Divination Techniques

Divinations can take place in anything from clouds to cards. Some of the signs seen in clouds were mentioned in Chapter 3, but there are many others, depending on the occasion and the message. The practitioner need only feel attuned in order to interpret cloud formations.

Often the images will appear unbidden, and you may hear a voice within telling you the meaning of what you see. When you quietly express your interpretation of visions, do not be surprised to see the clouds suddenly change and the images look towards you, perhaps to smile or to nod in agreement. It is not unusual for Witches to see and hear things others might miss or ignore.

Divination with Tea

Tea Leaf Reading. Divination through tea leaf reading is relatively simple. The listing of symbols in the previous chapter can be applied to any divination, including tea leaves, dreams, clouds, and wax. For tea leaf reading, the person receiving the reading (the *querent*) drinks a cup of tea prepared from the loose leaves. Other herbal ingredients may be added to the tea to concentrate on divination, or any tea beverage is acceptable if the reading is more spontaneous in nature. If you are planning a divination by tea leaves, any of the following herbs may be added to the basic tea brew (but certainly not all together): anise (to call spirits), bergamot (for success), chamomile (for meditation), elder flower (for divination), eyebright (for mental and psychic power), hyssop (for purification), mugwort (for divination), mullein (for divination), and rose hips (for psychic power and divination).

For tea leaf reading, the tea should be placed loosely in a ceramic or china teapot. Bring cold water to a boil in a kettle and then pour it into the pot. After steeping for five minutes, the tea may be poured into a ceramic or china cup. Milk and sweetener may be added, if desired, for they do not interfere with the reading. Once the person seeking the divination has nearly, but not completely, finished drinking the tea, the cup on its saucer is handed over to you for reading the leaves in the residue at the bottom of the cup. I have read of different techniques, but the simplest is to place the cup in the palm of the left hand while holding it with the right hand, and swirling the tea three times clockwise. You may want to add a chant of your own creation, such as:

> *Swirl the leaves and set the tea,*
> *Clear and true this reading see,*
> *Lord and Lady stand by me,*
> *Guide my sight, so mote it be!*

Set the cup back in the saucer before the querent, handle to your right, and when the tea leaves have settled, examine them for symbols.

Sometimes the querent has a specific question in mind, and the reading may be related in this sense.

The Power of Tea. Drinking a soothing cup of tea prior to any magical working can aid in your spells and divination. While teas help to set the mood and relax the practitioner, they can also be used in connection with spell work and general health treatments. It is a good practice to keep a large stock of herbs and teas in the cupboard (away from the light) for creating your own tea combinations. A base of a black tea such as China, English breakfast or Irish breakfast is a starting point, and the herbs of your choice are added from there. The tea leaves and herbs are placed loosely into the pot and set near the burner while the water is heating to a boil. This allows the pot to warm up.

Sometimes I swish a little hot water in the teapot from the kettle and drain it out before adding the tea. Once the kettle comes to a boil, the hot water is poured over the leaves and herbs and steeped for three to five minutes, depending on how strong you like your tea. I have read of herbal teas steeping for an average of ten minutes, but I feel that is excessive unless you are using only herbs and no base of black or green tea. With a strainer in hand, pour the tea out of the steeping pot into the serving pot, and keep the latter covered with a cozy while you drink your tea. I recommend using two pots because if you leave tea sitting in the pot with the leaves, it will turn bitter and the acid will build up. Add milk (never cream: it will curdle) and sugar or honey to taste and enjoy. As with anything, moderation is needed as most teas have diuretic qualities and some herbal teas may affect the bowels or other organs.

By blending your own bulk teas you can draw upon the powers of the herbs towards a particular goal. The many combinations are tasty as well as beneficial in drawing the natural energies of the devas into your own sphere and infusing yourself with their magical properties to aid in your workings. This next section discusses magical (rather than medical) teas that may be used in a Green practice. The base tea is generally a black tea to ward negativity and to add strength and power to the magical tea blend. The practitioner should have a particular spoon to use for adding teas to the pot, generally of wood, and the type decided upon for the features of the wood. I use a spoon of oak to represent the God as the Green Man. Remember that it is probably not a good idea to exceed two or three cups of tea in one day, no matter how delicious it is.

Herbs can be used for health, comfort, treatments, and divinations. They are added to spells in charms, candle magic, oils, and incenses, and they are used in bulk for sprinklings, aspersions, and magic packets. In oils, herbs are used for consecrations, anointings, blessings, altars, and cleansings.

Magical Teas. Blend the teas for a recipe in a plastic baggie or glass jar, then measure out one tablespoon per cup of tea. A small two-cup teapot will take two tablespoons of tea. If you are like me, however, two cups of tea equates to three because I prefer my tea with a lot of milk. Because the tea base is black tea leaves, the addition of milk and a sweetener makes for a very flavorful beverage. Unless you are making tea for a crowd, you really do not need more than one or two tablespoons of tea at any one time. Store in a closed jar in a cabinet away from light.

Tea for Divination

1 tablespoon China black,
   English breakfast or Irish
   breakfast tea
2 teaspoons lemon balm

1 teaspoon eyebright
1 tablespoon mugwort
1 tablespoon rose hips

Tea for Psychic Healing

1 tablespoon China black tea
1 teaspoon elder flower
1 teaspoon nettle

2 teaspoons burdock root
2 teaspoons mullein
2 teaspoons rose hips

Tea for Love (Spells)

1 tablespoon China black tea
1 teaspoon damiana
1 teaspoon raspberry leaves

2 teaspoons chamomile
1 tablespoon mullein
2 teaspoons rose hips

Tea for Meditation

1 tablespoon China black
   or English breakfast tea
2 teaspoons chamomile

1 teaspoon rose hips
2 teaspoons elder flower

Tea for Purification

1 tablespoon China black tea
2 teaspoons fennel
1 teaspoon valerian

1 teaspoon chamomile
2 teaspoons hyssop

Tea for Relaxation

1 tablespoon English breakfast tea
1 teaspoon elder flower
2 teaspoons rose hips

1 teaspoon chamomile
2 teaspoons hops
1 teaspoon valerian

Tea for Health (Spells)

1 tablespoon China black tea

2 teaspoons fennel

1 teaspoon mint

2 teaspoons rose hips

1 teaspoon elder flower

2 teaspoons hops

1 teaspoon mullein

1 teaspoon white oak

Tea for Protection (7 Herbal Powers)

1 tablespoon Irish or
   English breakfast tea

2 teaspoons elder flower

1 teaspoon linden flower (tila)

1 teaspoon valerian

2 teaspoons burdock root

1 teaspoon comfrey

1 teaspoon hyssop

2 teaspoons rose hips

Personal Recommendations. Besides magical teas, there are combinations that are simply a pleasant way to re-connect with the earth devas, the Goddess and the God. For this type of quiet closeness to nature, you might want to try these tasty combinations of herbal teas:

- English breakfast, rose hips, and hyssop
- Linden flower and chamomile
- China black, chamomile, and rose hips
- English breakfast, dandelion root, rose hips, chamomile
- English breakfast, elder flower, hops, and rose hips

Experiment with the ratios and develop the taste you like. For a very silky tea, I particularly like:

1 tablespoon English breakfast tea

1 teaspoon comfrey

1 teaspoon rose hips

½ teaspoon chamomile

¼ teaspoon elder flower

Divination with a Crystal Ball

Another type of divination is accomplished with a crystal ball. Usually the image this technique brings to mind involves a pure glass ball, but actually, the procedure is better if there is a large bubble inside the ball. I have a lovely six-inch diameter ball of lead crystal that is a blue-green color and filled with little bubbles, including a couple of strands. It reminds me of the sea and the sky, but even in this collection of bubbles, there is one that I focus on for readings. The practitioner should be alert and focused. Do not let your vision blur as this interferes with the divination. Concentrate on the bubble and think about what you want to see.

The first time I used my crystal ball, it took awhile for the vision to come, but subsequent use makes it easier. Initially, you may notice that clouds or smoke may pass by your sight, but stay focused on the clear bubble inside the crystal or on the center of the ball if there are no bubbles. Blink when you need to, and do not strain yourself—divination is a lot easier than you may imagine. Let the vision come to you, and when it does, it will be clear and inside the bubble, moving like a motion picture in color. When I asked the Lady for aid in using the ball because my eyes are at different strengths, she told me to focus with my left eye. The benefit of doing this was instantly apparent as the divination unfolded before me. Both eyes were open, but the left directed the primary focus. If you find you are having difficulty seeing in the ball, this might be a helpful hint.

Prior to using the crystal ball, it should be dedicated and charged (empowered) with an herbal wash of mugwort made by pouring boiled water over loose mugwort (in a teapot, for example), letting it cool, then washing the crystal ball with it. There is a dedication ritual for tools in Chapter 7 that is used in conjunction with the wash.

Divination with Cards

Divination by regular playing cards or Tarot cards can initially follow a set pattern of interpretations, but after a little practice, you should be able to see images. Again, intuition is a very important aspect of a good reading, and requires the reader to be relaxed and open to communication. Cards in particular present events as they exist at the time of the reading, but the querent can take that information and use it to alter the depicted events. Often there are choices that can be made and outcomes that can vary according to the choices. I have done readings, however, where the events had already progressed to such a degree that the outcome was fairly conclusive. In situations like this, it is up to the reader to be caring and sensitive in what is revealed.

With one subject, the querent did not know she was pregnant, but the cards did. I told her the possible outcome if things went as they were shown, and because the cards reflected her personality so well, her actions did indeed follow the depicted course of events. The material conclusion was a pleasant one for her, gaining a husband, family approval, and a healthy son all as predicted, but unfortunately she now feared the occult and blamed the reader for the visions, as though I had been the cause of her pregnancy!

It is important to remind the querent that the reading shows how things stand at the present time, and that things can be changed to some extent. In some ways the cards provide warnings, in others they show possibilities, but there are occasions when they can only show what has already occurred and the path upon which the querent has already set foot.

Some people advise that one should never read one's own cards, but most of those I have heard this from seem mainly concerned about generating negativity into their lives. When I discussed this opinion with another reader, she asked how anyone could feel confident about reading for others while feeling uncertain personally. If a reader is concerned about influencing the cards in self-readings, how can that person be sure of not projecting personal influences into the readings done for others? I consider this fear to be a vestige of insecurity from religious injunctions against divination. We do not need to live in fear of our ability to communicate with the Lady and the Lord, and when we do our readings, we should always invoke their aid in understanding what lies before us. They are our divine parents and want to guide us, but will not impose themselves, so we must call upon them. By all means, read your own cards, but with an open mind and a positive heart, for even if you see troubles in the future, you will have been forewarned and may meet, avert or subdue them by taking appropriate action.

If you are uncomfortable with the idea of reading your own cards or are unable to be objective, then of course you should have someone else do it for you. In that case, you may have to try several readers before you find someone who can read meaningfully for you. The idea of being so psychically saturated that a person is unable to do their own reading for fear of influencing the cards seems to me to reflect an inability to have an objective reading, for whatever reason. If you feel that you cannot view things in a positive manner or see warnings that you can respond to, then do not read your cards until you feel your psychic balance is restored.

I have done my own readings and I have had others read for me (it can be very relaxing to have a reading done—like going to the hairdresser, but more rewarding). Whenever there is something negative in the reading, I use that as a message to direct some positive energy into an area of my life or the lives of those dear to me. There is nothing wrong with forebodings in the cards simply because things can be changed. The important part is to remember and trust in the loving connection you have with the Divine and the elementals. That being established, what have you to fear?

For playing cards, there are a few little misunderstandings perpetrated by ignorant dramatic presentations. The Ace of Spades is **not** a death card, but a warning of abrupt, emotional changes (not the same as the Ace of Spades in the Tarot deck—all those Aces are power cards). In the Tarot deck, the Death card is **not** what the label states, but indicates the end of one thing and the start of another. The Devil card of the Tarot deck shows the problem of Judeo-Christian influence, for it is actually the Horned God and does not mean temptation or evil influence, but natural blessing. This card shows that the querent understands and accepts that he/she is part of nature and has the spirit of the God within. It is actually a very beautiful and spiritual card indicating a oneness with the earth, but the God of Nature has become maligned as a scary-looking devil in the cards created by Ceremonial magic orders. This is most likely because of the Ceremonial connection to the Judaic magical tradition of the medieval Kabbalah. The Rider-Waite deck, created for the Order of the Golden Dawn, has been an immensely influential deck, and because it is the basis for a number of later Tarot decks, the misconception about the Horned God has continued.

Playing cards' suites are spades, hearts, clubs, and diamonds and basically reflect strength and adversities (spades), emotions and intuition (hearts), work (clubs), and the material aspects of life (diamonds). Nevertheless, the vision of the reader should not be held to a strict interpretation by rote format. These suites in their Tarot form are swords (knives), cups (cauldrons), wands (rods), and pentacles (dish, disks) and cover the same basic categories as playing cards. Plain cards use the royal figures as people in the querent's life, and many Tarot cards have taken this same interpretation, but the Tarot has more cards than the playing deck and the royals have other meanings, as well.

My favorite deck is Ellen Cannon Reed's *The Witches Tarot*, and although she does incorporate the Kabbalah, her deck can easily be used without this reference. All cards that are used for divination should be dedicated with a good incense (like frankincense) and a sprinkling of an herb (such as rue, betony, cinquefoil, burdock, elder, lavender, marigold, mugwort, or wormwood) selected by the practitioner. The herbs may then be dusted off and either burned (**not** wormwood) with the incense, dropped into a candle flame (consecration ritual), or placed inside the box where the cotton cloth-wrapped cards will be kept when not in use. The color of the cloth can be picked to agree with your particular focus, but black, yellow, and purple are common choices. Most of my Tarot cards (I have six different sets) are wrapped in black to ward negativity, but I also have a couple of decks wrapped in green cloths to emphasize the herbal connection with the earth and basic level of the Craft.

The Tree of Life Spread. Various techniques can be used to read cards. One that has worked well for me for over thirty years with playing cards is to shuffle the deck, then lay it on the table and have the querent (who may or may not be concentrating on a particular question) knock on the deck once. I say, This is now your deck, and I reshuffle the cards and deal the cards in what I call the Tree of Life pattern. This name and spread simply came to me as a sudden inspiration when I was fifteen and had never heard of the Kabbalah, but there are many such formats that are universal. The Tree of Life motif is seen in Sumerian artifacts and is part of the continuing Dravidic tradition of India, so I consider it likely that the Tree of Life is another of the Green elements that runs through modern Pagan expressions.

Seven cards are laid face down in a line left to right, which I call the branches of the person's tree. Under the middle (fourth) card the eighth and ninth cards are laid to form the trunk of the tree. Moving right to left, four more cards are placed in a loop (the tenth, eleventh, twelfth, thirteenth and fourteenth cards) and form the roots of the tree. In the center of this circle is placed the fifteenth card, which is the heart of the tree. The deck is played out by returning to the start and laying cards down in the same sequence until cards run out, totaling four cards in slots one through seven and three in the rest.

The branches relate to people close to the querent and extended parts of the querent's life—how the person touches other people and is touched by outside influences. The trunk shows the nature, attitudes, and strengths of the querent. The roots show the querent's beliefs, foundations, and personal interactions, and the heart shows the most important matter before the querent at this time. For a younger person, the heart may reflect events affecting the heart of the family—the supporting parent, for example. It is basically a divination that shows interpersonal relationships. With the young woman who did not know she was pregnant, I interpreted the card at the heart of the tree to be a baby. For another individual, I saw his father at the heart of the tree (in three consecutive readings) with an impending illness that would cause initial alarm but not be fatal (the father had a mild heart attack that night).

THE TREE OF LIFE SPREAD

| 1 16, 31 46 | 2 17, 32 47 | 3 18, 33 48 | 4 19, 34 49 | 5 20, 35 50 | 6 21, 36 51 | 7 22, 37 52 |

8
23
38

9
24
39

14
29
44

10
25
40

15
30
45

13
28
43

12
27
42

11
26
41

To make the reading, the cards may first be turned over one at a time in the sequence dealt, and the reading builds up from there. The cards are seen in relation to each other in each entire sequence, in relation to the other cards occupying the same position, and finally in an overall picture. Sometimes, however, I have felt a rush of visions and have turned over all the cards in sequence, fanning the multiple card stacks in their proper position. Then I could evaluate the entire picture at once and make my interpretation. Many times, the card you turn will relate to the next card and so forth, so if you feel you need the others face up to make a competent reading, follow your intuition. You may feel inclined to deal the cards out directly for divination rather than lay them out and turn them, and this works equally well.

I have also used Tarot cards for this spread, playing out the entire deck with three cards left over from which I may receive a final impression. The Tarot in this type of spread becomes meaningful through the impressions received from the pictures on the cards and the relationship between the cards. I have sometimes done two readings in a row with the complete Tarot when requested, only to find that the relationships have remained the same. For this kind of Tarot reading, the vision presented is more important than the usual meanings ascribed to the individual cards.

The Celtic Cross Spread. A card spread that is more typically used in Tarot readings is called the Celtic Cross or Celtic Spread, and features a circled Solar Cross with a single column to the right. The cards are dealt into ten places, and while many readers will allot one card for each place, I use the royal cards as modifiers (as does Ellen Reed) so that there could be two or three cards at any one spot. I also do not use a designator card since I consider this superfluous, so the first card is placed vertically in the center of the reading. The second card crosses the first. The third card (and this is another difference from most writings on this particular layout) goes at the base of the cross, the fourth at the left arm, the fifth at the top, and the sixth at the right arm. This is because we are actually making a circle around the Solar Cross (representing the God) that will lead off into the line at the right of the Solar Cross. The other method of laying out the cards emulates the Roman Catholic ritual gesture of making the sign of the cross. Ellen Reed also uses the Witch's Circle instead of the Catholic Cross when she lays out this spread. The seventh card forms the base of the column next to the Celtic Cross, and the eighth, ninth and tenth cards are played out in a row base to top.

The first card shows the current atmosphere or influences. The second card shows what events are currently arising from those influences. The third card shows past events acting as a foundation for the querent's present situation, and the fourth card shows influences that are passing. The fifth card depicts the querent's preferences, and the sixth card shows arriving influences. The seventh card relates to the general life of the querent, and here is where matters relating to family, friends, domestic life and employment may turn up. The eighth card shows the querent's strong points and advantages, while the ninth card shows the matters the querent worries about or aspires to most. The tenth card shows the conclusion of the matter being considered or the final outcome of the situation thus far depicted.

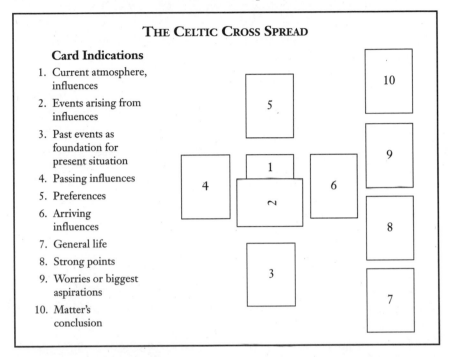

THE CELTIC CROSS SPREAD

Card Indications

1. Current atmosphere, influences
2. Events arising from influences
3. Past events as foundation for present situation
4. Passing influences
5. Preferences
6. Arriving influences
7. General life
8. Strong points
9. Worries or biggest aspirations
10. Matter's conclusion

The reading will depend upon what it is the person wants to learn. I have done general readings for a simple glance into the future to see how things are developing, and I have done specific readings relating to one question that was bothering the querent. The cards are meant for guidance, as an alternative way of stepping back from a situation and getting a new perspective. The readings are not the final word on events, but are used to offer possible methods for meeting a challenge or various routes to take in achieving a goal.

The cards of a playing deck have no up or down, but the Tarot can be read as upright or reversed, with the interpretation changing to fit the situation. One traditional method of shuffling the deck is for the querent to shuffle, then divide the deck face down into three stacks, right to left. The reader, sitting across from the querent, re-stacks the cards from the reader's middle, right, and left, and may then proceed to lay out the cards. Another variation has the querent shuffle, divide the deck face down into three parts, re-stack the cards middle, left, and right, and then spread the cards out in a line and randomly select the needed number of cards (such as ten for the Celtic Cross spread), placing each card face down in one stack. The rest of the deck is gathered up by the reader and set aside, and then the reader lays out the ten cards, turning each one over as the reading progresses from card one to card ten.

The method used is really immaterial, but it helps to be consistent in what you do. For example, some readers start with the top card of the stack as the first card of the reading, although it was actually the tenth card selected. Other readers will re-stack the selected cards so the first card selected is placed in the position of the first card read. This problem does not exist when the cards are not spread out for selection. Once you decide on a method, you should continue to use it to develop a clear reading style.

A basic explanation for the meanings applied to Tarot cards follows (the *R* indicates the reversed meaning):

Major Arcana (22 cards)

0	the Fool	innocence, enthusiasm, start of a quest; (R) the quest has been achieved, it is time to rest and decide on a new objective
1	the Magician	control over one's own destiny; (R) lack of confidence, hesitation
2	the High Priestess	intuition, seeking wisdom and meanings of mysteries; (R) knowledge received is tailored to suit one's ability to understand
3	the Empress	inspiration and competence, a project nears completion; (R) initial progress is slow, but one gains understanding
4	the Emperor	reason dominates; (R) vitality to take action to bring ideas to life
5	the High Priest (Hierophant)	spiritual truths and energy; (R) Divine guidance inspires actions
6	the Lovers	the greater perspective of unity results in trust and partnership; (R) appreciation of one's self worth allows one to reach out to others

7	the Chariot	establishing balance, control by willpower, project launched; (R) direction found and action taken with comprehension of goals
8	Strength	willpower, ability to overcome obstacles; (R) power tempered with kindness
9	the Hermit (Seeker, Wise One)	search for wisdom and enlightenment; (R) learning begins
10	the Wheel	(in some decks, this position is traded with Justice) destiny, seeking purpose, changes in life; (R) moving on to the next goal in life
11	Justice	fairness, virtue; (R) the reward is appropriate to the action
12	the Hanged Man	inner peace, suspended activity, wisdom not applied; (R) course of action decided upon, knowledge put to use
13	Death	change, end of one project and the start of a new one, casting off restrictions; (R) resisting change, self evaluation, teaching others
14	Temperance	balance, moderation, patience, trusting intuition; (R) emotion ruling reason, disharmony will end when unity regained
15	the Horned God (Horned One, Devil)	acceptance of harmony with nature; (R) bondage to form over substance, seeking spiritual freedom
16	the Tower	sudden change, old beliefs vanish with enlightenment; (R) self revelation
17	the Star (Stars)	opportunity, good prospects, hope, creativity, inspiration; (R) seeking creativity and success
18	the Moon	warning of deception, reflection of actions, trust intuition, (R) self denial, overcoming temptation, awareness of facades
19	the Sun	success, contentment, mental and spiritual growth; (R) success delayed, answer to problems discovered

| 20 | Judgement (Karma) | rebirth, atonement, potential fulfilled, appropriate reward received; (R) gaining knowledge from the past, learning from past mistakes |
| 21 | the World (the Universe) | achievement, union with the Goddess and the God, success, joy; (R) striving for greatness, seeking attainment |

Minor Arcana (56 cards)

The Aces are considered power cards in that what they express is done with great strength. The royal or face cards may be read at face value as depicting people whose personalities fit the description, as messages given with particular emphasis and possibly relating to particular people, or simply as modifiers of the next card. This last method is very rewarding and can result in a lot of detail about a subject. When using the modifier method in a spread (the Celtic Cross, for example) use the method of dealing the cards so that you deal from the stack rather than from ten pre-selected cards. Then, when you lay down a modifier card, place the next card beside it. If this is also a royal card, add another until you come to a non-royal card. Then read that place on the spread with all the cards now allotted to it. I have gotten some very precise readings using this method, and the Celtic Cross sometimes ends up with quite a few more than ten cards.

Wands (or Rods)

Ace	creative power, new beginning; (R) stagnation, decline
King	conscientiousness, plan is possible; (R) criticism, inaction
Queen	practical, concept formed, sincerity; (R) poor planning, envy
Prince	(Knight) journey, movement; (R) discord, plans change
Princess	(Page) completion, energy, message; (R) uncertainty
10	determination, fruition of plans; (R) difficulties, plans halted
9	pause, deeper awareness, readiness; (R) obstacles, delays
8	travel, quick action, learning; (R) deception, journey canceled
7	obstacles overcome, success; (R) dissipation of energy, doubts
6	triumph after difficulty, understanding; (R) vanity, disloyalty

5	conflict leads to change, renewal; (R) complexity needs caution
4	serenity, romance, stability; (R) dissatisfaction, disorganized
3	business success, negotiations; (R) end of trouble, fact-finding
2	fulfillment, forceful personality; (R) hollow gains, no growth

Swords (or Knives)

Ace	strength, power to achieve goals, action; (R) obstacles, inaction
King	authority, will and intellect, implementation of ideas decided; (R) tyranny, plans halted or methods undecided
Queen	determination, action taken; (R) impracticality, spitefulness
Prince	heroic, career, action begun; (R) ideas unformed, conceit
Princess	matter resolved, insight; (R) hindrance, cunning
10	misfortune, disappointment; (R) improvement through courage
9	worry, plans about to be realized; (R) deception, disgrace, doubt
8	indecision, actions require care; (R) improved health, fears end
7	creative action, frustration, artistic energy; (R) poor advice, postponement of plans
6	success after worries, journey, altruism; (R) hindrance, selfishness
5	force applied for good, courage; (R) empty gains, power misused
4	orderliness, rest, peace; (R) discretion in renewed activity
3	separation, strife; (R) regrets, confusion, need to understand
2	balance of opposing forces, harmony; (R) duplicity, wrong choices

Cups (or Cauldrons)

Ace	abundance, love, joy, inspiration; (R) emotional upset, delays
King	intuition, counselor, creative desire; (R) obstacles, immobility
Queen	nurturing, psychic, emotional ties; (R) emotional ambivalence
Prince	inspiration, opportunity; (R) fraud, unworkable ideas
Princess	emotional realization, artistic; (R) indiscretion, unfulfillment

10	contentment in home and family; (R) quarrel, loss of friendship
9	intuition accurate, self-satisfaction; (R) imperfect impressions
8	reason, old discarded for new; (R) continued effort leads to joy
7	gains in love, resolve, success; (R) fear of failure, delusion
6	loving acceptance, nostalgia; (R) resisting changes, egotism
5	anger, imperfections, useless regrets; (R) difficulties overcome
4	new possibilities, love, faithfulness; (R) apathy, discontentment
3	good luck, intuition takes form; (R) unappreciation, indulgence
2	balance, unity, strong intuition; (R) misunderstanding, delusion

Pentacles (or Dish or Disks)

Ace	material gains, growth, happiness; (R) immobility, empty wealth
King	sensible, worldliness, manifest ideas; (R) inability, corrupt
Queen	stability, culture, plans become reality; (R) neglect, delays
Prince	mature, responsible, implementation; (R) reckless, no gains
Princess	completion, study; (R) dissipation of energy, unrealistic
10	prosperity, stability, joy; (R) worries, changes, disruption
9	accomplishment, comfort, growth; (R) health cares, growth halted
8	increase by personal effort; (R) unambitious, vain, untrusting
7	gain by perseverance, goal achieved; (R) lack of achievement
6	gratification, wealth, sincerity, balance; (R) avarice, illness
5	loneliness, worries lessen by understanding; (R) relief, courage
4	endurance, security, materialism; (R) losses, fortunes reversed
3	work rewarded, goods acquired, pregnancy; (R) indifference, greed
2	effort for balance, energy to gain goals; (R) news, weakness

There are any number of books available on Tarot spreads, meditations, and even spells involving these cards. Card packs come with their own booklets of interpretations, most of which are fairly similar but may be focused on a particular viewpoint, such as the Kabbalah, Native American Shamanism, Wicca, Ceremonial Magic, Enochian Magic, and Greek or Egyptian Mythology. The practitioner, however, may find that certain images come to mind when looking at the pictures on the various cards, and this, rather than someone's booklet, is the best way to decide on interpretation. By lighting a white candle and burning a fragrant incense, the mood for divination is set and the images will likely flow.

Magical Practices the Herbal Way

Herbal Baths

Another facet of the Green element of the Craft involves the use of herbs in baths. This practice dates back thousands of years and is an excellent way to align the Witch with the powers of the herbal devas. The herbs infuse the warm water with their benefits which are then absorbed by the body. An herbal bath is ideally a magical experience affecting body, mind, heart, and spirit. Light a candle, burn incense, and let the scented waters work their magic into you.

For Peace

chamomile	hops
lavender	peppermint
rose	

For Energy

heather	lemon balm
rosemary	savory

For Comforting

calendula (marigold)	chamomile
lavender	mint
raspberry leaves	rosemary

For Relaxation

chamomile	dianthus
heather	jasmine flower
lemon balm	

Herbal Oils

Herbs are an essential part of the oils used in a Green practice of Witchcraft. Scented oils infuse the power of the herbs into an object or person and aid in creating a union of magical essence. Oils can be used to consecrate a magic tool and supply box, to aid in the empowerment of objects used in a spell, or to help open the practitioner to alternate states of awareness. The oils are generally applied with the fingertip of the power hand in the design of a pentagram (five-pointed, interlaced star), Solar Cross (an equal-arm cross representative of the God), or Spiral (representative of the Goddess). I like to use the symbols of the God and the Goddess together as this reminds me of the balance between them and me.

An anointing oil is used during the rituals of Sabbats and Esbats to mark the Solar Cross in a circle upon the forehead. This emblem marks the psychic center of the third eye and represents connection with the energy of the God. Consecration oil is used when dedicating Craft tools. Altar oil is used to prepare the altar for ritual and may be sprinkled with a sprig appropriate for the season, such as white heather at Imbolc, a stalk of wheat at Lughnassadh, or mistletoe at Yule. A blessing oil may be used for rites of passage, such as presentations, namings, handfastings, and passings. Cleansing oil is used to revitalize and refresh an area, purging it of any negativity that may have built up (this is particularly useful if there has been an unwelcome visitor or quarrels). To asperse a large area or one with furniture, a base of spring water rather than oil may be preferable to avoid accidental spotting. Spring water may be purchased bottled in nearly any grocery store these days.

The following examples of these oils are made by adding the ground herbs (use an electric herb grinder or a ceramic mortar and pestle for mixing the herbs as wood tends to absorb herbal oils) to a base of spring water, or an oil such as sunflower or safflower, and drops of essential oils. Bottle and store away from light. For other ideas and techniques on the various types of oils and ointments that can be created for specific magical purposes, I recommend Scott Cunningham's book *The Complete Book of Incense, Oils & Brews*.

Altar Oil

mix with mortar/pestle:	½ teaspoon rue
	½ teaspoon thyme
	½ teaspoon vervain
add:	3 drops oil of citronella
	1 drop oil of fir
	1 drop oil of rue
	2 drops oil of sandalwood
gently swirl with:	¼ cup spring or distilled water

You may asperse the altar with this oil using a white heather sprig.

Anointing Oil

mix with mortar/pestle:	1 star anise
	¼ teaspoon basil
	¼ teaspoon hyssop
	½ teaspoon rosemary
add:	3 drops oil of acacia
	2 drops oil of balsam of Peru
	1 drop oil of benzoin
	2 drops oil of rose
gently swirl with:	¼ cup sunflower or safflower oil

Astral Projection Oil

mix with mortar/pestle:	1 teaspoon jasmine
	1 teaspoon cinquefoil
	2 teaspoon mugwort
	1 teaspoon woodruff
add:	2 drops oil of acacia
	4 drops oil of benzoin
	3 drops oil of rue
	1 drop oil of sandalwood
gently swirl with:	¼ cup sunflower or safflower oil

Apply to temples, forehead, throat, pulse at wrists and inner elbows, back of knees, ankles, and soles of feet. You can also burn an incense of jasmine, sandalwood, or benzoin.

Blessing Oil

mix with mortar/pestle:	1 teaspoon lavender
	½ teaspoon rosemary
	1 teaspoon St. John's Wort
add:	2 drops oil of juniper berry
	2 drops oil of rose
	3 drops oil of vetivert
gently swirl with:	¼ cup sunflower or safflower oil

Cleansing Oil

mix with mortar/pestle:	1 teaspoon basil
	2 teaspoons rosemary
	1 teaspoon valerian
	1 teaspoon mugwort
add:	2 drops oil of balsam of Peru
	2 drops oil of benzoin
	1 drop oil of fir
	2 drops oil of lavender
	4 drops oil of rue
gently swirl with:	¼ cup sunflower or safflower oil

Consecration Oil

mix with mortar/pestle:	1 teaspoon fennel
	1 teaspoon tansy
	1 teaspoon rue
	1 teaspoon wormwood
	½ teaspoon yarrow
add:	2 drops oil of fir
	3 drops oil of rue
	2 drops oil of sandalwood
gently swirl with:	¼ cup sunflower or safflower oil

Spell Work Factors

The subject of spell work is a topic that has been worked over thoroughly in many books. Spells are generally done on a personal basis to effect changes advantageous to the Witch; however, there are times when other people will approach a practitioner of the Craft for assistance in attaining a particular goal. I have already mentioned payment and have described a few simple spells, but when it comes to important matters, there are certain dangers involved with working spells for other people. A primary difficulty is that a person must sincerely want the spell done.

I rarely do spells for other people anymore unless it is something I absolutely know that person wants. When my mother was dying of cancer the one thing she feared most was pain, so when she asked me to do a spell for her I had no qualms about doing so. Afterwards, the signs left in the two wax candles I used were a crescent moon in the candle before the Goddess and a sun symbol (a circle with a dot in the center) in the candle before the God. I read this as their blessing and the spell granted. My mother eventually passed on when her body deteriorated to where it could no longer function, but she never suffered pain and died peacefully in her sleep. This made me grateful that I had followed my inclinations early in life so that later I could be of help to someone I loved.

I have learned that people will say one thing and think another, and this will throw a spell off into a different direction. The result of asking for one thing but of mentally attaching conditions is that once those conditions are met, the spell will work, but not necessarily as the person originally wanted. I did a spell for a friend after giving her all the warnings of what can go wrong if she really did not want what she asked for. She assured me she would not stray from her determination, but of course she did. So the spell was cast, the divination afterwards showed the effect would take place within seven days, and in seven days her intended eloped with another woman. Her condition, she admitted later, was that she thought he should marry the woman of his choice. The spell simply moved him into action.

Timing Factors

The method I have used for determining the timing of an event comes from observing the spell remnants. With the above spell, I had used a red candle for the power of love and a marigold flower for marriage. When the spell was concluded and I was letting the candle burn for the remainder of the hour, a small hole appeared in the melted wax, which immediately began to bubble. The bubbles kept coming out of the little hole until the hole disappeared and in its place was a perfect little marigold flower done in candle wax. It remained there for the rest of the time the candle burned and stayed after I had snuffed the flame.

131

I do not move the candle holder around (in this case a small pottery cauldron), but use the directions as I face the candle to represent a clock face. North (top) is twelve o'clock, east (right) is three o'clock, south (bottom) is six o'clock, and west (left) is nine o'clock. The numbers on this imaginary clock face can represent hours, days, weeks, months, or years depending on the type of spell being worked. In this case, I was looking for some fast action, and when I saw the marigold form close to the one o'clock position, I could interpret that as one day or one week or one month, but I felt that one week was more likely, and that turned out to be an accurate assessment.

With other spells, the nature of the spell and the type of image or special occurrence located at some position of the laid-out spell is an indication of timing. In the case of the card reading I mentioned concerning the pregnant woman and her marriage, I accurately saw the month of the marriage and the month of the baby's birth because the cards presented visions to me of winter holidays with red and green tones that made me see December (she wed during Christmas vacation) and white and ice blue that made me see January (when the baby was born). So there are different ways to approach timing, but not all readings or spells are time-oriented.

Moon Factors

When performing a spell, the position of the moon is always a factor in your focusing:

waxing moon	growth and new projects
full moon	healing and empowerment
waning moon	releasing, banishing, and cleansing
new moon	divination

But if you need a spell now, and the moon is waning, think of it in reverse terms: instead of bringing good health, for example, think of cleansing yourself of the ailment; instead of drawing money, think of releasing poverty; instead of drawing love, think of banishing loneliness. Magic is a craft, a skill, and an art, and creativity in outlook will help you to be more flexible in your workings.

Precautions

What follows here are sample spells that have been used successfully, but like all magic, it is what you put into the spell that makes it work, not just a combination of ingredients. Remember, too, that every spell must be altered in some compatible way to make it your own. You need to address a specific need and work in an atmosphere that you find conducive to magic. Spells are generally cast within the circle, with the elementals and the deities on hand to add their power. Be sure you have blessed all those who have contributed to your spell work. When you gather an herb for a spell, leave a token gift.

The most important precaution is preserving yourself from unwanted karma by applying to your work the rules about negativity and getting back what you send. "Harm none" is still an excellent guideline. Although planetary astrology may not have been widespread in the Green-level practice, it may be used if it helps the modern Witch set the atmosphere for a spell that is planned sufficiently in advance. Prepare a ritual altar and circle before calling upon the elementals and the deities. Remember, too, that in the case of medical emergency or illness, seeing a doctor can be supplemented with raising positive energy to aid in your healing, but you do not want to ignore available medical help.

Runes

With runes, my usage is only as a type of shorthand borrowed from the Norse alphabet with generally accepted magical meanings attached. You could just as easily use Egyptian hieroglyphics, symbols of your own invention, or even spelled-out words in your own language. Scott Cunningham has a number of typical Wiccan symbols in his books *Wicca For the Solitary Practitioner* and *Living Wicca*, and I have already made a few other suggestions: the ogam of Celtic heritage can also be used for inscriptions, and *Buckland's Complete Book of Witchcraft* has several alphabets to choose from for magical inscriptions.

Health (I)

This spell is performed on a Thursday at the eighth hour after sunrise. Prepare in a dish an herbal powder consisting of 2 teaspoons lavender, 1 teaspoon thyme, 1 teaspoon allspice, 1 teaspoon coriander seed, and 1 willow leaf, saying to each as you do so:

> *I charge you by the sun and the moon to release your energy in my work!*

Prepare a light blue votive candle: inscribe with the symbols of Jupiter ♃ (or something that means health to you), the Goddess ☾, water ▽, victory ↑, the God ⚡, and healing energy ⟨, stating what each mark represents as it is inscribed. (Relate the elemental to the ailment: fire △ for fever, air ⊖ for sinuses, earth ▽ for warts, and so forth.) Rub lavender oil over the candle from top to bottom and back again and set in a heat-proof container on a heat-resistant surface before the Goddess image (or left side of altar). Light the candle and say:

I call upon thee, Great Goddess, to hasten my healing. Through this candle dedicated to health, inscribed with the symbols of the God and the Goddess, healing energy and victory over the watery confusion in my body, and with the herbs of healing whose energy may be released to my aid do I call upon thee. Cast aside my sickly imbalance I bid thee, that as I will, so mote it be!

Slowly add the herbal powder from the dish into the candle while envisioning the power of the herbs working for you as you say:

With the protective power of lavender, with the healing strength of thyme, allspice, and coriander seed, and with the protective and healing power of the willow do I infuse this spell with the power to work my will.

Let the candle burn until the liquefied wax is reduced by half, then snuff (with a snuffer) and as the wax hardens, interpret the signs or symbols left behind.

Health (II)

Arrange altar with ritual tools, bowl of water and bowl of salt. Light sandalwood incense and candles for the Goddess and the God (green and red or blue and orange) at the left and right sides of the altar. Anoint two yellow votive candles with rue oil and dedicate them to the healing of (name) in the names of the Lady and the Lord, (names you use), and through the elements as you name them:

Through the power of the Elemental Earth (sprinkle with salt), *through the power of the Elemental Air* (pass through incense smoke), *through the power of the Elemental Fire* (pass through the flames of both deity candles), *through the power of the Elemental Water* (sprinkle with blessed water) *this candle is dedicated to healing* (name).

Inscribe the candles with runic or other symbols for the Goddess ᛒ; the God ᛋ; protection ᚦ; victory ᛏ; healing ⚕ ; good fortune ᛖ ; healing by the sun wheel ᛉ ; love ᚹ ; and the God and Goddess and completion ᛉ. Place each inscribed candle in a heat-proof dish (votive holders are fine) on a heat-resistant surface. Light the candles, one from the Goddess candle (and set it in front of the Goddess representation, such as an image or symbol of the Lady) and one from the God candle (and set it in front of the God representation).

Add the following herbs into the flames of each votive candle, stating the action as you do it and envisioning the power of the herbs entering into the spell:

> *Ash bark for health and protection.*
> *St. John's Wort for health, protection, and strength.*
> *Tansy for health and the love of the Goddess.*
> *Woodruff for victory and the love of the God.*
> (Add here an herb for a particular ailment.)

Let the votive candles burn until liquid, and continue until it is reduced nearly to the bottom of the container. Snuff out the candles and look to see what signs or symbols are formed in the wax as it cools. **Never** hold the votive glass once the candle is liquid. It is very hot. Conclude as you would any ritual, blessing those who aided you and opening the circle.

Love

Can be performed the first Friday night of a full moon at 10 PM, or any Friday of a waxing moon at 8 AM, 3 PM, or 10 PM, but it will work equally well with any day and any hour. Again, do as you feel is right for you. **Warning:** Remember karma and free will, but this traditional spell just happens to work, and is useful to nudge someone into action.

This spell incorporates a mandala, or seal, which is an aspect of Green level practice used in Ceremonialism today. This is another of those universal elements of magical usage that can be found in the Indus, Babylonia, Native America, and China.

Set up altar and circle, calling upon the elementals and deities. Inscribe a red votive candle with runic or other symbols of your choice for joy ᚹ, victory ᛏ, the Goddess ᛒ, the God (and completion) ᛉ, love ᚹ , good fortune ᛖ , and union (sex magic) ᛉ. Be careful to copy this last one correctly if you use the runic symbol as you could end up with constraint, which will work against the spell!

On a square piece of parchment or red paper (a six-inch piece works well) draw two circles, one inside the other and inscribe it as follows:

zodiac sign of intended

planetary sign of intended

person's sign and planet

Place a small cauldron on the pentagram in the drawn circle. Set the red candle inside the cauldron, light it and say:

> *Red candle burn bright as* (name) *is possessed by burning love for me. Let* (his/her) *desire burn for me as nothing has been so desired before. Let* (him/her) *burn with love for me.*

(If you have some small thing of the intended's, you may drop it into the flame at this point and say, "This is (name) burning with love for me!")

Sprinkle into the candle flame ½ teaspoon yarrow and ½ teaspoon marjoram and say:

> *Bring the one I love to me and may the essence of these herbs incite* (name) *to love only me. One for love and one for marriage. Make two become one* (add a marigold flower to the flame). *So mote it be!*

Let the candle burn down (at least one hour) and check for signs. Put the candle out with a snuffer and let it cool. Remove the wax from the container, bury it in the earth and say:

Here goes the seed into the fertile soil, let the spell grow with naught to foil. So mote it be!

Money

This spell can be performed at 8 AM or 3 PM on a Wednesday, Thursday, or Sunday, symbolizing Mercury for skill and removal of debt, Jupiter for riches, or the sun for fortune and money.

Set up altar and circle, calling upon the elementals and deities, and use patchouli incense on the altar for the element of air. The herbs used are empowered by mixing them with the athame in a bowl and passing the bowl through the representations of the elements as you call upon them to charge the herbs with their power. Salt for earth, candle flame (the Lady and the Lord candles) for fire, incense for air, and blessed water for water.

The following herbs are combined and may be dropped into a green candle anointed with bergamot oil and then inscribed with symbols for the Lady ᛒ and the Lord ᛋ, victory ↑, good fortune ᚠ, prosperity ᚨ, wealth ᚷ, and completion ᛯ. Or, the combined herbs may be dropped into a simmering potpourri, such as are popular for scenting homes, and use a little candle underneath the pot to generate the heat.

1 teaspoon allspice (may be omitted for potpourri)
1 teaspoon bergamot
1 teaspoon comfrey
1 teaspoon chamomile
1 teaspoon cinquefoil
1 tablespoon whole cloves (may be omitted for potpourri)
1 teaspoon nutmeg
1 teaspoon mint
1 teaspoon marjoram

As the herbs are dropped into the hot water of a potpourri, say:

With the power of air is the spell carried, with the power of fire is the magic released, with the power of water is the will spread, and with the power of earth is the goal brought into being.

If using the candle method, drop the herbs into the flame and say:

With the power of air is the spell carried, and with the power of fire is the magic released.

With finger tip, dip into the bowl of altar water, let a drop fall into the melting candle wax of the votive, and say:

With the power of water is the will spread.

With the tip of the athame, take a bit of altar salt and drop it into the melting wax and say:

With the power of earth is the goal brought into being.

With wand in hand, move it in a circular motion three times counter-clockwise (matching the magnetic flow of the earth) over the pot or candle, direct the energy into it, and say:

Let this spell be spread into the air,
Grant that nothing may my work impair,
Bring success and wealth to me,
As this I spell, so mote it be!

Let the magic work for one hour, then snuff the candle and check the wax for signs and symbols. With the potpourri, put out the candle underneath and read the pattern of the herbs within as you would for tea leaves.

There are any number of spells the practitioner can construct from the basic elements of the Craft as presented in this work. Once you know the correspondences, you will develop your own feel for how to put a spell together. The above examples are meant merely to act as a guide for the individual, not as the end all of spell craft. Each person adds a little of their own personality into a spell and that is what makes it relevant and workable. In all things, ask for the guidance of the Lady and the Lord, and they will help you.

7

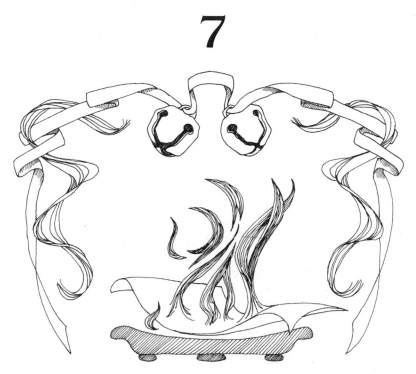

Green Rituals

The Green beliefs of Pagan traditions are rarely enumerated as such, although the recognition of this facet of Paganism is addressed in the northern tradition. The Green level of Witchcraft may be only a magical practice, in which case spells, divinations, and herbal lore could make up the sum of the Craft. But the Green level may also go beyond that to include a union with the Divine as Goddess and God, and with the elementals as extensions of the Divine and the practitioner. Green Witchcraft as a religion, then, presents basic concepts that are fairly standard in the practice of the Craft.

The idea of there having always been the One who is All is matched with the idea of All being from the One. This is pantheism as well as animism, and forms the core of ancient Pagan religions. The aspects of the Divine are considered separate and united as male, female, and both, and historically the Lord and the Lady have been depicted in various interchangeable or shared forms: Father Sky and Mother

Earth, Sky Goddess and Earth God, Triple Goddess and Wed to the Triple Goddess, Threefold God and Wed to the Threefold God, Lord and Lady of Greenwood, Lord of Abundance and Lady of Plenty, Queen of the Stars and King of the Universe, sun and moon, spirit and matter, life and passage, and cosmic dancers of energy and matter. The creative forces of nature are revered, with the Goddess and the God symbolizing the universal energies and materials from which comes all existence. The Goddess and the God are equal and omnipresent, for they are throughout the universe, the earth, and ourselves. Because it is the spiral dance of rebirth that brings us back to the source of our existence in the Goddess and the God, reincarnation is an accepted part of the religion.

Knowledge is the gift of the Goddess and the God so that we learn through our lives on earth and keep close to them. Magic is considered a natural means of working with natural energies to accomplish a goal, and this magic becomes infused as part of ordinary life to the practicing Witch. Although consciousness may be altered through visualization, meditation, ritual, music, and dance to better commune with the Divine and affect the magic, the communication is constant and altered states are not always necessary for contact with the Divine in nature.

Individual freedom and personal responsibility are also aspects of Green practice. Predestination or evil deities are not part of the religion, and are neither accepted nor blamed for the unpleasant things that happen in life. There is no orthodox liturgy, for the magic will naturally flow when we accept our oneness with the All and take responsibility for our lives.

Immanence, interconnection, and community are three core principles of Witchcraft. Because the Goddess and the God are manifested in all life, all existence is connected to be one living cosmos. The focus is on the growth of the whole through care for the earth, the environment, and each other. The mythology of the Lord and the Lady revolves around two themes: that of fertility and the passage of the seasons, and that of the life cycle which is often allegorically related to the changing of the seasons. Thus, the "sacrificed god" motif can be found in the corn (wheat) cycle, wherein the God willingly gives his life-force into the crops that humanity may be sustained. Yet this is also the motif of the "sacrificed goddess" as discussed in Joseph Campbell's *Primitive Mythology*, wherein the Goddess is mythologically cut apart and buried only to reappear as a life-sustaining crop, be it corn or coconut trees depending on the locale. In the most primitive societies, it is the Goddess who gives life. Mythology serves to relate the Divine to our lives.

The Triple Goddess is the maiden, mother, and crone (matron), whose consort is the Horned God, the creator, destroyer (hunter),and Lord of the beasts. All nature has both positive and negative aspects, and to be re-born, one must first die. The Goddess is seen as both life in her form as mother and death in her form as crone, yet both are the same. Death is a natural passage to new life and is not feared or labeled as evil. With nature there are both pleasant aspects and harsh aspects, but this is all part of the reality of the energy that flows in the earth, the universe, and the creatures of the earth, including humans. The transition from incarnation to incarnation is not feared, but understood.

Attuning to the Goddess and the God changes one forever and sparks new hope for the individual and for the planet. Fatalism is not part of Witchcraft, and the practitioner takes control of personal destiny. The dark aspects of the Goddess and the God as well as the bright aspects are accepted; they are both creation and destruction, abundant nature and destructive nature. Since all life is joined in the dual deity and to each other, life cannot be destroyed, only changed or moved into and out of the cauldron of life. Witchcraft as a religion is the worship or reverence of the life force represented in the dual deity as a conscious unity. This reverence may be expressed through ceremonies or rituals dedicated to cycles of fertility, planting and harvest, and solar and lunar phases.

The Green element of Witchcraft can be found in rituals of the full moon and new moon known today as the Esbats. These are times for communing with the Goddess and receiving learning from her. The Green Sabbats are composed of four solar festivals, and the White Sabbats are the four agricultural festivals. These eight Sabbats, along with the Esbats, form the main rituals. Twelfth Night can be celebrated as required or desired as either a Naming Day or time of re-dedication.

The names used to identify the Lord and the Lady depend on the practitioner, for they are one by whatever names they are known by, and they dwell within. They give life to be lived fully and with enjoyment, and we are reborn to learn until we are reunited with them. The Witch knows of the connection of all things, the immortality of life, and draws upon the power therein. In olden days such people were called Wise Ones, and the use of that wisdom was called the Craft.

. . . it is the spiral dance of rebirth that brings us back to the source of our exis-
tence in the Goddess and the God . . . Since all life is joined in the dual deity and
to each other, life cannot be destroyed, only changed or moved into and out of the
cauldron of life.

Rules of Conduct

The Rules of Conduct are stated as taught to me by my mother, with the exception of the use of the word "Witch" in the last rule. This is my interpretation of "someone who has the power." I did not invent these rules, but I have lived by them all my life. In practice, you may want to simplify things by remembering to harm none.

- To use the power, you must feel it in your heart and know it in your mind.
- Be careful what you do.
- Be careful who you trust.
- Do not use the power to hurt another for what is sent comes back.
- A Witch never uses the power against another Witch.

A Verbal Blessing of the Green Witch

Blessed be my feet, that take me on my path.
Blessed be my knees, that support me before the Divine.
Blessed be my abdomen, that gives me inner strength.
Blessed be my breast, that holds my heart true to them.
Blessed be my lips, that speak the secret names.
Blessed be my eyes, that see the beauty of their love.
Blessed be my mind, that seeks their knowledge and their wisdom.

Lesser Sabbats (Quarters)

Yule—(12/21) winter solstice
Ostara—(3/21) vernal (spring) equinox
Litha—(6/21) summer solstice
Mabon—(9/21) autumnal equinox

Greater Sabbats (Cross Quarters)

Samhain—(10/31) death/promise: end of the harvest season
Imbolc—(2/2) purification: preparing for the planting
Beltane—(5/1) fertility: planting
Lughnassadh—(8/1) bread: first harvest

The Altar

The Witch can practice the Green elements of the Craft alone, as a solitary; with a family group, in a family-style coven; or with others of like mind. The altar may be decorated according to the season and type of ritual, but the general setting is shown here. Add, subtract, or amend as you desire; I do with every ritual. There is no kiss or anointing involved in my use of the Sevenfold Blessing. The Blessing, the Rules of Conduct, and various activities may be incorporated as the practitioner sees fit (some ideas will be described in the individual Sabbat chapters). Although I have statues for my altar, candles or stones can easily be substituted.

I have several permanent altars in my home: two are centered around Shiva and Parvati, one is dedicated to Cerridwyn and Cernunnos (the statues may be purchased through mail order and the shop is listed in Appendix B), and one focuses on the Green Man and Hecate Triformus. Little shrines can be placed in any appropriate place about the house (I have one for Rhea as Snake Goddess) and can be dressed up for altar use.

GODDESS	BOTH	GOD
statue	candelabra	statue
statue	candle	snuffer
water bowl	censer	salt bowl
	—with handle or chain	
wine goblet	pentacle	incense
wand	cauldron	athame
bell	offering dish for cakes	bolline
supplies	Book of Rituals	supplies
—oils, herbs	—spell work materials	—matches, candles

The Circle

The circle serves to contain power and focus magic energy. Sweep the circle area with a besom clockwise (deosil). All circle movements start north, moving east, south, west, and back to north, saying as you do so:

As I sweep, may the besom chase away all negativity from within this circle that it be cleansed and ready for my work.

The circle may be large or small, delineated with a cord, drawn in the dirt, or simply visualized. The quarters of north, east, south, and west are defined by candles in heat-proof dishes; green for earth, yellow for air, red for fire, and blue for water. Have the circle candles and the altar ready prior to the ritual or ceremony, with the altar in the center of the circle so the practitioner faces north. Use the candle colors appropriate for the ritual (this will be specified).

Wear what feels appropriate—clothes, robes, jewelry, or skyclad. Prior to beginning the ritual, review what you want to do and have your tools ready.

Stay in the circle, or "cut" a doorway with the athame and seal the opening with the sign of the pentagram upon leaving and returning. If you really must leave the circle, remember your invited guests are there for you, and you should excuse yourself. Return as promptly as possible, otherwise end the ritual and begin anew at a better time.

An herbal bath prior to the ritual is recommended, and may include basil, fennel, lavender, rosemary, thyme, and vervain.

Use your "power hand" (usually the one you write with) in your work; for most people, this is the right hand.

"Mote" means "must" and either word may be used.

Basic Ceremony

Note: The basic ceremony is numbered for future references to the steps leading to and completing any ritual. The rituals are not numbered but should be followed in the order they are written.

When doing this ritual, have a flask or pitcher of wine or fruit juice on the altar to refill the goblet.

1. Sweep circle area; lay out circle and altar items; bathe and robe.

2. Light incense and altar candles (blue-white-yellow).

3. Ring bell three times (the bell and a striker are ancient tools of religion; Parvati is often depicted holding these items) and say:

   The circle is about to be cast and I freely stand within to greet my Lady and my Lord.

4. Take center candle (there are either three in a candelabra or one before each section of the altar) and light each candle of the circle moving north, then east, south, and west, and say:

(N) *I call upon light and earth at the north to illuminate and strengthen the circle.*

(E) *I call upon light and air at the east to illuminate and enliven the circle.*

(S) *I call upon light and fire at the south to illuminate and warm the circle.*

(W) *I call upon light and water at the west to illuminate and cleanse the circle.*

5. Take athame in hand, upraised, begin circle at north and move around the circle north to east to south to west, and say:

I draw this circle in the presence of the Goddess and the God where they may come and bless their child, (name).

Lower the athame at the north, and as you walk around the circle, envision a blue light shooting out from the point and forming the circle boundary, and say:

This is the boundary of the circle. Only love shall enter and leave.

6. Return to altar and ring bell three times.

7. Place point of athame in the salt and say:

Salt is life and purifying. I bless this salt to be used in this sacred circle in the names of the Goddess and the God, (names).

8. Pick up salt bowl and use tip of athame to drop three portions of salt into the water bowl. Set salt bowl back in its place.

9. Stir three times with athame and say:

Let the blessed salt purify this water that it may be blessed to use in this sacred circle. In the names of the Goddess and the God, (names), *I consecrate and cleanse this water.*

10. Take the salted water bowl in hand and sprinkle water from it as you move deosil around the circle (N-E-S-W-N) and say:

I consecrate this circle in the names of the Goddess and the God, (names). *The circle is conjured a circle of power that is purified and sealed. So mote it be!*

11. Return the water bowl to the altar and pick up censer; take it around the circle to cense it; return censer to altar.

12. Take anointing oil, make a Solar Cross ringed by a circle on your forehead, and say:

    I, (name) *am consecrated in the names of the Goddess and the God,* (names), *in this their circle.*

If working with family members or a Green-focused coven, open a door in the circle with the athame now for all to enter. Use anointing oil to trace a Solar Cross in a circle on their foreheads as each person enters, having said some kind of greeting, such as the Wiccan, "I come in perfect love and perfect trust." Then close the door with the athame. The text is for solitary use but may be thus altered for family or coven participation. The envisionings are suggestions only.

13. Take the wand, hold it aloft with both arms open and upraised at the north side of the circle (envision a powerful bull arriving) and say:

    I call upon you, Elemental Earth, to attend this rite and guard this circle, for as I have body and strength, we are kith and kin!

14. Lower wand, move to the east, raise up wand (see devas, fairies, or an eagle in flight) and say:

    I call upon you, Elemental Air, to attend this rite and guard this circle, for as I breathe and think, we are kith and kin!

15. Lower wand, move to the south, raise up wand (see a dragon) and say:

    I call upon you, Elemental Fire, to attend this rite and guard this circle, for as I consume life to live, we are kith and kin!

16. Lower wand, move to the west, hold wand aloft (see an undine, a sea serpent, or a dolphin) and say:

    I call upon you, Elemental Water, to attend this rite and guard this circle, for as I feel and my heart beats, we are kith and kin!

17. Return to altar and use wand to draw in the air above the altar the symbol of infinity (an 8 laying on its side), the sign of working between the worlds.

18. Set wand on altar, raise up athame in both hands overhead and say:

Hail to the elementals at the four quarters! Welcome Lady and Lord to this rite! I stand between the worlds with love and power all around!

19. Set down athame and pick up goblet of wine. Pour a little into the cauldron. This is a libation to the Divine in which they are honored by offering to them the first draught, then you take a sip. You may prefer to have a bowl specifically for the libation.

20. Ring bell three times.

Initiation/Re-dedication Ritual

Arms upraised, say:

Lady and Lord, (names), I call out to thee! I hold you in honor and know that I am one with all the things of the earth and sky. My kin are the trees and the herbs of the fields, the animals and stones through the seas and the hills. The fresh waters and deserts are built out of thee, and I am of you and you are of me.

Lower arms and say:

I call upon you to grant my desire. Let me rejoice in my oneness with all things and let me love the life that emanates from my Lady and my Lord into all things. I know and accept the creed: that if I do not have that spark of love within me, I will never find it outside myself, for love is the law and love is the bond. This do I honor when I give honor to the Lady and the Lord.

Kiss your right palm, hold your hand high, and say:

My Lady and my Lord, known to me as (names), I stand before you both and dedicate myself to your honor. I will defend and protect thy spark within me and seek thy protection and defense of me. You are my life and I am of you. I accept and will ever abide by the principal of harming none, for what is sent returns. So mote it be!

Grasp the goblet of wine, slowly pour the remainder of wine into the cauldron, and say:

As this wine drains from the cup, so shall the blood drain from my body should I ever turn away from the Lady and the Lord or harm those in kinship with their love, for to do so would be to break trust, to cast aside the love of the Goddess and the God, and to break my own heart. Yet through their continued love I know they would heal my heart and spirit that I might again journey through the cauldron of rebirth to embrace the love they freely give. So mote it be!

Dip forefinger into the anointing oil and again make the sign of the Solar Cross over the third eye (center of forehead). Then make the sign of the pentagram over the heart, followed by the Sacred Triangle (for the triple quality of both Deities) touching solar plexus, right breast, left breast, solar plexus.

For a Re-dedication Ritual, usually done at Imbolc and/or Litha, at this point you would proceed to Cakes and Wine. For the Initiation Ritual, continue with the following Call of Recognition.

Raise arms, open them wide, and say:

As a sign of my rebirth and initiation into the Craft, I take for myself a new name. As I study the Craft that I may be called Witch, I shall be known as (name). *Know now my name, my Lady and my Lord, and see me as this name and as part of you both. So mote it be!*

Lower your arms and meditate for a time on your new path begun and being in the Old Religion. Let your feelings flow from your body and let the touch of the Goddess and the God enter. Raise both hands high and say:

I am blessed by the Goddess and the God, known to me as (names), *by their attendance at my initiation! Know that I am your child,* (Craft name), *and receive me into your guidance!*

Refill goblet and proceed to Cakes and Wine. You could use white bread and strawberry jam and a light rosé wine for this part.

This ritual may be adapted for changing the Craft name, for adding a coven name, and for adding another Craft name. Some Witches have several Craft names for different circumstances and perhaps a coven name, but it is the working name that is never revealed as it defines the Witch and is a trust from the Divine.

21. **Cakes and Wine**—Ring bell three times. Feet spread and arms upraised, say:

    I acknowledge my needs and offer my appreciation to that which sustains me! May I ever remember the blessings of my Lady and my Lord.

22. Feet together, take up goblet in left hand and athame in right. Slowly lower the point of the athame into the wine and say:

    As male joins female for the benefit of both, let the fruits of their union promote life. Let the earth be fruitful and let her wealth be spread throughout all lands.

23. Lay down the athame and drink from the goblet. Replace the goblet on the altar and pick up the athame. Touch the point of the athame to the cake in the offering dish and say:

    This food is the blessing of the Lady and the Lord given freely to me. As freely as I have received, may I also give food for the body, mind, and spirit to those who seek such of me.

24. Eat the cake (or bread), finish the wine, and say:

    As I enjoy these gifts of the Goddess and the God, (names), may I remember that without them I would have nothing. So mote it be!

25. When all is finished, hold athame in your power hand level over the altar and say:

    Lord and Lady, I am blessed by your sharing this time with me, watching and guarding me, and guiding me here and in all things. I came in love and I depart in love.

26. Raise up athame in a salute and say:

    Love is the law and love is the bond. Merry did I meet, merry do I part, and merry will I meet again. Merry meet, merry part, and merry meet again! The circle is now cleared. So mote it be!

27. Kiss the flat of the blade and set the athame on the altar. Take up the snuffer and go to the north quarter, raise up arms and say:

Depart in peace, Elemental Earth. My blessings take with you!

28. Lower arms, snuff the candle, envision the Elemental Power departing. Go to the east, raise up arms and say:

Depart in peace, Elemental Air. My blessings take with you!

29. Lower arms, snuff the candle, envision the Elemental Power departing. Go to the south, raise up arms and say:

Depart in peace, Elemental Fire. My blessings take with you!

30. Lower arms, snuff the candle, envision the Elemental Power departing. Go to the west, raise up arms and say:

Depart in peace, Elemental Water. My blessings take with you!

31. Lower arms, snuff the candle, envision the Elemental Power departing. Return to altar and set down snuffer. Raise up arms and say:

Beings and powers of the visible and invisible, depart in peace! You aid in my work, whisper in my mind, and bless me from the Otherworld, and there is harmony between us. My blessings take with you. The circle is cleared.

32. Take up athame, go to the north quarter, point athame down and move widdershins (counter-clockwise) around circle (N-W-S-E-N). Envision the blue light drawing back into the athame and say:

The circle is open yet the circle remains as its magical power is drawn back into me.

33. When you return to the north, having walked the circle, raise up the athame so the blade touches your forehead and envision the blue light swirling around back into you. Return to altar and say:

The ceremony is ended. Blessings have been given and blessings have been received, and may the peace of the Goddess and the God remain in my heart. So mote it be!

Set down the athame. Put away all magical tools and clear the altar except for candles or any objects that need to burn out or work for a stated time (such as candle magic). The cauldron or libation bowl contents are poured onto the earth (if not out in the yard, then into a flowerpot containing soil and perhaps a hardy, leafy green plant).

Dedication Ritual

Sweep circle area. Lay out circle and altar items, which will include a piece of parchment, writing instrument, ink, and an extra white candle in a safe container (something you can handle without getting burned), a needle, and a dish of soil. Review this ritual, then bathe and robe. Light incense and altar candles (blue-white-yellow). Ring bell three times and say:

> *The circle is about to be cast and I freely stand within to greet my Lady and my Lord.*

Take center candle from altar and light each candle of the circle moving north, then east, south, and west, and say:

> (N) *I call upon light and earth at the north to illuminate and strengthen the circle.*
>
> (E) *I call upon light and air at the east to illuminate and enliven the circle.*
>
> (S) *I call upon light and fire at the south to illuminate and warm the circle.*
>
> (W) *I call upon light and water at the west to illuminate and cleanse the circle.*

Take athame in hand, upraised, begin circle at north and move around the circle north to east to south to west, and say:

> *I draw this circle in the presence of the Goddess and the God where they may come and bless their child,* (name).

Lower the athame at the north, and as you walk around the circle, envision a blue light shooting out from the point and forming the circle boundary, and say:

> *This is the boundary of the circle. Only love shall enter and leave.*

Return to altar and ring bell three times. Place point of athame in the salt and say:

> *Salt is life and purifying. I bless this salt to be used in this sacred circle in the names of the Goddess and the God,* (names).

Pick up salt bowl and use tip of athame to drop three portions of salt into the water bowl and set salt bowl back in its place. Stir three times with athame and say:

> *Let the blessed salt purify this water that it may be blessed to use in this sacred circle. In the names of the Goddess and the God,* (names), *I consecrate and cleanse this water.*

Take the salted water bowl in hand and sprinkle water from it as you move deosil around the circle (N-E-S-W-N) and say:

> *I consecrate this circle in the names of the Goddess and the God,* (names). *The circle is conjured a circle of power that is purified and sealed. So mote it be!*

Return the water bowl to the altar and pick up censer; take it around the circle to cense it; return censer to altar. Take anointing oil, make a Solar Cross ringed by a circle on your forehead, and say:

> *I,* (name) *am consecrated in the names of the Goddess and the God,* (names), *in this their circle.*

The following text is for solitary use but may be altered for family or coven participation. The envisionings are suggestions only.

Take the wand and hold it aloft, with both arms open and upraised, at the north of the circle (envision a powerful bull arriving) and say:

> *I call upon you, Elemental Earth, to attend this rite and guard this circle, for as I have body and strength, we are kith and kin!*

Lower wand and move to east, raise up wand (see devas, fairies, or an eagle in flight) and say:

> *I call upon you, Elemental Air, to attend this rite and guard this circle, for as I breathe and think, we are kith and kin!*

Lower wand and move to the south, raise up wand (see a dragon) and say:

> *I call upon you, Elemental Fire, to attend this rite and guard this circle, for as I consume life to live, we are kith and kin!*

Lower wand and move to the west, hold wand aloft (see an undine, a sea serpent, or a dolphin) and say:

> *I call upon you, Elemental Water, to attend this rite and guard this circle, for as I feel and my heart beats, we are kith and kin!*

Return to altar and use wand to draw in the air above the altar the symbol of infinity (an 8 laying on its side), the sign of working between the worlds. Set wand on altar, raise up athame in both hands overhead and say:

> *Hail to the elementals at the four quarters! Welcome Lady and Lord to this rite! I stand between the worlds with love and power all around!*

Set down athame and pick up goblet of wine. Pour a little into the cauldron. Ring bell three times. Address the Goddess and the God and tell them that you want to dedicate yourself to them.

Take your time in each phase of this rite, and feel free to create it from your own heart. What is presented here is only a sample which you may adapt to suit your own needs as your intuition leads you, but the four elements are invoked by your actions in the process of a dedication.

Air—Make a promise to try to live up to your potential, open your mind to the Ancient Ones, and develop your magical skills.

Fire—Light the extra white candle and then place it on the ground (floor) near you, but not too close (to avoid accidents).

Earth—Lie down on your back, close your eyes and visualize yourself sinking into the earth.

At this point things should start happening, but don't be alarmed. You will feel like the ground beneath you is in motion, and this is your signal to let all of your negative feelings drain out of you and into the earth below. The sensation may leave you feeling empty and you may even cry, but that should be expected. The symbolism here is that you are letting your body die and your spirit is moving into the Land of Shadows, and crying at parting is normal.

Water—Visualize the sacred waters of the earth—the seas, springs, and snow/rain, rivers—washing over you and cleansing your spirit. You are now floating in the waters of life, and you are at peace. When you are relaxed, you will feel yourself blessed with the water. The Lady may speak your new name at this point (although for me this came later, so if you hear no voice, after you have performed this visualization, just continue, but do not rush matters—take the time you need).

Spirit—Slowly move yourself into a fetal position and prepare to be reborn into the light. Sit up gently with your knees drawn up and your arms folded around them, and again, relax. Think about the God as fire, sun, hunter, and protector.

Visualize yourself being born into the light as you open your eyes and look at the candle. If you envision connecting lines to the quarters and center of this ritual—E,S,N,W,C—you can see that the infinity symbol has been created, so you are personally the gateway between the worlds.

Rise now and take the candle up with you and set it in the center of the altar. If you did not receive your name prior to your rebirth (as was the case for me), continue the dedication by closing your eyes and calling upon the Goddess and the God:

> **Great Lady and Great Lord, I call upon you to receive my dedication unto you. I, whom you have guided under the name of** (Craft name) **do ask you to give me a new name, one that is secret between thee and me. As parents name their children, so do I, as your child, seek thy naming of me. Tell me, my Lady and my Lord, what is my name.**

They will come and name you. The Lady showed me my name visually, pronounced it for me, and then, at my request (it was totally unfamiliar to me) spelled it out for me letter by letter. Later I looked it up in the dictionary, for it is a noun, and the definition matched perfectly the vision I was given of it. I treasure the name for the beautiful gift that it is, and the memory of the dedication is like a jewel that sparkles with an inner light.

Afterwards, you may ask for their secret names. If you forget to do this, you can do so at any time; the connection is now firm and is always there. The experience of coming face to face with the Lady and the Lord is such that you might feel too overwhelmed to engage in questioning of them. Still, you have but to ask and they will reveal their secret names to you. This is for you alone—you do not share this with anyone, not even with other Witches. The Ancient Ones are giving you something like a private access line to them, a sacred trust, and while others may have received the same names, if you spread this gift around, it is a breach of trust. Do not be swayed by someone saying it is okay between Witches to reveal names given to you: it is not, and this could be a clue to you that you have experienced a wonder someone else has not.

Now acknowledge receipt of their gift, open your eyes, and write on a piece of paper your promise (which you composed and spoke earlier under "Air") and word it with your new name:

> **I** (working name) **do make my promise...**

Kiss the paper and burn it in the flame of the extra white candle. Pull out a few of your hairs and burn them in the flame. With a clean needle or the tip of your athame or bolline—you can sterilize it in the flame—prick the little finger of your left hand and squeeze a few drops of blood onto the earth. If you are indoors, have a little dish of soil which you can later empty into the yard or use a flower pot if you have no yard.

Some people may object to the use of even a few drops of blood in a ritual and may want to substitute something else, but as I see it, by the time you have met the Lady and the Lord, it is unlikely that you will want anything to come between you and them. The tokening of hair and blood is an ancient custom that indicates the seriousness of your pledge. A dedication is not something done lightly or as a matter of form, but is done with a sincerity of heart and purpose to experience fully a new way of life. I cannot guarantee that anything less than the intimacy of your own sacred fluid is acceptable, but you can always ask them if they will take a substitute and if so, what. My feeling is that they have given us our bodies (symbolized by hair) and our lives (symbolized by blood) and that if we are to be one with them, we must be expected to give as we receive. This is the Law of Return on a personal relationship. The hair is earth, the blood is water, the promise is air, and the flame they enter is fire. By dedication to the Lady and the Lord, you are kith and kin to the elementals as well. They are personified through you and it would be hard to consider them as impersonal forces after such a union. The working name is **never** revealed as it *defines* the Witch and is a trust from the Divine.

Cakes and Wine—Ring bell three times. Feet spread and arms upraised, say:

> *I acknowledge my needs and offer my appreciation to that which sustains me! May I ever remember the blessings of my Lady and my Lord.*

Feet together, take up goblet in left hand and athame in right. Slowly lower the point of the athame into the wine and say:

> *As male joins female for the benefit of both, let the fruits of their union promote life. Let the earth be fruitful and let her wealth be spread throughout all lands.*

Lay down the athame and drink from the goblet. Replace the goblet on the altar and pick up the athame. Touch the point of the athame to the cake in the offering dish and say:

This food is the blessing of the Lady and the Lord given freely to me. As freely as I have received, may I also give food for the body, mind, and spirit to those who seek such of me.

Eat the cake (or bread), finish the wine, and say:

As I enjoy these gifts of the Goddess and the God, (N and N), *may I remember that without them I would have nothing. So mote it be!*

When all is finished, hold athame in your power hand level over altar and say:

Lord and Lady, I am blessed by your sharing this time with me, watching and guarding me, and guiding me here and in all things. I came in love and I depart in love.

Raise up athame in a salute and say:

Love is the law and love is the bond. Merry did I meet, merry do I part, and merry will I meet again. Merry meet, merry part, and merry meet again! The circle is now cleared. So mote it be!

Kiss the flat of the blade and set the athame on the altar. Take up the snuffer and go to the north quarter, raise up arms, and say:

Depart in peace, Elemental Earth. My blessings take with you!

Lower arms and snuff the candle, envision the Elemental Power departing. Go to the east, raise up arms, and say:

Depart in peace, Elemental Air. My blessings take with you!

Lower arms and snuff the candle, envision the Elemental Power departing. Go to the south, raise up arms, and say:

Depart in peace, Elemental Fire. My blessings take with you!

Lower arms and snuff the candle, envision the Elemental Power departing. Go to the west, raise up arms, and say:

Depart in peace, Elemental Water. My blessings take with you!

Lower arms and snuff the candle, envision the Elemental Power departing. Return to altar and set down snuffer. Raise up arms and say:

Beings and powers of the visible and invisible, depart in peace! You aid in my work, whisper in my mind, and bless me from the Otherworld, and there is harmony between us. My blessings take with you. The circle is cleared.

Take up athame, go to the north quarter, point athame down and move widdershins (counter-clockwise) around circle (N-W-S-E-N) and envision the blue light drawing back into the athame, and say:

The circle is open yet the circle remains as its magical power is drawn back into me.

When you return to the north, having walked the circle, raise up the athame so the blade touches your forehead and envision the blue light swirling around back into you. Return to altar and say:

The ceremony is ended. Blessings have been given and blessings have been received, may the peace of the Goddess and the God remain in my heart. So mote it be!

Set down the athame. Put away all magical tools and clear the altar. The dish of soil with the blood drops and the contents of the cauldron or libation bowl is poured onto the earth (if not out in the yard, then into a flowerpot containing soil and perhaps a hardy, leafy green plant).

Rites of Passage

Besides the Esbats, Initiation/Re-dedication, and Dedication, there are other events in a Witch's life that are celebrated with festivities other than the eight Sabbats. These are called rites of passage and include Presenting or Wiccaning (when a newborn is presented to the coven or to the Deities); Naming Day or Coming of Age (a rite of puberty), Handfasting or Jumping the Broom (marriage); Handparting (divorce); and Passing into Summerland or Crossing the Bridge (a memorial service for the deceased).

In a coven setting there are generally prescribed formats for these rites, but in a solitary tradition the observances are much more subject to individuality. Even so, a rite of passage is usually added into the Sabbat or Esbat ceremony, with the actual wordings and actions planned by the people involved. In the case of a Handfasting, unless it is performed by an ordained priest or priestess of Wicca who has the proper licensing by the state (and more Wiccans are achieving this status every day), the ritual is not legally binding.

Unless the Priestess or Priest is licensed, the wedding couple must also have a civil ceremony in addition to the Handfasting if they want to enter into a legal status of matrimony. The ramifications of wedded legality affect such things as income taxes, inheritance, insurance, and community property, so you need to be aware of the type of official qualifications of any Wiccan Priest or Priestess officiating a Handfasting. With a Handparting, a civil court must be involved for a legal status of divorce to be entered into the records, otherwise, the marriage remains legal, which prevents a person from re-marriage and in most states means that a spouse is responsible for the partner's debts. In all cases of marriage and divorce, you need to work within the civil laws.

Wiccaning (Presenting)

For a Wiccaning, the newborn child is brought into the circle and presented to the Lady and the Lord. After step 20 of the basic ceremony, a parent may hold up the child and say:

>*Loving Lady and gracious Lord, behold the harvest of my love, named* (name). *Watch over and bless this child, bringing love and joy to all* (his/her) *days.*

One parent may now anoint the child's brow with oil in the Solar Cross within a circle. Then pat a bit of the salted water on the baby's head, pass the baby over the incense burner through the smoke, and say:

>*May the elementals cherish you and guard you. May the Lady and the Lord guide you and teach you. May you live and grow in harmony with the earth, the stars, and the unity of the Divine.*

Proceed to Cakes and Wine, and then to step 21 of the basic ceremony. Altar decorations may include flowers such as Baby's Breath and yellow baby roses. The food may include white cake and you may also have presents for the child that reflect the Craft, such as a quilt in a design of forest animals, a stuffed animal toy, etc.

Naming Day (Coming of Age)

The Naming Ceremony can be simplicity itself and need not take place during a Sabbat ritual. Any details you want to create will most likely work just fine. Some covens have this ritual, others do not. For a solitary practitioner, the family is more likely to compose the circle, and the child about to enter adulthood may be brought into the circle and led through a ritual that describes the life myth of the God and the Goddess and evokes the elementals. Then the child may be blindfolded and led on a quest to communicate with nature by the voices of the adults acting out roles of the Lord and Lady of Greenwood and their relationship to the elementals. The child may be guided to notice sounds and sensations in natural surroundings, and may be given some task to perform that will impart a sense of satisfaction or accomplishment. The child is led back to the coven site, the blindfold is removed, and he/she is welcomed into the circle as an adult. The new adult announces the chosen Craft name when being led through the Initiation ritual.

The family circle becomes in many ways a small coven, led by the parents, so it would be up to them to decide how to handle the ritual. The newly-named adult member of the circle may read the rite from the Book of Rituals. Ideally, there should be at least one male and one female in the family circle, but if not, it is easy to adjust the ritual to accommodate the reality. Waxing to full moon is usually the best time for this ceremony if not using Twelfth Night.

The child may be brought to a circle defined by the elemental candles with the altar set up and arranged inside. Gifts may be hidden under the altar. An adult (mother or father) may say:

> **This is my child,** (name)**, who is moving into adulthood and seeks entrance into the circle to stand before the Lady and the Lord.**

The other parent or adult may ask:

> **Do you come of your own free will to the circle?**

The child answers in the affirmative. The adult may ask:

> **Are you willing to follow the Path of Initiation?**

The child answers in the affirmative. The adult may say:

> **Let this child enter before the Lady and the Lord.**

The child is then brought into the circle, the circle is cast with the basic ceremony steps 1–20, but do not anoint the child. At this point the adults review the life cycle of the Lord and the Lady.

Adult female:

> **The Lord is born at Yuletide with the returning of the sun. The Lady and all the earth rejoices at his return.**

Adult male:

The Lady rests at Imbolc and prepares for the coming of the spring. Her son grows strong and plays the games of childhood.

Adult female:

Together they walk the fields and woods at Ostara, and all nature awakens as they pass.

Adult male:

With Beltane they sport and play, and all the land rejoices with life and vigor.

Adult female:

At Litha they are one and the promise of the harvest gives hope of sustenance to their children of the earth.

Adult male:

The Lord enriches the grain and gives his life for the creatures of the earth at Lughnassadh, yet the promise remains within the Lady.

Adult female:

With Mabon, the Lord and Lady give us of their bounty and the Lord moves into his dark realm where he offers peace and rest to those whose life's cycle is ended.

Adult male:

In Samhain the veil between the worlds is thinnest, and the Lady as Crone stands by the Lord in the Land of Shadows, yet still she holds the promise within her and we bide the turning of the wheel with her.

Adult female:

At Yule the cycle is renewed and the Lord returns with the sun. The wheel of the seasons is the wheel of life, and as the one turns, so turns the other. You are in the turning of the wheel.

Both adults (one may recite, the other may anoint the third eye, making the sign of the Solar Cross at the end of the recitation):

Blessed be thy feet, that take you on your path.
Blessed be thy knees, that support you before the Divine.
Blessed be thy abdomen, that gives you inner strength.
Blessed be thy breast, that holds your heart true to the Lady
and the Lord.
Blessed be thy lips, that speak the sacred names.

Note: Not secret names as this is bestowed by the Lady and the Lord at the Dedication, after which the blessing changes.

Blessed be thy eyes, that see the beauty of their love.
Blessed be thy mind, that seeks their knowledge and their
wisdom. (Anoint at third eye.)

The child is now blindfolded, the adults take up whatever they will need (such as bread and meat, a feather fan, and a candle and matches) and a doorway is cut into the circle for all to exit. This is done with the athame by cutting the circle to the left of you, up and over your head, and down the other side to the ground on the right of you. You should visualize this as a door, which you then push open and exit the circle, standing by the invisible door. Once everyone is outside, you close the door, and seal it with a pentagram drawn with the athame. When you return, you will work the pentagram backwards with the athame to unseal the doorway, enter inside and when everyone has passed through the door, you visualize closing it and reseal it with the sign of the pentagram drawn with the athame.

In determining the nature of the Coming of Age activities, the adults will consider how to make the most of their surroundings. In the ceremony, the child may be led to appreciate the four elements and their relationship with the Goddess and the God, with the parents (or other members of the circle) sharing or trading off roles. One adult may lead while the other dances around the child reciting a role, then swap places and continue like this until all is done. Lead the blindfolded child barefoot to the site of a natural water (river, lake, pond, sea, or spring). As you approach, you would demonstrate the elementals.

Earth—The female may say:

I am the Earth Mother from whose body you were formed.
Know me in the feel of the ground beneath your feet, in the
touch of the trees against your hand. (Guide the child's hand to touch a tree.)

The male may say:

I am the Lord of the Wildwood and the grain whose life fills the wilderness and gives you bread. Know me in the animals and the grain you eat, for all life consumes life. (Give the child a taste of bread and bite of a meat, like beef jerky—vegetarians may want to alter this to read: "Know me in the animals you protect and the grain you eat," and give the child bread and perhaps an animal friend to pet.)

Air—The male may say:

I am the God of the Sky whose breath gives you life. Know me when you inhale my essence. (Fan the child's face.)

Fire—The male may then say:

I am the Lord of the Dance, know me in the fire of the sun and in the energy that moves you through your life. (Here you could take the child by both hands and lead him/her in a merry, energetic circular romp, or you could move the child into direct sunlight and let the child feel it on his/her face, or if you carry a torch or light a candle, you could carefully wave it around the child so the heat could be felt.)

Water—The female may say when you reach the site:

I am the Goddess whose water of life flows through your body. Listen to my voice in the current of the (sea, river, lake, etc.). (Pause for the child to hear the sound of water.)

Spirit—The female may say:

I am the Goddess who is from the beginning of time and will be to the end of time. My power and my love brings forth the fruitfulness of the earth and all that are born thereof. (Kiss the child on the cheek.)

Move back to the location of the circle to continue the rite. It is important to remember that a child is not simply directed into the circle, but must decide to participate. There are Witches whose children follow their own separate paths and others whose entire family is Wiccan. It is the child becoming adult who makes the oaths and pours out the wine in the ritual of Initiation, but the parents may then perform the anointing. The new adult follows this by announcing the chosen Craft name, and they pause to let their feelings of oneness in the Craft permeate them. The parents may then perform the Call of Recognition which may be reworded for a Naming Day as follows:

> *We are blessed by the Goddess and the God, known to us as* (names), *by their attendance at this Initiation. Know that* (given name) *is your child,* (Craft name), *and receive him/her into your guidance!*

After this, the child is kissed by the members of the circle and given gifts of tools (such as an athame or bolline) and/or a token of the Craft (such as a conch shell or deer antlers). They proceed to Cakes and Wine together, and the new adult may now participate in the actions and food of the communion.

If you are limited to an indoor ceremony, the child could be led around the house, being brushed with a leafy tree branch, fanned, warmed by a candle, and taken to a sink or tub of running water. The Initiation that involves the Naming Day rite is traditionally held on January 6 (today called Epiphany or Twelfth Night) no matter what the moon, but I mention the waxing to full moon time frame since the Rite of Passage for coming of age can also take place around the child's thirteenth birthday or upon first menses.

Handfasting (Jumping the Broom)

This ritual may be inserted after a Sabbat but before the Cakes and Wine. Flowers for the altar may be according to season, favorite colors, and/or white. Have a besom against the altar, two wreaths of flowers (marigolds included) and decorate the wand with colorful ribbons (yellow and white or pink and pale green). Have a white pillar-style candle that may be decorated for the wedding, and a white satin cord on the altar. Although the Green form of the Craft is basically a solitary one these days, the wording may be adjusted for a group ceremony or a commemoration of a civil ceremony by the couple.

Ring the bell three times and say:

> *Today we are gathered for a Handfasting ceremony between* (names) *before the Lady and the Lord of Greenwood.*

The male partner may say:

Before the Lady and the Lord of Greenwood do I pledge to love and honor this woman, that we be in the image of the Divine, two who are one.

The female partner may say:

Before the Lady and the Lord of Greenwood do I pledge to love and honor this man, that we be in the image of the Divine, two who are one.

Either the officiating person or the two individuals hold up high the flower wreaths, one before each partner or each other:

The flowers of the field in the circle of life give testament to the joy of love and unity.

Place the wreaths on the heads of the partners. Take up the wand and hand it to the partners to hold together between them, then wrap the cord around their hands. They may say to each other one at a time:

With the wand of life do I pledge myself unto you in the bonds of matrimony. Let there always be joy between us as we live together in perfect love and perfect trust.

Remove the cord and place the wand on the altar. They may exchange rings, saying:

This ring is the symbol of the love and the honor I give unto you. With this circle do I bind myself to the one I love.

Together the couple lights the candle from the center candle of the altar and set it in the cauldron. The officiator may say:

Before the Lady and the Lord, before the elementals, before your friends and family are you now wed. Two are made one.

The bride and the groom now jump the broomstick as the besom is held on either side by a member of the circle (or laid upon two footstools). The officiator may say:

May the Lady and the Lord bless you and keep you both in their love. May they shower you with their bounty and may you bring forth fruit from the cauldron of life.

Ring the bell three times and proceed to Cakes and Wine, which is the wedding feast typical of most marriages. Traditional foods include a white cake, perhaps with a silver ring hidden inside as a Wishing Ring for whomever finds it (warn the guests so they eat their cake carefully), champagne (elder if you can find it), fruit and nuts (candied almonds), and a spread of various favorite foods. Maypole dancing ensues.

Handparting

A Handparting is done if there is no acrimony in the divorce, otherwise, the civil ceremony will have to suffice. This ritual is not a necessary one at the dissolution of a marriage, but if both parties are willing, it may help them to visualize the end of the relationship and still retain their bonds of friendship. The ritual may take place after step 20 of the basic ceremony, and is normally not done on a Sabbat. Because partings are an emotional event, a ritual must necessarily be simple.

Ring bell three times and say:

> *Today we are gathered to witness the parting of hands and shedding of the bonds of matrimony between* (names).

The couple stand together holding hands and the officiator may say:

> *Do you seek the parting of your hands that you may both live apart and yet remain as friends?*

The couple may say:

> *We seek to part our hands and live our separate lives by the love and the grace of the Lady and the Lord.*

The officiator takes both hands into his/her own and pulls the hands apart. The couple stands with hands at their sides, and the officiator may say:

> *This union is ended, but like all things, one ending is a new beginning. The wheel turns on and we turn with it. I call upon the Lady and the Lord,* (names), *to keep you both always in their love.*

Ring the bell nine times. Proceed to Cakes and Wine. I refer to males and females for suggested role playing rather than Priests and Priestesses because in the Green level, a Witch is a Witch, and all are equal before the Divine.

Passing into Summerland

Since death is seen in Wicca as crossing over to Summerland to rest until the next incarnation, the time is not so sad for the Witch as it is an expression of fond memories, letting go of any regrets, and well-wishing for the next incarnation. The ceremony may begin after step 20 of the basic ceremony. Have rue on the altar to burn and a white candle in a fireproof bowl.

Ring the bell three times and say:

Today I bid farewell to (name of deceased). *I remember the good times and the less happy times, for all life has both pleasant and unpleasant experiences. I release the negative and hold onto the positive.*

Light the white candle and say:

Like the flame of this candle will the memory of (name) *light up my heart and my mind.*

Take the rue, drop it slowly into the candle flame, and say:

As the rue burns, it takes away the power of any negative memories about (name). *I will treasure the good and put aside the ill.*

Raise arms upwards and say:

Great Lady and Great Lord, give rest and refreshment to (name) *that he/she may be brought into your love and journey again through the cauldron of life.*

Lower arms, ring the bell nine times, and say:

Farewell, dear (name). *My love and blessings take with you to your rest. May you soon rejoin the dance of life.*

Proceed to Cakes and Wine. Traditional foods for a memorial service include pomegranates or apples, raisin bread, pork dishes, acorn squash, and dark wine. If celebrating with others, this is the time to share memories and feast in the name of the deceased, for this is like a wake.

8

The Esbats

Preparing Your Altar

- Candles are blue-white-orange or green-white-red.
- Incense may be bay, sandalwood or frankincense.
- Have any spell work materials ready on the altar.

Full Moon Esbat Rite

Sweep circle area; lay out circle and altar items; bathe and robe. Light incense and altar candles. Ring bell three times and say:

> *The circle is about to be cast and I freely stand within to greet my Lady and my Lord.*

Take center candle (there are either three in a candelabra or one before each section of the altar) and light each candle of the circle moving north, then east, south, and west, and say:

(N) *I call upon light and earth at the north to illuminate and strengthen the circle.*

(E) *I call upon light and air at the east to illuminate and enliven the circle.*

(S) *I call upon light and fire at the south to illuminate and warm the circle.*

(W) *I call upon light and water at the west to illuminate and cleanse the circle.*

Take athame in hand upraised and begin circle at north. Move around the circle north to east to south to west, and say:

I draw this circle in the presence of the Goddess and the God where they may come and bless their child, (name).

Lower the athame at the north, and as you walk around the circle, envision a blue light shooting out from the point and forming the circle boundary, and say:

This is the boundary of the circle. Only love shall enter and leave.

Return to altar and ring bell three times. Place point of athame in the salt and say:

Salt is life and purifying. I bless this salt to be used in this sacred circle in the names of the Goddess and the God, (names).

Pick up salt bowl and use tip of athame to drop three portions of salt into the water bowl and set salt bowl back in its place. Stir three times with athame and say:

Let the blessed salt purify this water that it may be blessed to use in this sacred circle. In the names of the Goddess and the God, (names), *I consecrate and cleanse this water.*

Take the salted water bowl in hand and sprinkle water from it as you move deosil around the circle (N-E-S-W-N) and say:

I consecrate this circle in the names of the Goddess and the God, (names). *The circle is conjured a circle of power that is purified and sealed. So mote it be!*

Return the water bowl to the altar and pick up censer; take it around the circle to cense it; return censer to altar. Take anointing oil and make a Solar Cross ringed by a circle on your forehead, and say:

I, (name) *am consecrated in the names of the Goddess and the God,* (names), *in this their circle.*

If working with family members or a Green-focused coven, open a door in the circle with the athame now for all to enter. Use anointing oil to trace a Solar Cross in a circle on their foreheads as each person enters, having said some kind of greeting, such as the Wiccan, "I come in perfect love and perfect trust." Then close the door with the athame. The text is for solitary use but may be thus altered for family or coven participation. The envisionings are suggestions only.

Take the wand and hold it aloft, with both arms open and upraised, at the north of the circle (envision a powerful bull arriving) and say:

I call upon you, Elemental Earth, to attend this rite and guard this circle, for as I have body and strength, we are kith and kin!

Lower wand and move to the east, raise up wand (see devas, fairies, or an eagle in flight) and say:

I call upon you, Elemental Air, to attend this rite and guard this circle, for as I breathe and think, we are kith and kin!

Lower wand and move to the south, raise up wand (see a dragon) and say:

I call upon you, Elemental Fire, to attend this rite and guard this circle, for as I consume life to live, we are kith and kin!

Lower wand and move to the west, hold wand aloft (see an undine, a sea serpent, or a dolphin) and say:

I call upon you, Elemental Water, to attend this rite and guard this circle, for as I feel and my heart beats, we are kith and kin!

Return to altar and use wand to draw in the air above the altar the symbol of infinity (an 8 lying on its side), the sign of working between the worlds. Set wand on altar , raise up athame in both hands overhead, and say:

Hail to the elementals at the four quarters! Welcome Lady and Lord to this rite! I stand between the worlds with love and power all around!

Set down athame and pick up goblet of wine. Pour a little into the cauldron. This is a libation to the Divine in which they are honored by offering to them the first draught, then you take a sip. You may prefer to have a bowl specifically for the libation. Ring bell three times. Raise the wand in greeting, and say:

> *I,* (Craft or working name), *who am your child, stand between the worlds and call upon my Lady and my Lord,* (names), *to hold communion with me.*

Ring bell three times and say:

> *If it harms none, do what you will. Thus runs the Witch's Rede. Once more I affirm my joy of life and union with the Lady and the Lord. I honor the God and the Goddess,* (names), *for the favors they have bestowed upon me, and ask their blessings upon me.* (Instead of the Rede, you could say, "I acknowledge that what I send returns to me and conduct my Craft accordingly," or address your own thoughts.)

Set the salted water on the pentacle, hold the athame over it, and say:

> *Great Mother, bless this creature of water and of earth to your service. May I always remember the cauldron waters of rebirth and the many forms and beings of the blessed earth. Of water and earth am I.*

Hold water bowl aloft and say:

> *Great Mother, I honor you!* [You are showing your respect for the Lady and the element that represents her in this ritual.]

Replace the water bowl in the proper place on the altar. Place censer on the pentacle, hold athame over it, and say:

> *Great Father, bless this creature of fire and of air to your service. May I always remember the sacred fire that dances within every creation and hear the voices of the Divine. Of fire and air am I.*

Raise the censer aloft and say:

> *Great Father, I honor you!*

Return censer to the proper place on the altar. Raise the cup of wine aloft and say:

> *Power and grace; beauty and strength are in the Lady and the Lord both. Patience and love, wisdom and knowledge. I honor you both!*

Pour a libation into the cauldron and take a sip of wine. Stand at the altar, facing north, open arms upraised and feet apart, say:

> *Behold the Great Lady, who travels the sky; the stars shine around her and light up the night.*

Take up wand and say:

> *Lovely Lady known by so many names, but known to me as* (names), *with* (God's names) *at your side, honor and reverence I give to you and invite you to join with me on this, your special night. Descend, my Lady, and speak with your child, whom you have named* (name, if given a working name or Craft name).

At this time you may hear her speak something pertinent to you, or if you needed guidance on a matter, she will instruct you. Replace the wand on the altar. You may now do any spell work, divinations, consecrations, etc. at this time.

Consecration of a Tool

Tools used in the practice of the Craft may be consecrated to that purpose, although this is not a necessity, as any kitchen witch will attest. The tool is placed on the altar and should be used soon after consecration to soak up some energy from the ceremony. You should have a red candle on the altar that will be lit from the center candle representing both of the Deities, and also a bowl of fresh water (not salted).

Inscribe the tool with magical signs and runes indicating somewhere your Craft (not your working) name. Consecrate by the elementals (earth, air, fire, and water) by touching the tool to the pentacle; passing it through incense smoke; passing it through the flame of the red candle; and sprinkling it with water from the bowl, saying:

> *In the names of the Goddess and the God,* (names), *I consecrate this* (name of item) *to be used in my practice of the Craft. I charge this by the Element Earth* (touch the pentacle); *by the*

Element Air (pass through smoke)*; by the Element Fire* (pass through flame)*; and by the Element Water* (sprinkle with water). *This tool is now by powers bond to aid me in my work. So mote it be!*

With arms spread and upraised, say:

You are the Mother of All; Maiden, Mother, and Crone. You are at life's beginning and at its end. You dwell within us all for you are life and love, and thus do you make me life and love. With love are we united, one to another. So mote it be!

Cakes and Wine—Ring bell three times. Feet spread and arms upraised, say:

I acknowledge my needs and offer my appreciation to that which sustains me! May I ever remember the blessings of my Lady and my Lord.

Feet together, take up goblet in left hand and athame in right. Slowly lower the point of the athame into the wine and say:

As male joins female for the benefit of both, let the fruits of their union promote life. Let the earth be fruitful and let her wealth be spread throughout all lands.

Lay down the athame and drink from the goblet. Replace the goblet on the altar and pick up the athame. Touch the point of the athame to the cake in the offering dish and say:

This food is the blessing of the Lady and the Lord given freely to me. As freely as I have received, may I also give food for the body, mind, and spirit to those who seek such of me.

Eat the cake, finish the wine, and say:

As I enjoy these gifts of the Goddess and the God, (names), *may I remember that without them I would have nothing. So mote it be!*

When all is finished, hold athame in your power hand level over altar and say:

Lord and Lady, I am blessed by your sharing this time with me, watching and guarding me, and guiding me here and in all things. I came in love and I depart in love.

Raise up athame in a salute and say:

*Love is the law and love is the bond. Merry did I meet, merry do
I part, and merry will I meet again. Merry meet, merry part,
and merry meet again! The circle is now cleared. So mote it be!*

Kiss the flat of the blade and set the athame on the altar. Take up the
snuffer and so to the north quarter, raise up arms, and say:

Depart in peace, Elemental Earth. My blessings take with you!

Lower arms and snuff the candle, envision the Elemental Power
departing. Go to the east, raise up arms, and say:

Depart in peace, Elemental Air. My blessings take with you!

Lower arms and snuff the candle, envision the Elemental Power
departing. Go to the south, raise up arms, and say:

Depart in peace, Elemental Fire. My blessings take with you!

Lower arms and snuff the candle, envision the Elemental Power
departing. Go to the west, raise up arms, and say:

Depart in peace, Elemental Water. My blessings take with you!

Lower arms and snuff the candle, envision the Elemental Power
departing. Return to altar and set down snuffer. Raise up arms and say:

*Beings and powers of the visible and invisible, depart in peace!
You aid in my work, whisper in my mind, and bless me from
the Otherworld, and there is harmony between us. My blessings
take with you. The circle is cleared.*

Take up athame, go to the north quarter, point athame down and
move widdershins (counter-clockwise) around circle (N-W-S-E-N),
envision the blue light drawing back into the athame and say:

*The circle is open yet the circle remains as its magical power is
drawn back into me.*

When you return to the north having walked the circle, raise up the
athame so the blade touches your forehead and envision the blue light
swirling around back into you. Return to altar and say:

*The ceremony is ended. Blessings have been given and blessings
have been received, may the peace of the Goddess and the God
remain in my heart. So mote it be!*

Set down the athame. Put away all magical tools and clear the altar except for candles or any objects that need to burn out or work for a stated time (such as candle magic). The cauldron or libation bowl contents are poured onto the earth (if not out in the yard, then into a flowerpot containing soil and perhaps a hardy, leafy green plant).

Preparing Your Altar

- Candles are: blue-white-orange or green-white-red.

- Incense may be bay, sandalwood or frankincense.

- Have any spell work materials ready on the altar.

New Moon Esbat Rite

Sweep circle area; lay out circle and altar items; bathe and robe. Light incense and altar candles. Ring bell three times and say:

> *The circle is about to be cast and I freely stand within to greet my Lady and my Lord.*

Take center candle (there are either three in a candelabra or one before each section of the altar) and light each candle of the circle moving north, then east, south, and west, and say:

> (N) *I call upon light and earth at the north to illuminate and strengthen the circle.*
> (E) *I call upon light and air at the east to illuminate and enliven the circle.*
> (S) *I call upon light and fire at the south to illuminate and warm the circle.*
> (W) *I call upon light and water at the west to illuminate and cleanse the circle.*

Take athame in hand, upraised, begin circle at north and move around the circle north to east to south to west, and say:

> *I draw this circle in the presence of the Goddess and the God where they may come and bless their child,* (name).

Lower the athame at the north, and as you walk around the circle, envision a blue light shooting out from the point and forming the circle boundary, and say:

This is the boundary of the circle. Only love shall enter and leave.

Return to altar and ring bell three times.

Place point of athame in the salt and say:

Salt is life and purifying. I bless this salt to be used in this sacred circle in the names of the Goddess and the God, (names).

Pick up salt bowl and use tip of athame to drop three portions of salt into the water bowl and set salt bowl back in its place.

Stir three times with athame and say:

Let the blessed salt purify this water that it may be blessed to use in this sacred circle. In the names of the Goddess and the God, (names), I consecrate and cleanse this water.

Take the salted water bowl in hand and sprinkle water from it as you move deosil around the circle (N-E-S-W-N) and say:

I consecrate this circle in the names of the Goddess and the God, (names). The circle is conjured a circle of power that is purified and sealed. So mote it be!

Return the water bowl to the altar and pick up censer; take it around the circle to cense it; return censer to altar. Take anointing oil and make a Solar Cross ringed by a circle on your forehead, and say:

I, (name), am consecrated in the names of the Goddess and the God, (names), in this their circle.

If working with family members or a Green-focused coven, open a door in the circle with the athame now for all to enter. Use anointing oil to trace a Solar Cross in a circle on their foreheads as each person enters, having said some kind of greeting, such as the Wiccan, "I come in perfect love and perfect trust." Then close the door with the athame. The text is for solitary use but may be thus altered for family or coven participation. The envisionings are suggestions only.

Take the wand and hold it aloft, with both arms open and upraised, at the north of the circle (envision a powerful bull arriving) and say:

I call upon you, Elemental Earth, to attend this rite and guard this circle, for as I have body and strength, we are kith and kin!

Lower wand and move to the east, raise up wand (see devas, fairies, or an eagle in flight) and say:

> *I call upon you, Elemental Air, to attend this rite and guard this circle, for as I breathe and think, we are kith and kin!*

Lower wand and move to the south, raise up wand (see a dragon) and say:

> *I call upon you, Elemental Fire, to attend this rite and guard this circle, for as I consume life to live, we are kith and kin!*

Lower wand and move to the west, hold wand aloft (see an undine, a sea serpent, or a dolphin) and say:

> *I call upon you, Elemental Water, to attend this rite and guard this circle, for as I feel and my heart beats, we are kith and kin!*

Return to altar and use wand to draw the symbol of infinity (an 8 lying on its side) in the air above the altar, the sign of working between the worlds. Set wand on altar , raise up athame in both hands overhead, and say:

> *Hail to the elementals at the four quarters! Welcome Lady and Lord to this rite! I stand between the worlds with love and power all around!*

Set down athame and pick up goblet of wine. Pour a little into the cauldron. This is a libation to the Divine in which they are honored by offering to them the first draught, then you take a sip. You may prefer to have a bowl specifically for the libation. Ring bell three times. Raise the wand in greeting and say:

> *I,* (Craft or working name), *who am your child, stand between the worlds and call upon my Lady and my Lord,* (names), *to hold communion with me.*

Ring bell three times and say:

> *If it harms none, do what you will. Thus runs the Witch's Rede. Once more I affirm my joy of life and union with the Lady and the Lord. I honor the God and the Goddess,* (names), *for the favors they have bestowed upon me, and ask their blessings upon me.* (Instead of the Rede, you could say, "I acknowledge that what I send returns to me and conduct my Craft accordingly," or address your own thoughts.)

Set the salted water on the pentacle, hold the athame over it, and say:

Great Mother, bless this creature of water and of earth to your service. May I always remember the cauldron waters of rebirth and the many forms and beings of the blessed earth. Of water and earth am I.

Hold water bowl aloft and say:

Great Mother, I honor you! (You are showing your respect for the Lady and the element that represents her in this ritual.)

Replace the water bowl in the proper place on the altar. Place censer on the pentacle, hold athame over it, and say:

Great Father, bless this creature of fire and of air to your service. May I always remember the sacred fire that dances within every creation and hear the voices of the Divine. Of fire and air am I.

Raise the censer aloft and say:

Great Father, I honor you!

Return censer to the proper place on the altar. Raise the cup of wine aloft and say:

Power and grace; beauty and strength are in the Lady and the Lord both. Patience and love; wisdom and knowledge. I honor you both!

Pour a libation into the cauldron and take a sip of wine. Stand with head bowed and arms crossed over chest; chant the name of the Goddess (such as Hecate), then proceed:

As (names you use for the Goddess) *known, this is the moon of my Lady as crone, Lady of darkness, of wisdom, of mysteries shown. The wheel turns through birth, death, and rebirth, and every end is a new beginning. You are the passage from life to life. You are she who is at the beginning and the end of all time. You, with your Lord* (God's name) *at your side, abide in us all. So mote it be!*

Enjoy a moment of reverent silence to consider the mysteries and your special closeness to the Goddess of the Witches. You may now do any spell work appropriate for the new moon.

Cakes and Wine—Ring bell three times. Feet spread and arms upraised, say:

> *I acknowledge my needs and offer my appreciation to that which sustains me! May I ever remember the blessings of my Lady and my Lord.*

Feet together, take up goblet in left hand and athame in right. Slowly lower the point of the athame into the wine and say:

> *As male joins female for the benefit of both, let the fruits of their union promote life. Let the earth be fruitful and let her wealth be spread throughout all lands.*

Lay down the athame and drink from the goblet. Replace the goblet on the altar and pick up the athame. Touch the point of the athame to the cake in the offering dish and say:

> *This food is the blessing of the Lady and the Lord given freely to me. As freely as I have received, may I also give food for the body, mind, and spirit to those who seek such of me.*

Eat the cake, finish the wine, and say:

> *As I enjoy these gifts of the Goddess and the God,* (names), *may I remember that without them I would have nothing. So mote it be!*

When all is finished, hold athame in your power hand level over altar and say:

> *Lord and Lady, I am blessed by your sharing this time with me; watching and guarding me, and guiding me here and in all things. I came in love and I depart in love.*

Raise up athame in a salute and say:

> *Love is the law and love is the bond. Merry did I meet, merry do I part, and merry will I meet again. Merry meet, merry part, and merry meet again! The circle is now cleared. So mote it be!*

Kiss the flat of the blade and set the athame on the altar. Take up the snuffer and go to the north quarter, raise up arms, and say:

> *Depart in peace, Elemental Earth. My blessings take with you!*

Lower arms and snuff the candle, envision the Elemental Power departing. Go to the east, raise up arms, and say:

Depart in peace, Elemental Air. My blessings take with you!

Lower arms and snuff the candle, envision the Elemental Power departing. Go to the south, raise up arms, and say:

Depart in peace, Elemental Fire. My blessings take with you!

Lower arms and snuff the candle, envision the Elemental Power departing. Go to the west, raise up arms, and say:

Depart in peace, Elemental Water. My blessings take with you!

Lower arms and snuff the candle, envision the Elemental Power departing. Return to altar and set down snuffer. Raise up arms and say:

Beings and powers of the visible and invisible, depart in peace! You aid in my work, whisper in my mind, and bless me from the Otherworld, and there is harmony between us. My blessings take with you. The circle is cleared.

Take up athame, go to the north quarter, point athame down and move widdershins (counter-clockwise) around circle (N-W-S-E-N), envision the blue light drawing back into the athame, and say:

The circle is open yet the circle remains as its magical power is drawn back into me.

When you return to the north having walked the circle, raise up the athame so the blade touches your forehead and envision the blue light swirling around back into you. Return to altar and say:

The ceremony is ended. Blessings have been given and blessings have been received, may the peace of the Goddess and the God remain in my heart. So mote it be !

Set down the athame. Put away all magical tools and clear the altar except for candles or any objects that need to burn out or work for a stated time (such as candle magic). The cauldron or libation bowl contents is poured onto the earth (if not out in the yard, then into a flowerpot containing soil and perhaps a hardy, leafy green plant).

9

Yule Sabbat
December 21

The year begins at different times depending upon the tradition. It can be Samhain, Yule, Imbolc, or Ostara, but my family has always used the Yule holidays as the turning of the wheel of the year with the departure of the Holly King (known today as the Dark Lord, old Saint Nick, and Father Time) and arrival of the Oak King (known today as the Sun King, Jesus, and the New Year's Baby). Incenses shown are only suggestions; you may prefer to drop herbs onto a charcoal block.

As I have mentioned previously, in my childhood our family observances would have been considered a secular form of the socially acceptable holidays of Christmas, Easter, and Thanksgiving. In addition, it was easy to celebrate May Day, Summer, and Halloween as these were already in the secular realm. Nevertheless, for us these times had earth-centered meanings that can be used for the Green-level practice of the Craft as easily as the accepted Sabbat dates used in contemporary Witchcraft.

Years after I put aside the trappings of Christianity in my search for a basic form of religious expression, I subsequently adopted the Sabbats of the Craft and have been very satisfied with this. You may want to follow a different course or blend Witchcraft with the mainstream to feel yourself united with society as a whole. At the worst, you may be considered a secular Christian or a humanist. At the best, you may help affect the acceptance of the Craft by your example of kinship with the earth and her inhabitants. The Sabbat rituals shown form the framework for my own practice of the Craft, yet I always improvise, add, or subtract by inspiration.

As a child, going outside to gaze at the full moon and being told the various names for the moons (which are still found today in almanacs) and perhaps singing a song like "Shine On Silver Moon" or playing "Moonlight Sonata" formed the family's basic recognition of the changing faces of the moon. Sometimes there were stories, other times simply a nighttime romp out-of-doors when all the neighbors were in their homes. This was a time filled with its own essence and sense of closeness to the mystery of magical presence. The new moon was acknowledged for the absence of moonlight in the night sky, but everything was casually done as a naturalist observing the surroundings as if for the first time. The odors and atmosphere of the evening air were always different from that of the daylight hours, and it was enough to take the time to pause and partake of nature.

If you celebrate a Sabbat on a full or new moon, you may begin with the Esbat and moon rite, and insert the Sabbat ritual before going on to the Cakes and Wine. Prepare in advance with the appropriate altar decor and candles. There are suggested Sabbat activities given with each Sabbat, and while spells are generally not conducted at a Sabbat, they may be if in conjunction with an Esbat. Seasonal decorations may be used around the circle along with the four candle settings for the quarters. Incenses and altar candles may vary by Sabbat, and some suggestions are given with each Sabbat.

Preparing Your Altar

- Altar candles should be red-green-red.
- Circle candles remain the usual colors for the elementals (green, yellow, red, and blue).

- Incense may be bayberry.

- Circle may be decorated with holly, mistletoe, ivy, pine, pine cones, etc. A Yule Log (half of a log cut to set on the altar, has three holes in it to hold candles, decorated with greenery and pine cones) may substitute for a candle holder.

- Place ash twigs in the cauldron.

Instructions for the Ceremony

Sweep circle area; lay out circle and altar items; bathe and robe. Light incense and altar candles. Ring bell three times and say:

The circle is about to be cast and I freely stand within to greet my Lady and my Lord.

Take center candle from altar and light each candle of the circle moving north, then east, south, and west, and say:

(N) *I call upon light and earth at the north to illuminate and strengthen the circle.*

(E) *I call upon light and air at the east to illuminate and enliven the circle.*

(S) *I call upon light and fire at the south to illuminate and warm the circle.*

(W) *I call upon light and water at the west to illuminate and cleanse the circle.*

Take athame in upraised hand, begin circle at north and move around the circle north to east to south to west, and say:

I draw this circle in the presence of the Goddess and the God where they may come and bless their child, (name).

Lower the athame at the north. As you walk around the circle, envision a blue light shooting out from the point and forming the circle boundary, and say:

This is the boundary of the circle. Only love shall enter and leave.

Return to altar and ring bell three times. Place point of athame in the salt and say:

Salt is life and purifying. I bless this salt to be used in this sacred circle in the names of the Goddess and the God, (names).

Pick up salt bowl and use tip of athame to drop three portions of salt into the water bowl and set salt bowl back in its place. Stir three times with athame and say:

> *Let the blessed salt purify this water that it may be blessed to use in this sacred circle. In the names of the Goddess and the God,* (names), *I consecrate and cleanse this water.*

Take the salted water bowl in hand, sprinkle water from it as you move deosil around the circle (N-E-S-W-N), and say:

> *I consecrate this circle in the names of the Goddess and the God,* (names). *The circle is conjured a circle of power that is purified and sealed. So mote it be!*

Return the water bowl to the altar and pick up censer; take it around the circle to cense it; return censer to altar. Take anointing oil and make a Solar Cross ringed by a circle on your forehead and say:

> *I,* (name) *am consecrated in the names of the Goddess and the God,* (names), *in this their circle.*

If working with family members or a Green-focused coven, open a door in the circle with the athame now for all to enter, then close the door with the athame. The text is for solitary use but may be thus altered for family or coven participation.

Take the wand and hold it aloft, with both arms open and upraised, at the north of the circle (envision a powerful bull arriving) and say:

> *I call upon you, Elemental Earth, to attend this rite and guard this circle, for as I have body and strength, we are kith and kin!*

Lower wand and move to east, raise up wand (see devas, fairies, or an eagle in flight) and say:

> *I call upon you, Elemental Air, to attend this rite and guard this circle, for as I breathe and think, we are kith and kin!*

Lower wand and move to the south, raise up wand (see a dragon) and say:

> *I call upon you, Elemental Fire, to attend this rite and guard this circle, for as I consume life to live, we are kith and kin!*

Lower wand and move to west, hold wand aloft (see an undine, a sea serpent, or a dolphin) and say:

*I call upon you, Elemental Water, to attend this rite and guard
this circle, for as I feel and my heart beats, we are kith and kin!*

Return to altar and use wand to draw the symbol of infinity (an 8
lying on its side) in the air above the altar, the sign of working between
the worlds. Set wand on altar, raise up athame in both hands overhead,
and say:

*Hail to the elementals at the four quarters! Welcome Lady
and Lord to this rite! I stand between the worlds with love
and power all around!*

Set down athame and pick up goblet of wine. Pour a little into the
cauldron. This is a libation to the Divine in which they are honored by
offering to them the first draught, then you take a sip. You may prefer
to have a bowl specifically for the libation. Ring bell three times. Raise
up arms and say:

*Blessed are the Lord and the Lady who turn the mighty wheel of
the year. Welcome the Yule for the turning point of winter is here
at last. The end of the solar year has come; a new year has begun.*

Arms down, take up wand and hold it aloft and say:

*This is a new beginning, and I send my power forth to join
with the energies of the Sun God that the sun's rebirth
rekindles my strength.*

Place wand back on the altar. Take the middle candle and light the
kindling in the cauldron, and say:

*This new fire is lit to bid farewell to the Dark Lord of the solar
night and greet the rebirth of the sun. May my power be added
to the strength of the newborn Lord, and his to mine.*

Return candle; take up the athame in both hands, hold aloft and say:

*Hail to the Sun God! Hail the movement of time eternal! Hail
the death and rebirth of Yule! Hail the God* (name)*!*

Return the athame to the altar and ring the bell three times. With
candles in Yule Log, light the candles at the start of the ritual, and
when the ritual is ended, let the candles burn very low and then snuff
the reds, replace them with green candles and light them from the still-
lit green in the middle. Then snuff the green, replace it with a red candle and light it fresh and say:

*May the Yule Log bring light and may all good enter here.
Good health, good cheer, good fortune in the coming year! For
as I will, so mote it be!*

Cakes and Wine—Ring bell three times. Feet spread and arms
upraised, say:

*I acknowledge my needs and offer my appreciation to that
which sustains me! May I ever remember the blessings of my
Lady and my Lord.*

Feet together, take up goblet in left hand and athame in right.
Slowly lower the point of the athame into the wine and say:

*As male joins female for the benefit of both, let the fruits of
their union promote life. Let the earth be fruitful and let her
wealth be spread throughout all lands.*

Lay down the athame and drink from the goblet. Replace the goblet
on the altar and pick up the athame. Touch the point of the athame to
the cake in the offering dish and say:

*This food is the blessing of the Lady and the Lord given freely to
me. As freely as I have received, may I also give food for the
body, mind, and spirit to those who seek such of me.*

Eat the fruitcake (or other Yule food), finish the wine, and say:

As I enjoy these gifts of the Goddess and the God, (names),
*may I remember that without them I would have nothing.
So mote it be!*

When all is finished, hold athame in your power hand level over altar
and say:

*Lord and Lady, I am blessed by your sharing this time with
me, watching and guarding me, and guiding me here and in
all things. I came in love and I depart in love.*

Raise up athame in a salute and say:

*Love is the law and love is the bond. Merry did I meet, merry do
I part, and merry will I meet again. Merry meet, merry part,
and merry meet again! The circle is now cleared. So mote it be!*

Kiss the flat of the blade and set the athame on the altar. Take up the snuffer and go to the north quarter, raise up arms, and say:

Depart in peace, Elemental Earth. My blessings take with you!

Lower arms and snuff the candle, envision the Elemental Power departing. Go to the east, raise up arms, and say:

Depart in peace, Elemental air. My blessings take with you!

Lower arms and snuff the candle, envision the Elemental Power departing. Go to the south, raise up arms, and say:

Depart in peace, Elemental fire. My blessings take with you!

Lower arms and snuff the candle, envision the Elemental Power departing. Go to the west, raise up arms, and say:

Depart in peace, Elemental Water. My blessings take with you!

Lower arms and snuff the candle, envision the Elemental Power departing. Return to altar and set down snuffer. Raise up arms and say:

Beings and powers of the visible and invisible, depart in peace! You aid in my work, whisper in my mind, and bless me from the Otherworld, and there is harmony between us. My blessings take with you. The circle is cleared.

Take up athame, go to the north quarter, point athame down and move widdershins (counter-clockwise) around circle (N-W-S-E-N). Envision the blue light drawing back into the athame and say:

The circle is open yet the circle remains as its magical power is drawn back into me.

When you return to the north having walked the circle, raise up the athame so the blade touches your forehead and envision the blue light swirling around back into you. Return to altar and say:

The ceremony is ended. Blessings have been given and blessings have been received, may the peace of the Goddess and the God remain in my heart. So mote it be!

Set down the athame. Put away all magical tools and clear the altar except for candles or any objects that need to burn out or work for a stated time (such as candle magic). The cauldron or libation bowl contents are poured onto the earth (if not out in the yard, then into a flow-erpot containing soil and perhaps a hardy, leafy green plant).

Traditional foods for the Yule Sabbat include nuts, fruits mixed in a fruitcake or plum pudding, game or pork dishes, and wassail, so the celebration can be followed by a simple or very elaborate feast.

Yule Activities

There are a number of Yuletide activities that can be experienced out-side or in conjunction with the Sabbat. Many will be familiar because they have been borrowed by mainstream religions.

- Sing pagan solstice carols (Deck the Halls, The Holly and the Ivy, Joy to the World, Tannenbaum, Wassailing Song, Green Groweth the Holly, Lord of the Dance, and a number of carols that have been re-adapted to their original pagan themes—see samples below).

- Decorate the Solstice, or Yule, Tree.

- String popcorn and cranberries and hang them on an outdoor tree for the birds.

- Decorate pine cones with glue and glitter as symbols of the fairies and place these on the Yule Tree.

- Hang little bells on the Yule Tree to call the spirits and fairies.

- Glue the caps onto acorns and attach red string to hang on the Yule Tree.

- For personalized wrapping paper, cut a pattern on a halved potato, then dip it into tempera paint and onto plain wrapping tissue paper.

- Wassail: 2 cups cranberry juice, ¼ cup grenadine, 1 cup orange juice, ¼ cup rum (optional).

- For prosperity, burn ash wood.

- Yule Blessings—Wreath on the door, Mistletoe indoors, food and clothing donations, sunflower seeds outside for birds, ring the bells to greet the Solstice Morn, and perform magic for a peaceful planet.

- Gather up the Yule greens after Twelfth Night and save. At Imbolc, burn the greens to banish winter and usher in spring.

- Consecrate the Yule Tree—Asperse with salted water, pass smoke of incense through the branches, and walk around the tree with a lighted candle and say:

  By fire and water, air and earth,
  I consecrate this tree of rebirth.

- Legend of Santa Claus—Santa is the Holly King, the sleigh is the Solar Chariot, the eight reindeer are the eight Sabbats, their horns represent the Horned God, the North Pole symbolizes the Land of Shadows and the dying solar year, and the gifts are meant both to welcome the Oak King as the sun reborn and as a reminder of the gift of the Holly King who must depart for the Oak King to rule.

Some Familiar Yuletide Songs With Pagan Lyrics

God Rest Ye Merry Pagan Folk

God rest ye merry pagan folk, let nothing you dismay.
Remember that the sun returns, upon this solstice day!
The growing dark is ended now, and spring is on its way.
O, tidings of comfort and joy, comfort and joy!
O, tidings of comfort and joy!

The winter's worst still lies ahead, fierce tempest, snow and rain!
Beneath the blanket on the ground, the spark of life remains!
The sun's warm rays caress the seeds, to raise life's songs again!
O, tidings of comfort and joy, comfort and joy!
O, tidings of comfort and joy!

Within the blessed apple lies, the promise of the queen
For from this pentacle shall rise, the orchards fresh and green.
The earth shall blossom once again, the air be sweet and clean!
O, tidings of comfort and joy, comfort and joy!
O, tidings of comfort and joy!

O, Come All Ye Faithful

O, come all ye faithful, joyful and triumphant!
O, come ye, oh, come ye to greet the sun!
Join in the Yuletide, turning of the solstice fire.
O, come let us invoke him
O, come let us invoke him,
O, come let us invoke him
Lord of the Light.

Yea, Lord we greet thee, born again at solstice!
Yule fire and candle flame, to light your way.
Come to thy Lady, fill the earth with love anew!
O, come let us invoke him,
O, come let us invoke him,
O, come let us invoke him,
Lord of the Light.

Joy to the World

Joy to the world, the sun has come!
Let Earth receive her Lord!
Let every heart, prepare him room,
And all of nature sing, and all of nature sing,
And all, and all of nature sing!

Welcome the Lord, who brings us Light!
The Lady gives him birth!
His warming light, brings joy into our hearts!
And wakes the sleeping earth, and wakes the sleeping earth,
And wakes, and wakes the sleeping earth!

We light the fires, to greet the sun;
Our light, our life, our Lord!
Let every voice, join in with life's song!
And merry turns the wheel, and merry turns the wheel,
And merry, and merry the wheel turns!

10

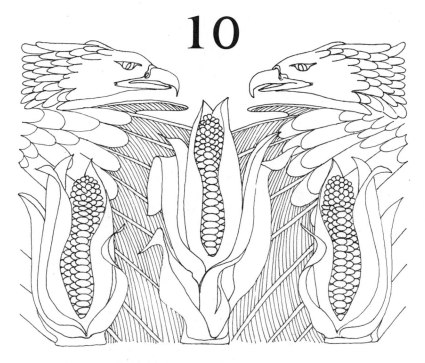

Imbolc Sabbat
February 2

Preparing Your Altar

- Altar candles should be white.

- Incense may be benzoin or vanilla.

- Circle may be decorated with white flowers.

- Circle candles remain the usual colors for the elementals (green, yellow, red, and blue).

- Lay your besom upon the altar.

- Have a white votive candle in the cauldron.

- Have rosemary and bay to burn.

- Have extra wine.

Instructions for the Ceremony

Sweep circle area; lay out circle and altar items; bathe and robe. Light incense and altar candles. Ring bell three times and say:

> *The circle is about to be cast and I freely stand within to greet my Lady and my Lord.*

Take center candle from altar and light each candle of the circle moving north, then east, south, and west, and say:

> (N) *I call upon light and earth at the north to illuminate and strengthen the circle.*
>
> (E) *I call upon light and air at the east to illuminate and enliven the circle.*
>
> (S) *I call upon light and fire at the south to illuminate and warm the circle.*
>
> (W) *I call upon light and water at the west to illuminate and cleanse the circle.*

Take athame in hand upraised, begin circle at north and move around the circle north to east to south to west, and say:

> *I draw this circle in the presence of the Goddess and the God where they may come and bless their child,* (name).

Lower the athame at the north, and as you walk around the circle, envision a blue light shooting out from the point and forming the circle boundary, and say:

> *This is the boundary of the circle. Only love shall enter and leave.*

Return to altar and ring bell three times. Place point of athame in the salt and say:

> *Salt is life and purifying. I bless this salt to be used in this sacred circle in the names of the Goddess and the God,* (names).

Pick up salt bowl and use tip of athame to drop three portions of salt into the water bowl and set salt bowl back in its place. Stir three times with athame and say:

> *Let the blessed salt purify this water that it may be blessed to use in this sacred circle. In the names of the Goddess and the God,* (names), *I consecrate and cleanse this water.*

Take the salted water bowl in hand and sprinkle water from it as you move deosil around the circle (N-E-S-W-N) and say:

I consecrate this circle in the names of the Goddess and the God, (names). *The circle is conjured a circle of power that is purified and sealed. So mote it be!*

Return the water bowl to the altar and pick up censer; take it around the circle to cense it; return censer to altar. Take anointing oil and make a Solar Cross ringed by a circle on your forehead and say:

I, (name), *am consecrated in the names of the Goddess and the God,* (names), *in this their circle.*

If working with family members or a Green-focused coven, open a door in the circle with the athame now for all to enter. Use anointing oil to trace a Solar Cross in a circle on their foreheads as each person enters, having said some kind of greeting, such as the Wiccan, "I come in perfect love and perfect trust." Then close the door with the athame. The text is for solitary use but may be thus altered for family or coven participation.

Take the wand and hold it aloft with both arms open and upraised at the north of the circle (envision a powerful bull arriving) and say:

I call upon you, Elemental Earth, to attend this rite and guard this circle, for as I have body and strength, we are kith and kin!

Lower wand and move to the east, raise up wand (see devas, fairies, or an eagle in flight) and say:

I call upon you, Elemental Air, to attend this rite and guard this circle, for as I breathe and think, we are kith and kin!

Lower wand and move to the south, raise up wand (see a dragon) and say:

I call upon you, Elemental Fire, to attend this rite and guard this circle, for as I consume life to live, we are kith and kin!

Lower wand and move to the west, hold wand aloft (see an undine, a sea serpent, or a dolphin) and say:

I call upon you, Elemental Water, to attend this rite and guard this circle, for as I feel and my heart beats, we are kith and kin!

Return to altar and use wand to draw the symbol of infinity (an 8 lying on its side) in the air above the altar, the sign of working between the worlds. Set wand on altar, raise up athame in both hands overhead, and say:

> *Hail to the elementals at the four quarters! Welcome Lady and Lord to this rite! I stand between the worlds with love and power all around!*

Set down athame and pick up goblet of wine. Pour a little into the cauldron. This is a libation to the Divine in which they are honored by offering to them the first draught, then you take a sip. You may prefer to have a bowl specifically for the libation. Ring bell three times and say:

> *This is the mid-winter Feast of Lights. The spring lies within sight and the seed is prepared for sowing.*

Ring bell five times and say:

> *With my besom in my hand I will sweep out that which is no longer needed so as to purify my surroundings and prepare for new growth.*

Take up besom and say:

> *Clear out the old and let the new enter. Life starts anew at this time of cleansing.*

Sweep the circle with outward motions as you walk deosil (clockwise) around the circle, starting and ending at the north. Return besom to the altar. Light cauldron candle, drop the rosemary and bay into the flame, and say:

> *I call upon the power of these herbs that their scent released in this cauldron's fire purify me, my surroundings, and the tools of my Craft. With this rite I am reaffirmed in my Craft and made ready for the renewal of life in the coming of spring.*

Wave the end of the besom over the cauldron and say:

> *May this besom be cleansed that nothing cast out of the circle return with it or cling to it. So mote it be!*

Set aside besom and say:

> *As I have purified all within this circle, I am now ready to re-dedicate myself to my Lady and my Lord.*

Re-dedication Ritual

Arms upraised, say:

Lady and Lord, (names), *I call out to thee! I hold you in honor and know that I am one with all the things of the earth and sky. My kin are the trees and the herbs of the fields, the animals and stones through the seas and the hills. The fresh waters and deserts are built out of thee, and I am of you and you are of me.*

Lower arms and say:

I call upon you to grant my desire. Let me rejoice in my oneness with all things and let me love the life that emanates from my Lady and my Lord into all things. I know and accept the creed: that if I do not have that spark of love within me, I will never find it outside myself, for love is the law and love is the bond! And this do I honor when I give honor to the Lady and the Lord.

Kiss your right palm, hold your hand high, and say:

My Lady and my Lord, known to me as (names), *I stand before you both and dedicate myself to your honor. I will defend and protect thy spark within me and seek thy protection and defense of me. You are my life and I am of you. I accept and will ever abide by the principal of harming none, for what is sent returns. So mote it be!*

Take up the goblet of wine, slowly pour the remainder of wine into the cauldron, and say:

As this wine drains from the cup, so shall the blood drain from my body should I ever turn away from the Lady and the Lord or harm those in kinship with their love, for to do so would be to break trust, to cast aside the love of the Goddess and the God, and to break my own heart. Yet through their continued love I know they would heal my heart and spirit that I might again journey through the cauldron of rebirth to embrace the love they freely give. So mote it be!

Dip forefinger into the anointing oil and again make the sign of the Solar Cross over the third eye (center of forehead). Then make the sign of the pentagram over the heart, followed by the Sacred Triangle (for the triple quality of both Deities) touching solar plexus, right breast, left breast, solar plexus. Refill the goblet for Cakes and Wine.

Cakes and Wine—Ring bell three times. Feet spread and arms upraised, say:

> *I acknowledge my needs and offer my appreciation to that which sustains me! May I ever remember the blessings of my Lady and my Lord.*

Feet together, take up goblet in left hand and athame in right. Slowly lower the point of the athame into the wine and say:

> *As male joins female for the benefit of both, let the fruits of their union promote life. Let the earth be fruitful and let her wealth be spread throughout all lands.*

Lay down the athame and drink from the goblet. Replace the goblet on the altar and pick up the athame. Touch the point of the athame to the cake in the offering dish and say:

> *This food is the blessing of the Lady and the Lord given freely to me. As freely as I have received, may I also give food for the body, mind, and spirit to those who seek such of me.*

Eat the food, finish the wine, and say:

> *As I enjoy these gifts of the Goddess and the God,* (names), *may I remember that without them I would have nothing. So mote it be!*

When all is finished, hold athame in your power hand level over altar and say:

> *Lord and Lady, I am blessed by your sharing this time with me, watching and guarding me, and guiding me here and in all things. I came in love and I depart in love.*

Raise up athame in a salute and say:

> *Love is the law and love is the bond. Merry did I meet, merry do I part, and merry will I meet again. Merry meet, merry part, and merry meet again! The circle is now cleared. So mote it be!*

Kiss the flat of the blade and set the athame on the altar. Take up the snuffer and go to the north quarter, raise up arms, and say:

Depart in peace, Elemental Earth. My blessings take with you!

Lower arms and snuff the candle, envision the Elemental Power departing. Go to the east, raise up arms, and say:

Depart in peace, Elemental Air. My blessings take with you!

Lower arms and snuff the candle, envision the Elemental Power departing. Go to the south, raise up arms, and say:

Depart in peace, Elemental Fire. My blessings take with you!

Lower arms and snuff the candle, envision the Elemental Power departing. Go to the west, raise up arms, and say:

Depart in peace, Elemental Water. My blessings take with you!

Lower arms and snuff the candle, envision the Elemental Power departing. Return to altar and set down snuffer. Raise up arms and say:

Beings and powers of the visible and invisible, depart in peace! You aid in my work, whisper in my mind, and bless me from the Otherworld, and there is harmony between us. My blessings take with you. The circle is cleared.

Take up athame, go to the north quarter, point athame down and move widdershins (counter-clockwise) around circle (N-W-S-E-N). Envision the blue light drawing back into the athame and say:

The circle is open yet the circle remains as its magical power is drawn back into me.

When you return to the north having walked the circle, raise up the athame so the blade touches your forehead and envision the blue light swirling around back into you. Return to altar and say:

The ceremony is ended. Blessings have been given and blessings have been received, may the peace of the Goddess and the God remain in my heart. So mote it be!

Set down the athame. Put away all magical tools and clear the altar except for candles or any objects that need to burn out or work for a stated time (such as candle magic). The cauldron or libation bowl contents are poured onto the earth (if not out in the yard, then into a flowerpot containing soil and perhaps a hardy, leafy green plant).

Traditional foods are from dairy products and spiced with onion, leek, shallot, garlic, and olive; the wine may be spiced and foods may contain raisins. Bread puddings and creamy soups are typical.

Imbolc Activities

Here are a few suggestions for Imbolc activities, some of which can be incorporated into the Sabbat celebration or simply as something to make the day more special, especially for children.

- Burn the Yule greens to send winter on its way.

- Make the Bride's Bed using the Corn (or Wheat) Doll made the previous Lughnassadh. Dress the doll in white or blue with a necklace that represents the seasons. Lay it in a long basket adorned with ribbons; light white candles on either side of the basket, and say:

> *Welcome the bride both maiden and mother; rest and prepare*
> *for the time of the seed; cleansed and refreshed from labors*
> *behind her; with the promise of spring she lays before me.*

Next morning, remove the dress and scatter the wheat outdoors (or if you use corn, hang it up in a tree for the squirrels and the birds). This can be seen in terms of the Lady's recovery from the birthing bed and readiness to begin the turning of the seasons anew.

The Imbolc Corn Doll represents the mother nurturing her son, who will grow and become her husband. This is the earth and the sun, which is still weak but gaining in strength. I have a doll from Brazil made of hemp with an apron having a front pocket labeled *fosforo* (meaning "matches") and this, too, is a Bride Doll of Imbolc. Her hair is decorated with flowers, and she carries the light in her pocket as a mother holds a babe in her lap. Pagan imagery can be found in many items of folk art.

- On Imbolc Eve, leave buttered bread in a bowl indoors for the fairies who travel with the Lady of Greenwood. Next day, dispose of it as the "essence" will have been removed.

- Place three ears of corn on the door as symbol of the Triple Goddess and leave until Ostara.

- Light a white candle and burn sandalwood.

- Cleanse the area where you do card readings or scrying with a censer burning rosemary or vervain and say:

  By the power of this smoke I wash away the negative influences that this place be cleansed for the Lady and her babe.

- Cleanse the altar and equipment, do a self-purification rite with the elemental tools representing earth (salt) for body; air (incense) for thoughts; fire (candle flame) for will; and water (water) for emotions.

- Make dream pillows for everyone in the family.

- Create a Solar Cross from palm fronds, enough to place one in each room of the house. Place a red pillar-style candle center to the front door; with palms in hand, light the candle and open the door and say:

  We welcome in the Goddess and seek the turning of the wheel away from winter and into spring.

Close door; take up the candle and go to each room of the house and say:

  Great Lady enter with the sun and watch over this room!

Leave a Solar Cross in the room and proceed thusly throughout the house. This is great for the kids as you can divide up the tasks for each to do—one can hold the palms, another can open doors, another can carry the candle, and so forth. The last room should be the kitchen and here you say:

  Mother of the earth and the sun,
  Keep us safe and keep us warm,
  As over our home you extend your blessing.

11

Ostara Sabbat
March 21

Preparing Your Altar

- Altar candles should be light green.

- Incense may be jasmine.

- Decorate circle with spring wildflowers; have a bundle on the altar.

- Circle candles remain the usual colors for the elementals (green, yellow, red, and blue).

- Have an earthenware or wooden bowl containing soil on the altar.

- Place a large seed of some kind on the pentacle.

- Have a sheet (or piece) of parchment paper, ink, and a writing tool on the altar.

Instructions for the Ceremony

The text is for solitary use but may be thus altered for family or coven participation. The envisionings are suggestions only.

Sweep circle area; lay out circle and altar items; bathe and robe. Light incense and altar candles. Ring bell three times and say:

The circle is about to be cast and I freely stand within to greet my Lady and my Lord.

Take center candle from altar and light each candle of the circle moving north, then east, south, and west, and say:

(N) *I call upon light and earth at the north to illuminate and strengthen the circle.*

(E) *I call upon light and air at the east to illuminate and enliven the circle.*

(S) *I call upon light and fire at the south to illuminate and warm the circle.*

(W) *I call upon light and water at the west to illuminate and cleanse the circle.*

Take athame in upraised hand, begin circle at north and move around the circle north to east to south to west, and say:

I draw this circle in the presence of the Goddess and the God where they may come and bless their child, (name).

Lower the athame at the north, and as you walk around the circle, envision a blue light shooting out from the point and forming the circle boundary, and say:

This is the boundary of the circle. Only love shall enter and leave.

Return to altar and ring bell three times. Place point of athame in the salt and say:

Salt is life and purifying. I bless this salt to be used in this sacred circle in the names of the Goddess and the God, (names).

Pick up salt bowl and use tip of athame to drop three portions of salt into the water bowl and set salt bowl back in its place. Stir three times with athame and say:

Let the blessed salt purify this water that it may be blessed to use in this sacred circle. In the names of the Goddess and the God, (names), I consecrate and cleanse this water.

Take the salted water bowl in hand and sprinkle water from it as you move deosil around the circle (N-E-S-W-N):

I consecrate this circle in the names of the Goddess and the God, (names). The circle is conjured a circle of power that is purified and sealed. So mote it be!

Return the water bowl to the altar and pick up censer; take it around the circle to cense it; return censer to altar. Take anointing oil, make a Solar Cross ringed by a circle on your forehead, and say:

I, (name) am consecrated in the names of the Goddess and the God, (names), in this their circle.

If working with family members or a Green-focused coven, open a door in the circle with the athame now for all to enter. Use anointing oil to trace a solar cross in a circle on their foreheads as each person enters, having said some kind of greeting, such as the Wiccan, "I come in perfect love and perfect trust." Then close the door with the athame.

Take the wand and hold it aloft, with both arms open and upraised, at the north of the circle (envision a powerful bull arriving) and say:

I call upon you, Elemental Earth, to attend this rite and guard this circle, for as I have body and strength, we are kith and kin!

Lower wand and move to the east, raise up wand (see devas, fairies, or an eagle in flight) and say:

I call upon you, Elemental Air, to attend this rite and guard this circle, for as I breathe and think, we are kith and kin!

Lower wand and move to the south, raise up wand (see a dragon) and say:

I call upon you, Elemental Fire, to attend this rite and guard this circle, for as I consume life to live, we are kith and kin!

Lower wand, move to the west, hold wand aloft (see an undine, a sea serpent, or a dolphin) and say:

I call upon you, Elemental Water, to attend this rite and guard this circle, for as I feel and my heart beats, we are kith and kin!

Return to altar and use wand to draw the symbol of infinity (an 8 lying on its side) in the air above the altar, the sign of working between the worlds. Set wand on altar, raise up athame in both hands overhead, and say:

> *Hail to the elementals at the four quarters! Welcome Lady and Lord to this rite! I stand between the worlds with love and power all around!*

Set down athame and pick up goblet of wine. Pour a little into the cauldron. This is a libation to the Divine in which they are honored by offering to them the first draught, then you take a sip. You may prefer to have a bowl specifically for the libation. Ring bell three times and say:

> *I call upon me the blessings of the Ancient Ones as merry do we meet at this springtime rite. Lady and Lord, hear your child,* (name), *for I am here to celebrate with you and for you as we greet the spring together!*

Take up flowers from the altar and moving deosil around the circle (start at the north), drop the flowers inside around the circle. Ring bell three times and say:

> *Springtime is the time to sow the seed, and it is the time for me to plant what I want to grow. This season brings hope and joy; expectations for desires realized; and inspiration for new ideas. My life is brought into balance and I am reborn with the earth's renewal. I welcome thee, beautiful spring!*

Visualize the seed on the altar as what you want to plant—a quality, an opportunity, a creation, or whatever—so the seed represents the idea in the mind. Ring bell one time, then write on parchment the seed idea. Light the parchment from the center altar candle. Drop the burning ashes into the bowl of earth on the pentacle, and say:

> *Lady and Lord, receive the seed of my desire and let it grow and prosper that it may ripen and bear fruit.*

Use the athame to mix ashes into the soil. Take the wand, and with it upraised, move (dance) around the circle three times to raise the energy. Return to the altar with the wand still upraised, and say:

> *By the power instilled in this raised wand will the seed be planted in the ready soil. Blessed be the wand of spring and blessed be the earth that receives it!*

Kiss the tip of the wand, transferring the raised energy into it, then make an indentation in the center of the soil with it and visualize the energy entering. Set down the wand. Hold the seed aloft, concentrate energy into it (infusing it with your idea), place it in the furrow and close the soil over it, and say:

> *This seed is planted in the mother's womb to be part of the earth, of life, and of me. Let this seed and what it represents grow to manifestation. As I will it, so mote it be!*

Cakes and Wine—Ring bell three times. Feet spread and arms upraised, say:

> *I acknowledge my needs and offer my appreciation to that which sustains me! May I ever remember the blessings of my Lady and my Lord.*

Feet together, take up goblet in left hand and athame in right. Slowly lower the point of the athame into the wine and say:

> *As male joins female for the benefit of both, let the fruits of their union promote life. Let the earth be fruitful and let her wealth be spread throughout all lands.*

Lay down the athame and drink from the goblet. Replace the goblet on the altar and pick up the athame. Touch the point of the athame to the cake in the offering dish and say:

> *This food is the blessing of the Lady and the Lord given freely to me. As freely as I have received, may I also give food for the body, mind, and spirit to those who seek such of me.*

Eat the food, finish the wine, and say:

> *As I enjoy these gifts of the Goddess and the God, (names), may I remember that without them I would have nothing. So mote it be!*

When all is finished, hold athame in your power hand level over altar and say:

> *Lord and Lady, I am blessed by your sharing this time with me, watching and guarding me, and guiding me here and in all things. I came in love and I depart in love.*

Raise up athame in a salute and say:

Love is the law and love is the bond. Merry did I meet, merry do I part, and merry will I meet again. Merry meet, merry part, and merry meet again! The circle is now cleared. So mote it be!

Kiss the flat of the blade and set the athame on the altar. Take up the snuffer and go to the north quarter, raise up arms, and say:

Depart in peace, Elemental Earth. My blessings take with you!

Lower arms and snuff the candle, envision the Elemental Power departing. Go to the east, raise up arms, and say:

Depart in peace, Elemental Air. My blessings take with you!

Lower arms and snuff the candle, envision the Elemental Power departing. Go to the south, raise up arms, and say:

Depart in peace, Elemental Fire. My blessings take with you!

Lower arms and snuff the candle, envision the Elemental Power departing. Go to the west, raise up arms, and say:

Depart in peace, Elemental Water. My blessings take with you!

Lower arms and snuff the candle, envision the Elemental Power departing. Return to altar and set down snuffer. Raise up arms and say:

Beings and powers of the visible and invisible, depart in peace! You aid in my work, whisper in my mind, and bless me from the Otherworld, and there is harmony between us. My blessings take with you. The circle is cleared.

Take up athame, go to the north quarter, point athame down and move widdershins (counter-clockwise) around circle (N-W-S-E-N). Envisioning the blue light drawing back into the athame and say:

The circle is open yet the circle remains as its magical power is drawn back into me.

When you return to the north having walked the circle, raise up the athame so the blade touches your forehead and envision the blue light swirling around back into you. Return to altar and say:

The ceremony is ended. Blessings have been given and blessings have been received, may the peace of the Goddess and the God remain in my heart. So mote it be!

Set down the athame. Put away all magical tools and clear the altar except for candles or any objects that need to burn out or work for a stated time (such as candle magic). The cauldron or libation bowl contents are poured onto the earth (if not out in the yard, then into a flowerpot containing soil and perhaps a hardy, leafy green plant).

Traditional foods for Ostara are seeds and sprouts, sweet wine or wine with honey in it, hard-boiled eggs (decorated), yellow cake with poppy seeds, and banana nut bread.

After the Sabbat is concluded, you may want to transplant your seed into the garden or place it in an indoor flower pot. As it grows, your idea seed should also grow into being. I have on occasion used seeds I found on the ground and then planted outside after the Sabbat. Two of these seeds became magnificent green plants of tree-like proportions, so I like to use what nature provides.

Ostara Activities

Here are a few suggestions for activities that may be part of the Sabbat celebration or something to do during the day:

- Have a traditional breakfast of buns, ham, and eggs.

- Toss the crushed eggshells into the garden and say:

  For fairy, for flowers, for herbs in the bowers,
  The shells pass fertility with springtime showers.

- Wear green clothing.

- Bless seeds planted in the garden.

- Eat an egg you have empowered with a quality you desire.

- Color hard-boiled eggs and add the symbols for the Fertility God, the Goddess, the Sun God, unity, fire, water, agriculture, prosperity and growth, strength and wisdom, spring, love and affection, and protection.

- Consecrate the eggs:

  In the name of the Goddess of spring, (name),
  And the ever-returning God of the sun, (name),
  By the powers of the four elements—earth, air, fire, and water,
  I do consecrate these eggs of Ostara.

Point the athame at the eggs, make the sign of the pentagram, and see the energy flow through the blade into the eggs, and say:

New life lies within as new life shall enter the soil. Let those who seek this life find it and consume it, for all life feeds on life.

The eggs may be hidden and Ostara Egg Hunt commences. We like to make deviled eggs with them since we tend to decorate quite a few.

- Natural dyes can be made from herbs:

green	coltsfoot and bracken
yellow-green	carrot tops
yellow	turmeric
orange	onion skin
red	madder root
blue	blueberries
bright blue	red cabbage

- Make Hot Cross Buns to honor the union of the earth and sun for spring. Slash the "X" with the bolline and bless the cakes.

- On Ostara Eve, light a purple or violet candle and burn patchouli incense. Carry them both through the house, and say:

  Farewell to wintry spirits and friends;
  On morrow we greet the spirits of spring.
  Our blessings to thee as your way you wend;
  And merry we'll meet next winter again.

  Blow out the candle and say:

  Merry meet, merry part, and merry meet again!

12

Beltane Sabbat

May 1

Preparing Your Altar

- Altar candles should be dark green.

- Incense may be lilac.

- Circle may be decorated with seasonal flowers.

- Circle candles remain the usual colors for the elementals (green, yellow, red, and blue).

- Cauldron contains a dark green candle; have a dish for the libation.

- Have woodruff on the altar to burn.

- Have wood chips from birch, oak, rowan (ash), willow, hawthorn, hazel, apple, vine, and fir on the altar to burn.

Instructions for the Ceremony

The text is for solitary use but may be thus altered for family or coven participation. The envisionings are suggestions only.

Sweep circle area; lay out circle and altar items; bathe and robe. Light incense and altar candles. Ring bell three times and say:

> *The circle is about to be cast and I freely stand within to greet my Lady and my Lord.*

Take center candle and light each candle of the circle moving north, then east, south, and west, and say:

> (N) *I call upon light and earth at the north to illuminate and strengthen the circle.*
>
> (E) *I call upon light and air at the east to illuminate and enliven the circle.*
>
> (S) *I call upon light and fire at the south to illuminate and warm the circle.*
>
> (W) *I call upon light and water at the west to illuminate and cleanse the circle.*

Take athame in upraised hand, begin circle at north and move around the circle north to east to south to west, and say:

> *I draw this circle in the presence of the Goddess and the God where they may come and bless their child,* (name).

Lower the athame at the north, and as you walk around the circle, envision a blue light shooting out from the point and forming the circle boundary, and say:

> *This is the boundary of the circle. Only love shall enter and leave.*

Return to altar and ring bell three times. Place point of athame in the salt and say:

> *Salt is life and purifying. I bless this salt to be used in this sacred circle in the names of the Goddess and the God,* (names).

Pick up salt bowl and use tip of athame to drop three portions of salt into the water bowl and set salt bowl back in its place. Stir three times with athame and say:

> *Let the blessed salt purify this water that it may be blessed to*

*use in this sacred circle. In the names of the Goddess and the
God,* (names), *I consecrate and cleanse this water.*

Take the salted water bowl in hand and sprinkle water from it as you
move deosil around the circle (N-E-S-W-N) and say:

I consecrate this circle in the names of the Goddess and the God,
(names). *The circle is conjured a circle of power that is purified
and sealed. So mote it be!*

Return the water bowl to the altar and pick up censer; take it around
the circle to cense it; return censer to altar. Take anointing oil, make a
Solar Cross ringed by a circle on your forehead, and say:

I, (name) *am consecrated in the names of the Goddess and the
God,* (names), *in this their circle.*

If working with family members or a Green-focused coven, open a
door in the circle with the athame now for all to enter. Use anointing
oil to trace a Solar Cross in a circle on their foreheads as each person
enters, having said some kind of greeting, such as the Wiccan, "I come
in perfect love and perfect trust." Then close the door with the athame.

Take the wand and hold it aloft with both arms open and upraised at
the north of the circle (envision a powerful bull arriving) and say:

*I call upon you, Elemental Earth, to attend this rite and guard
this circle, for as I have body and strength, we are kith and kin!*

Lower wand and move to the east, raise up wand (see devas, fairies,
or an eagle in flight) and say:

*I call upon you, Elemental Air, to attend this rite and guard
this circle, for as I breathe and think, we are kith and kin!*

Lower wand and move to the south, raise up wand (see a dragon)
and say:

*I call upon you, Elemental Fire, to attend this rite and guard
this circle, for as I consume life to live, we are kith and kin!*

Lower wand and move to west, hold wand aloft (see an undine, a sea
serpent, or a dolphin) and say:

*I call upon you, Elemental Water, to attend this rite and guard
this circle, for as I feel and my heart beats, we are kith and kin!*

Return to altar and use wand to draw the symbol of infinity (an 8 lying on its side) in the air above the altar, the sign of working between the worlds. Set wand on altar and raise up athame in both hands overhead and say:

Hail to the elementals at the four quarters! Welcome Lady and Lord to this rite! I stand between the worlds with love and power all around!

Set down athame and pick up goblet of wine. Pour a little into the cauldron. This is a libation to the Divine in which they are honored by offering to them the first draught, then you take a sip. You may prefer to have a bowl specifically for the libation. Ring bell three times and say:

The Goddess of summer walks through the land with the God of the forest, and the dark time of winter is behind me.

Ring bell seven times and say:

The animals breed and the plants pollinate, as the May Queen and Green Man bestow their blessings upon the earth and earth's creatures. I, who am their child, (name), *rejoice with them and ask that their happy union become the example for all humanity to live in love and harmony.*

Light the candle in the cauldron and say:

The dark days are cleared away that the May Day can now begin!

Drop some of the woodruff into the flame and say:

May the light of May fire bring happiness and peace, and may the victory of the King of the Wood come into my life that I may dwell in the joy of the Lady and the Lord. So mote it be!

As you state the properties of each, drop wood chips one by one into the flame (be careful, and it is always good to use a small cauldron that can be covered with a snuffer in case things get out of hand—you don't need to use a lot of chips, just a little for the symbology):

I burn thee birch to honor the Goddess;
And now add thee oak to honor the God.
Thou rowan I add for a magical life;
And add thee willow to celebrate death.
Thou hawthorne I burn for fairies near me;

Thou hazel I burn for wisdom you bring.
I add thee good apple to bring to me love;
And thou vine whose fruit is symbol of joy.
Fir you are added as the symbol of rebirth;
Your sweet savor reminds me of my immortality.
My blessings I give to all of thee,
and thy blessings I call from thee upon me.
So as I will, so mote it be!

Hold up the goblet in both hands and say:

I greet the time of unions and give honor to the Lord and the
Lady for their fruitfulness!

Take a sip from the goblet and set back on the altar.

Note: Do not add libation to the hot cauldron. Use a separate bowl for this.

Cakes and Wine—Ring bell three times. Feet spread and arms upraised, say:

I acknowledge my needs and offer my appreciation to that
which sustains me! May I ever remember the blessings of my
Lady and my Lord.

Feet together, take up goblet in left hand and athame in right. Slowly lower the point of the athame into the wine and say:

As male joins female for the benefit of both, let the fruits of
their union promote life. Let the earth be fruitful and let her
wealth be spread throughout all lands.

Lay down the athame and drink from the goblet. Replace the goblet on the altar and pick up the athame. Touch the point of the athame to the cake in the offering dish and say:

This food is the blessing of the Lady and the Lord given freely to
me. As freely as I have received, may I also give food for the
body, mind, and spirit to those who seek such of me.

Eat the food, finish the wine, and say:

As I enjoy these gifts of the Goddess and the God, (names), *may*
I remember that without them I would have nothing. So mote
it be!

When all is finished, hold athame in your power hand level over altar and say:

Lord and Lady, I am blessed by your sharing this time with me, watching and guarding me, and guiding me here and in all things. I came in love and I depart in love.

Raise up athame in a salute and say:

Love is the law and love is the bond. Merry did I meet, merry do I part, and merry will I meet again. Merry meet, merry part, and merry meet again! The circle is now cleared. So mote it be!

Kiss the flat of the blade and set the athame on the altar. Take up the snuffer and go to the north quarter, raise up arms and say:

Depart in peace, Elemental Earth. My blessings take with you!

Lower arms and snuff the candle, envision the Elemental Power departing. Go to the east, raise up arms and say:

Depart in peace, Elemental Air. My blessings take with you!

Lower arms and snuff the candle, envision the Elemental Power departing. Go to the south, raise up arms and say:

Depart in peace, Elemental Fire. My blessings take with you!

Lower arms and snuff the candle, envision the Elemental Power departing. Go to the west, raise up arms and say:

Depart in peace, Elemental Water. My blessings take with you!

Lower arms and snuff the candle, envision the Elemental Power departing. Return to altar and set down snuffer. Raise up arms and say:

Beings and powers of the visible and invisible, depart in peace! You aid in my work, whisper in my mind, and bless me from the Otherworld, and there is harmony between us. My blessings take with you. The circle is cleared.

Take up athame, go to the north quarter, point athame down and move widdershins around circle (N-W-S-E-N). Envision the blue light drawing back into the athame and say:

The circle is open yet the circle remains as its magical power is drawn back into me.

When you return to the north having walked the circle, raise up the athame so the blade touches your forehead and envision the blue light swirling around back into you. Return to altar and say:

> *The ceremony is ended. Blessings have been given and blessings have been received, may the peace of the Goddess and the God remain in my heart. So mote it be!*

Set down the athame. Put away all magical tools and clear the altar except for candles or any objects that need to burn out or work for a stated time (such as candle magic). The cauldron or libation bowl contents are poured onto the earth (if not out in the yard, then into a flowerpot containing soil and perhaps a hardy, leafy green plant). Be sure to carefully extinguish the flame in the cauldron.

Traditional foods are those flavored with flowers, such as cookies made with rose extract and custards containing marigold or nasturtium, oatmeal cakes and wine flavored with flower petals of rose or nasturtium, or dandelion wine. Also, fruity wine, spiced pears, and cinnamon bread with raisins, almonds, and almond paste may be used.

Beltane Activities

Here are some Beltane activities that could be included at the Sabbat or during the day:

- Make paper baskets by folding a square piece of decorated paper diagonally and gluing or tying a handle of yarn through punched holes. Then place a few spring flowers inside the basket and place on the front doorknobs of your friends' and neighbors' houses.

   The kids will especially enjoy this because you have to do it undetected and not let on when people wonder who brought them the May flowers. I learned this as a child from my mother and used to go out early in the morning to place the baskets, but I also know that in some areas, it is a fairly common practice.

   A variation we also did was to cut colored construction paper into strips and weave two color strips together to form a square, then proceed as usual. I always preferred yellow and light green.

- Make a wish as you jump over a bonfire (or a campfire—May Day is a fine day to go camping).

- String beads or flowers for a blessing:

    May the God and the Goddess and the power of the elementals bless me now and always be with me.

- Make Beltane Bread. Preheat oven to 375 degrees, and combine:
    - 4 cups sifted flour
    - ½ cup ground almonds
    - 2 cups sugar
    - 1 tube almond paste
    - ½ teaspoon baking powder
    - 1 teaspoon cinnamon
    - 5 eggs

When dough is worked to medium soft, shape into flattened balls and place on ungreased cookie sheet. Bake until golden brown, about 20 minutes. Cool, ice with white Solar Cross. You could try this as a single loaf. I also like to make an almond biscuit with biscuit mix, almond extract, sugar, cinnamon, and eggs, but in smaller proportions. (A lot of my cooking is unmeasured, which doesn't help for making recipes.)

13

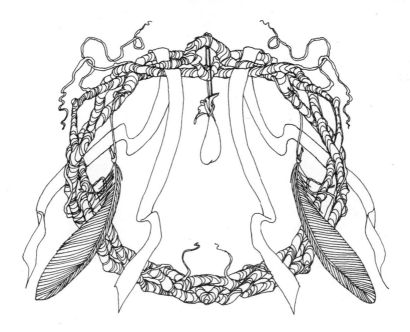

Litha Sabbat
June 21

Preparing Your Altar

- Altar candles should be blue.

- Incense may be lavender or musk.

- Circle may be decorated with summer flowers and fruit.

- Circle candles remain the usual colors for the elementals (green, yellow, red, and blue).

- Have a small amount of water in the cauldron. Do not fill the altar water bowl completely; leave room to add the water from the cauldron.

- Have a red votive candle in a heat-proof bowl on the altar.

- Have nine herbs and a bowl on the altar: betony wood (or basil), chamomile, fennel (or lavender), lemon balm (or dianthus), mullein, rue, St. John's Wort, thyme, and vervain.

Instructions for the Ceremony

The text is for solitary use but may be thus altered for family or coven participation. The envisionings are suggestions only.

Sweep circle area; lay out circle and altar items; bathe and robe. Light incense and altar candles. Ring bell three times and say:

> **The circle is about to be cast and I freely stand within to greet my Lady and my Lord.**

Take center candle from altar, light each candle of the circle and move around the circle north, then east, south, and west, and say:

- (N) **I call upon light and earth at the north to illuminate and strengthen the circle.**
- (E) **I call upon light and air at the east to illuminate and enliven the circle.**
- (S) **I call upon light and fire at the south to illuminate and warm the circle.**
- (W) **I call upon light and water at the west to illuminate and cleanse the circle.**

Take athame in upraised hand, begin circle at north and move around the circle north to east to south to west, and say:

> **I draw this circle in the presence of the Goddess and the God where they may come and bless their child,** (name).

Lower the athame at the north, and as you walk around the circle, envision a blue light shooting out from the point and forming the circle boundary, and say:

> **This is the boundary of the circle. Only love shall enter and leave.**

Return to altar and ring bell three times. Place point of athame in the salt and say:

> **Salt is life and purifying. I bless this salt to be used in this sacred circle in the names of the Goddess and the God,** (names).

Pick up salt bowl and use tip of athame to drop three portions of salt into the water bowl and set salt bowl back in its place. Stir three times with athame and say:

> *Let the blessed salt purify this water that it may be blessed to use in this sacred circle. In the names of the Goddess and the God,* (names)*, I consecrate and cleanse this water.*

Take the salted water bowl in hand and sprinkle water from it as you move deosil around the circle (N-E-S-W-N) and say:

> *I consecrate this circle in the names of the Goddess and the God,* (names)*. The circle is conjured a circle of power that is purified and sealed. So mote it be!*

Return the water bowl to the altar and pick up censer; take it around the circle to cense it; return censer to altar. Take anointing oil, make a Solar Cross ringed by a circle on your forehead, and say:

> *I,* (name) *am consecrated in the names of the Goddess and the God,* (names)*, in this their circle.*

If working with family members or a Green-focused coven, open a door in the circle with the athame now for all to enter. Use anointing oil to trace a Solar Cross in a circle on their foreheads as each person enters, having said some kind of greeting, such as the Wiccan, "I come in perfect love and perfect trust." Then close the door with the athame.

Take the wand and hold it aloft with both arms open and upraised at the north of the circle (envision a powerful bull arriving) and say:

> *I call upon you, Elemental Earth, to attend this rite and guard this circle, for as I have body and strength, we are kith and kin!*

Lower wand and move to the east, raise up wand (see devas, fairies, or an eagle in flight) and say:

> *I call upon you, Elemental Air, to attend this rite and guard this circle, for as I breathe and think, we are kith and kin!*

Lower wand and move to the south, raise up wand (see a dragon) and say:

> *I call upon you, Elemental Fire, to attend this rite and guard this circle, for as I consume life to live, we are kith and kin!*

Lower wand and move to the west, hold wand aloft (see an undine, a sea serpent, or a dolphin) and say:

> *I call upon you, Elemental Water, to attend this rite and guard this circle, for as I feel and my heart beats, we are kith and kin!*

Return to altar and use wand to draw the symbol of infinity (an 8 lying on its side) in the air above the altar, the sign of working between the worlds. Set wand on altar and raise up athame in both hands overhead and say:

> *Hail to the elementals at the four quarters! Welcome Lady and Lord to this rite! I stand between the worlds with love and power all around!*

Set down athame and pick up goblet of wine. Pour a little into the cauldron. This is a libation to the Divine in which they are honored by offering to them the first draught, then you take a sip. You may prefer to have a bowl specifically for the libation. Ring bell three times and say:

> *I celebrate life on this midsummer day! Sadness is cast aside and joy flows within as the high summer now begins.*

Take red candle and light it from the center altar candle. Hold it up in your right hand and say:

> *The light of the sun, the God of Life, shines round me and in me for all the world to see.*

Set candle in bowl and place on pentacle. With finger tips, sprinkle water from the cauldron upon the altar and say:

> *The Lord and Lady of the Greenwood have made their pact. The Lord rises into the Lady and prepares to descend into the corn, in both ways to be born again of the mother.*

Pour the water from the cauldron into the purified water bowl and say:

> *The life that enters the Lady's care is sanctified and purified in her love.*

Ring bell nine times. Raise arms upward and say:

> *As the sun moves on his course, so the course of life moves closer to death that life may come again. Soon will the Lord of the Corn move into his realm to become the Lord of Shadows, but now he shares with me the joy of his life and his love.*

Arms down, take up the athame and hold it over the candle and say:

As the God and Goddess share their light and life with me,
so do I share with others and offer comfort as is meet.

Set down athame, put herbs in the bowl, and mix with the athame. Add the herbs to the candle and say:

I call upon the powers imbued in these herbs that the midsummer
fire be empowered. Herbs of the earth; symbols of the planets, of
life and of love, your scent fills the air and drives away care.

Set down athame, hands (palms down) rest upon the altar, and say:

Lord and Lady, you fill my life with your bountiful love and gifts.
I call upon thee both for your continued blessings and offer my
petition to thee both that your love and caring remain with me
always. May I pass this joy to others. So mote it be!

Re-dedication Ritual

Optional, but I like to do this. If you do not do a re-dedication with this Sabbat, then you should proceed to Cakes and Wine.

With wand held aloft, say:

At this time of midsummer joy, I re-affirm my love for my
Lord and my Lady through my re-dedication.

Arms upraised, say:

Lady and Lord, (names), *I call out to thee! I hold you in honor*
and know that I am one with all the things of the earth and
sky. My kin are the trees and the herbs of the fields; the animals
and stones through the seas and the hills. The fresh waters and
deserts are built out of thee, and I am of you and you are of me.

Lower arms and say:

I call upon you to grant my desire. Let me rejoice in my
oneness with all things and let me love the life that emanates
from my Lady and my Lord into all things. I know and accept
the creed: that if I do not have that spark of love within me,
I will never find it outside myself, for love is the law and love
is the bond! And this do I honor when I give honor to the Lady
and the Lord.

Kiss your right palm, hold your hand high, and say:

My Lady and my Lord, known to me as (names), *I stand before you both and dedicate myself to your honor. I will defend and protect thy spark within me and seek thy protection and defense of me. You are my life and I am of you. I accept and will ever abide by the principal of harming none, for what is sent returns. So mote it be!*

Take up the goblet of wine, slowly pour the remainder of wine into the cauldron, and say:

As this wine drains from the cup, so shall the blood drain from my body should I ever turn away from the Lady and the Lord or harm those in kinship with their love, for to do so would be to break trust, to cast aside the love of the Goddess and the God, and to break my own heart. Yet through their continued love I know they would heal my heart and spirit that I might again journey through the cauldron of rebirth to embrace the love they freely give. So mote it be!

Dip forefinger into the anointing oil and again make the sign of the Solar Cross over the third eye (center of forehead). Then make the sign of the pentagram over the heart, followed by the Sacred Triangle (for the triple quality of both Deities) touching solar plexus, right breast, left breast, solar plexus. Refill the goblet for Cakes and Wine.

Cakes and Wine—Ring bell three times. Feet spread and arms upraised, say:

I acknowledge my needs and offer my appreciation to that which sustains me! May I ever remember the blessings of my Lady and my Lord.

Feet together, take up goblet in left hand and athame in right. Slowly lower the point of the athame into the wine and say:

As male joins female for the benefit of both, let the fruits of their union promote life. Let the earth be fruitful and let her wealth be spread throughout all lands.

Lay down the athame and drink from the goblet. Replace the goblet on the altar and pick up the athame. Touch the point of the athame to the cake in the offering dish and say:

This food is the blessing of the Lady and the Lord given freely to me. As freely as I have received, may I also give food for the body, mind, and spirit to those who seek such of me.

Eat the cake, finish the wine, and say:

As I enjoy these gifts of the Goddess and the God, (names), *may I remember that without them I would have nothing. So mote it be!*

When all is finished, hold athame in your power hand level over the altar and say:

Lord and Lady, I am blessed by your sharing this time with me; watching and guarding me, and guiding me here and in all things. I came in love and I depart in love.

Raise up athame in a salute and say:

Love is the law and love is the bond. Merry did I meet, merry do I part, and merry will I meet again. Merry meet, merry part, and merry meet again! The circle is now cleared. So mote it be!

Kiss the flat of the blade and set the athame on the altar. Take up the snuffer and go to the north quarter, raise up arms and say:

Depart in peace, Elemental Earth. My blessings take with you!

Lower arms and snuff the candle, envision the Elemental Power departing. Go to the east, raise up arms and say:

Depart in peace, Elemental Air. My blessings take with you!

Lower arms and snuff the candle, envision the Elemental Power departing. Go to the south, raise up arms and say:

Depart in peace, Elemental Fire. My blessings take with you!

Lower arms and snuff the candle, envision the Elemental Power departing. Go to the west, raise up arms and say:

Depart in peace, Elemental Water. My blessings take with you!

Lower arms and snuff the candle, envision the Elemental Power departing. Return to altar and set down snuffer. Raise up arms and say:

Beings and powers of the visible and invisible, depart in peace! You aid in my work, whisper in my mind, and bless me from the Otherworld, and there is harmony between us. My blessings take with you. The circle is cleared.

Take up athame, go to the north quarter, point athame down and move widdershins around circle (N-W-S-E-N). Envision the blue light drawing back into the athame and say:

The circle is open yet the circle remains as its magical power is drawn back into me.

When you return to the north, having walked the circle, raise up the athame so the blade touches your forehead, and envision the blue light swirling around back into you. Return to altar and say:

The ceremony is ended. Blessings have been given and blessings have been received, may the peace of the Goddess and the God remain in my heart. So mote it be!

Set down the athame. Put away all magical tools and clear the altar except for candles or any objects that need to burn out or work for a stated time (such as candle magic). The cauldron or libation bowl contents are poured onto the earth (if not out in the yard, then into a flowerpot containing soil and perhaps a hardy, leafy green plant).

Traditional foods include red wine, sweet breads (which contain glands from veal), herb bread, and pastries.

Litha Activities

The following are some suggestions for Litha activities, some of which you may want to incorporate into the Sabbat, while others would be more suitable during the day.

- Tie a sprig of rowan, a sprig of rue, and three flowers of St. John's Wort with red thread and hang over the door.

- Make amulets (simple charms) of protection out of herbs such as rue and rowan. If you make new amulets each year you can dispose of the old in the midsummer fire, but we like to simply recharge the old one for another year until it starts to deteriorate, then burn it.

- Create a pouch for psychic dreams (mugwort and bay leaves in a cloth of lavender, blue, or yellow and sewn with red thread) and place under your pillow.

- Make a Solar Wheel as a terrific family project—everyone can make one for their bedroom. Wind palm or grape vine into a circle, twisting as you go. Cut two short lengths of stem to be just a bit larger than the diameter of the circle and place one across the back horizontally and the other vertically crossing in back of the horizontal one and coming forward to the front of the circle to secure both, then adorn with symbols of the elementals (stone, feather, ashes in a pouch or a small candle, and a shell) and festoon with yellow ribbons. Hang in a tree outside or indoors as a reminder of the God's protection.

- Make a Witch's Ladder (another fun family project) using three colored yarns (red, black, and white for the Triple Goddess) braided together to be three feet long. Add nine feathers all the same color for a specific charm (such as green for money) or various colors for a more diverse charm, tie ends and hang up. Colors are red for vitality, blue for peace and protection, yellow for alertness and cheer, green for prosperity, brown for stability, black for wisdom, black and white for balance, patterned for clairvoyance, and iridescent for insight.

- You can burn the old Yule wreath in the Litha fire.

- Make a rue protection pouch out of white cotton. Add two or three sprigs of rue, bits of whole grain wheat bread, a pinch of salt, and two star anise seeds and hang indoors (can do one for each bedroom).

- Tie vervain, rosemary, and hyssop with white thread and dip the tips into a bowl of spring water (you can buy bottled spring water in grocery stores) and sprinkle the water about the house to chase out negativity, or sprinkle your tools to cleanse and purify.

- Gather herbs like St. John's Wort, vervain, and yarrow.

- Soak thyme in olive oil, then lightly anoint your eyelids to see the fairy folk at night.

- Tie a bunch of fennel with red ribbons and hang over the door for long life and the protection of the home.

- Look for the fairy folk under an elder tree, but don't eat their food or you'll have to remain with them for seven years (which I suppose would be a lot of fun unless you have other plans!).

14

Lughnassadh Sabbat
August 1

Preparing Your Altar

- Altar candles should be yellow.

- Incense may be frankincense.

- Circle may be decorated with summer flowers and grains.

- Circle candles remain the usual colors for the elementals (green, yellow, red, and blue).

- Have a loaf of multigrain or whole cracked wheat bread on the altar.

Instructions for the Ceremony

Sweep circle area; lay out circle and altar items; bathe and robe. Light incense and altar candles. Ring bell three times and say:

The circle is about to be cast and I freely stand within to greet my Lady and my Lord.

Take center candle from altar, light each candle of the circle moving north, then east, south, and west, and say:

(N) *I call upon light and earth at the north to illuminate and strengthen the circle.*

(E) *I call upon light and air at the east to illuminate and enliven the circle.*

(S) *I call upon light and fire at the south to illuminate and warm the circle.*

(W) *I call upon light and water at the west to illuminate and cleanse the circle.*

Take athame in upraised hand, begin circle at north and move around the circle north to east to south to west, and say:

I draw this circle in the presence of the Goddess and the God where they may come and bless their child, (name).

Lower the athame at the north, and as you walk around the circle, envision a blue light shooting out from the point and forming the circle boundary, and say:

This is the boundary of the circle. Only love shall enter and leave.

Return to altar and ring bell three times. Place point of athame in the salt and say:

Salt is life and purifying. I bless this salt to be used in this sacred circle in the names of the Goddess and the God, (names).

Pick up salt bowl and use tip of athame to drop three portions of salt into the water bowl and set salt bowl back in its place. Stir three times with athame and say:

Let the blessed salt purify this water that it may be blessed to use in this sacred circle. In the names of the Goddess and the God, (names), *I consecrate and cleanse this water.*

Take the salted water bowl in hand and sprinkle water from it as you move deosil around the circle (N-E-S-W-N) and say:

> *I consecrate this circle in the names of the Goddess and the God,* (names). *The circle is conjured a circle of power that is purified and sealed. So mote it be!*

Return the water bowl to the altar and pick up censer; take it around the circle to cense it; return censer to altar. Take anointing oil, make a Solar Cross ringed by a circle on your forehead, and say:

> *I,* (name) *am consecrated in the names of the Goddess and the God,* (names), *in this their circle.*

If working with family members or a Green-focused Coven, open a door in the circle with the athame now for all to enter. Use anointing oil to trace a Solar Cross in a circle on their foreheads as each person enters, having said some kind of greeting, such as the Wiccan, "I come in perfect love and perfect trust." Then close the door with the athame. The text is for solitary use but may be thus altered for family or coven participation.

Take the wand and hold it aloft with both arms open and upraised at the north of the circle (envision a powerful bull arriving) and say:

> *I call upon you, Elemental Earth, to attend this rite and guard this circle, for as I have body and strength, we are kith and kin!*

Lower wand and move to the east, raise up wand (see devas, fairies, or an eagle in flight) and say:

> *I call upon you, Elemental Air, to attend this rite and guard this circle, for as I breathe and think, we are kith and kin!*

Lower wand and move to the south, raise up wand (see a dragon) and say:

> *I call upon you, Elemental Fire, to attend this rite and guard this circle, for as I consume life to live, we are kith and kin!*

Lower wand and move to the west, hold wand aloft (see an undine, a sea serpent, or a dolphin) and say:

> *I call upon you, Elemental Water, to attend this rite and guard this circle, for as I feel and my heart beats, we are kith and kin!*

Return to altar and use wand to draw the symbol of infinity (an 8 lying on its side) in the air above the altar, the sign of working between the worlds. Set wand on altar and raise up athame in both hands overhead and say:

Hail to the elementals at the four quarters! Welcome Lady and Lord to this rite! I stand between the worlds with love and power all around!

Set down athame and pick up goblet of wine. Pour a little into the cauldron. This is a libation to the Divine in which they are honored by offering to them the first draught, then you take a sip. You may prefer to have a bowl specifically for the libation. Ring bell three times and say:

I celebrate this day the First Harvest, the Festival of Bread.

Chant or sing and dance around the circle to the Shaker tune, "Gift to Be Simple" (known in the Craft as "Lord of the Dance"):

Dance, dance, wherever you may be;
When you dance with the Lord, he will dance with thee.
Turn, turn, a circle you may form;
And the Lord of the Dance is the Lord of the Corn!

Stop at the altar and with upraised arms sing or chant:

Down, down, into the earth he'll go;
Giving life to the grain that in spring we'll sown.
He rules the Shadowland till Yule;
When his sun is reborn and he joins us anew!

Ring bell seven times and say:

Great is the power of the God of the sun and the Goddess of the earth from whom spring all life!

Take up wand, hold it upraised over the bread, and say:

The harvest of the corn that sustains us is brought through death and rebirth. The Lord of the Corn leaves the side of the earth mother that his power may be passed into the land for his children to live. Blessed be the God of the Corn, whose love for his children knows no bounds! In the Land of Shadows will he abide with the Lady as crone, awaiting the time of his joyous rebirth.

Lower the wand to touch the bread and say:

May (God's name—Lugh) *bless this bread that I eat in the honor of the cycle of life that created it and me.*

Set wand on altar, tear off a small portion of bread and drop into the cauldron, then eat a bite. The rest may be saved to be served later to others. With palms up, raise arms level over the altar and say:

My Lord and my Lady, (names), *I am blessed by your gifts from the soil. These first grains are the promise of life to come, and remind me that I am one with the All. So mote it be!*

Ring bell three times.

Cakes and Wine—Ring bell three times. Feet spread and arms upraised, say:

I acknowledge my needs and offer my appreciation to that which sustains me! May I ever remember the blessings of my Lady and my Lord.

Feet together, take up goblet in left hand and athame in right. Slowly lower the point of the athame into the wine and say:

As male joins female for the benefit of both, let the fruits of their union promote life. Let the earth be fruitful and let her wealth be spread throughout all lands.

Lay down the athame and drink from the goblet. Replace the goblet on the altar and pick up the athame. Touch the point of the athame to the cake in the offering dish and say:

This food is the blessing of the Lady and the Lord given freely to me. As freely as I have received, may I also give food for the body, mind, and spirit to those who seek such of me.

Eat the cake, finish the wine, and say:

As I enjoy these gifts of the Goddess and the God, (names), *may I remember that without them I would have nothing. So mote it be!*

When all is finished, hold athame in your power hand level over the altar and say:

Lord and Lady, I am blessed by your sharing this time with me; watching and guarding me, and guiding me here and in all things. I came in love and I depart in love.

Raise up athame in a salute and say:

Love is the law and love is the bond. Merry did I meet, merry do I part, and merry will I meet again. Merry meet, merry part, and merry meet again! The circle is now cleared. So mote it be!

Kiss the flat of the blade and set the athame on the altar. Take up the snuffer and go to the north quarter, raise up arms and say:

Depart in peace, Elemental Earth. My blessings take with you!

Lower arms and snuff the candle, envision the Elemental Power departing. Go to the east, raise up arms and say:

Depart in peace, Elemental Air. My blessings take with you!

Lower arms and snuff the candle, envision the Elemental Power departing. Go to the south, raise up arms and say:

Depart in peace, Elemental Fire. My blessings take with you!

Lower arms and snuff the candle, envision the Elemental Power departing. Go to the west, raise up arms and say:

Depart in peace, Elemental Water. My blessings take with you!

Lower arms and snuff the candle, envision the Elemental Power departing. Return to altar and set down snuffer. Raise up arms and say:

Beings and powers of the visible and invisible, depart in peace! You aid in my work, whisper in my mind, and bless me from the Otherworld, and there is harmony between us. My blessings take with you. The circle is cleared.

Take up athame, go to the north quarter, point athame down and move widdershins around circle (N-W-S-E-N). Envision the blue light drawing back into the athame and say:

The circle is open yet the circle remains as its magical power is drawn back into me.

When you return to the north having walked the circle, raise up the athame so the blade touches your forehead and envision the blue light swirling around back into you. Return to altar and say:

The ceremony is ended. Blessings have been given and blessings have been received, may the peace of the Goddess and the God remain in my heart. So mote it be!

Set down the athame. Put away all magical tools and clear the altar except for candles or any objects that need to burn out or work for a stated time (such as candle magic). The cauldron or libation bowl contents are poured onto the earth (if not out in the yard, then into a flowerpot containing soil and perhaps a hardy, leafy green plant).

Traditional foods for this Sabbat include multigrain bread, blackberry pie and a dark, fruity wine (I like to use blackberry wine for this occasion).

Lughnassadh Activities

The following are a few suggestions for activities that may be incorporated into the Sabbat ritual or engaged in during the day.

- Make sand candles to honor the Goddess and the God of the sea.

  If you do not live near a beach, you can achieve the same effect by putting sand in a large box, adding water, and working from there. This is definitely a porch or kitchen floor job, and I recommend newspapers under your work area for easy clean-up.

  —Melt wax from old candles (save the stubs from altar candles) in a coffee can set in a pot of boiling water.

  —Add any essential oil you want for scent.

  —Scoop out a candle mold in wet sand (you can make a cauldron by scooping out the sand and using a finger to poke three "feet" in the sand).

  —Hold the wick (you can get these ready-made in arts and crafts stores) in the center and gently pour in the melted wax.

  —Wait until it hardens, then slip your fingers under the candle and carefully lift it out and brush off the excess sand.

- String Indian corn on black thread for a necklace.

- If the Sabbat falls on a rainy day, you could collect rainwater in a glass or earthenware container, add dried mugwort, and use to empower objects.

- Create and bury a Witch's Bottle. This is a glass jar with sharp, pointy things inside to keep away harm. You can use needles, pins, thorns, thistles, nails, and bits of broken glass; it's a good way to dispose of broken crockery, old sewing equipment, and the pins that come in new clothes. Bury it near the entry to the house (like next to the driveway or the front door) or inside a large planter.

- Do a Harvest Chant when serving the corn bread at dinner:

  The Earth Mother grants the grain,
  The Horned God goes to his domain.
  By giving life into her grain,
  The God dies then is born again.

- Make a Corn Dolly to save for next Imbolc (although we keep the same ones and have one in the entry hall and one in the kitchen as a symbolic Guardian Goddess and Hearth Goddess). Double over a bundle of wheat and tie it near the top to form a head. Take a bit of the fiber from either side of the main portion and twist into arms that you tie together in front of the dolly. Add a small bouquet of flowers to the "hands," and then you can decorate the dolly with a dress and bonnet.

- Bake corn bread sticks. You can find an iron mold shaped like little ears of corn in kitchen supply shops. Preheat oven to 425 degrees.

      1 cup flour
      ½ cup corn meal
      ¼ cup sugar
      ¾ teaspoon salt
      2 teaspoons baking powder
      2 eggs
      1 cup milk
      ¼ cup shortening

  Sift dry ingredients together. Add eggs, milk, and shortening, and beat until smooth. Pour into molds and bake for 20-25 minutes.

- Collect blackberries and make a fresh pie marked with the Solar Cross (equal-armed cross).

- Have a magical picnic with libations to the earth of bread and wine.

- Sprout wheat germ in a terra cotta saucer (these can be found in nurseries for use under terra cotta flower pots). The sprouts can be added to homemade bread or used as an offering. Children enjoy planting the seeds and watching them grow, too.

> *God of the grain,*
> *Lord of rebirth.*
> *Return in spring,*
> *Renew the earth.*

A Corn Man Wheel

- Make a Solar Wheel or a Corn Man Wheel:

    —Turn a wire hanger into a circle (standard circle material for wreaths, too), keeping the hook to hang it by.

    —Make a small cardboard disk to glue the corn tips onto. You can decorate it with any design, for example, a pentagram or sun.

—Place ears of Indian "squaw" corn (it is smaller than regular corn and fits easily on a coat hanger) with the tips in the center of the circle and secure with hot glue to the cardboard disk. Use eight ears for a Solar Wheel, or five ears for a Corn Man. If all the ears of corn meet just right you won't need the disk, but if they are uneven the disk is helpful.

—Wrap a bit of the husks of each ear around the wire on either side of the ear of corn, leaving some to stand out free from the corn.

—Let dry overnight and hang on the front door.

15

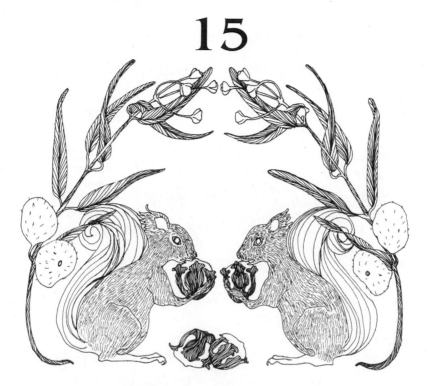

Mabon Sabbat
September 21

Preparing Your Altar

- Altar candles should be brown or cinnamon.

- Incense may be pine, sage, sweetgrass, or myrrh.

- Circle may be decorated with autumn flowers, acorns, gourds, corn sheaves, and fall leaves.

- Donate canned goods for those in need.

- Have nutbread in a dish on the altar.

- Circle candles remain the usual colors for the elementals (green, yellow, red, and blue).

Instructions for the Ceremony

Sweep circle area; lay out circle and altar items; bathe and robe. Light incense and altar candles. Ring bell three times and say:

> *The circle is about to be cast and I freely stand within to greet my Lady and my Lord.*

Take center candle from altar and light each candle of the circle moving north, then east, south, and west, and say:

(N) *I call upon light and earth at the north to illuminate and strengthen the circle.*

(E) *I call upon light and air at the east to illuminate and enliven the circle.*

(S) *I call upon light and fire at the south to illuminate and warm the circle.*

(W) *I call upon light and water at the west to illuminate and cleanse the circle.*

Take athame in upraised hand, begin circle at north and move around the circle north to east to south to west, and say:

> *I draw this circle in the presence of the Goddess and the God where they may come and bless their child,* (name).

Lower the athame at the north, and as you walk around the circle envision a blue light shooting out from the point and forming the circle boundary, and say:

> *This is the boundary of the circle. Only love shall enter and leave.*

Return to altar and ring bell three times. Place point of athame in the salt and say:

> *Salt is life and purifying. I bless this salt to be used in this sacred circle in the names of the Goddess and the God,* (names).

Pick up salt bowl and use tip of athame to drop three portions of salt into the water bowl and set salt bowl back in its place. Stir three times with athame and say:

> *Let the blessed salt purify this water that it may be blessed to use in this sacred circle. In the names of the Goddess and the God,* (names), *I consecrate and cleanse this water.*

Take the salted water bowl in hand and sprinkle water from it as you move deosil around the circle (N-E-S-W-N) and say:

> *I consecrate this circle in the names of the Goddess and the God,* (names). *The circle is conjured a circle of power that is purified and sealed. So mote it be!*

Return the water bowl to the altar and pick up censer; take it around the circle to cense it; return censer to altar. Take anointing oil, make a Solar Cross ringed by a circle on your forehead, and say:

> *I,* (name) *am consecrated in the names of the Goddess and the God,* (names), *in this their circle.*

If working with family members or a Green-focused Coven, open a door in the circle with the athame now for all to enter. Use anointing oil to trace a Solar Cross in a circle on their foreheads as each person enters, having said some kind of greeting, such as the Wiccan, "I come in perfect love and perfect trust." Then close the door with the athame. The text is for solitary use but may be thus altered for family or coven participation. The envisionings are suggestions only.

Take the wand and hold it aloft with both arms open and upraised at the north of the circle (envision a powerful bull arriving) and say:

> *I call upon you, Elemental Earth, to attend this rite and guard this circle, for as I have body and strength, we are kith and kin!*

Lower wand and move to the east, raise up wand (see devas, fairies, or an eagle in flight) and say:

> *I call upon you, Elemental Air, to attend this rite and guard this circle, for as I breathe and think, we are kith and kin!*

Lower wand and move to the south, raise up wand (see a dragon) and say:

> *I call upon you, Elemental Fire, to attend this rite and guard this circle, for as I consume life to live, we are kith and kin!*

Lower wand and move to the west, hold wand aloft (see an undine, a sea serpent, or a dolphin) and say:

> *I call upon you, Elemental Water, to attend this rite and guard this circle, for as I feel and my heart beats, we are kith and kin!*

Return to altar and use wand to draw in the air the symbol of infinity (an 8 lying on its side) above the altar, the sign of working between the worlds. Set wand on altar, raise up athame in both hands overhead and say:

Hail to the elementals at the four quarters! Welcome Lady and Lord to this rite! I stand between the worlds with love and power all around!

Set down athame and pick up goblet of wine. Pour a little into the cauldron. This is a libation to the Divine in which they are honored by offering to them the first draught, then you take a sip. You may prefer to have a bowl specifically for the libation. Ring bell three times and say:

This day I celebrate the Second Harvest, that of fruits, nuts and the vines, and I remember those who struggle without. As I accept the gifts of the Lord and the Lady so do I pass along what I may to those who have need.

Ring bell three times and say:

The wheel of the year is ever turning, through sun tides and moon tides, through seasons and harvests, for plants and for people; for all life moves within the wheel of the year from life to death to life again. The balance and the harmony of the dance of life is the spiral dance of energy eternal.

Hold up the dish of nutbread and a cup of wine and say:

I ask the blessing of the Lady and the Lord, (names), *upon this food that the harvest be bountiful.*

Ring bell three times and say:

The Lord of Shadows rules in his Shadowland, yet his love holds true, and with him my own dance will one day move the Other Way. As this harvest moves onward to the last harvest, I call upon the Lady and the Lord to bless this beautiful season and my life within it.

Take up wand and move to the north of the circle. Raise wand and say:

Hail to thee, Elemental Earth! Your steadfastness helps me to maintain the things of my home, my health, and my comfort. I honor you!

Lower wand and move to the east. Raise wand and say:

Hail to thee, Elemental Air! Your inspiration helps me to learn and understand. I honor you!

Lower wand and move to the south. Raise wand and say:

Hail to thee, Elemental Fire! Your energy helps me with the drive to accomplish my goals. I honor you!

Lower wand and move to the west. Raise wand and say:

Hail to thee, Elemental Water! Your gentle flow helps me maintain calm and balance in my relationships with others. I honor you!

Return to altar. Touch canned goods with wand and say:

In the names of the Lord and the Lady, and with the aid of the elementals, I bless these fruits of the harvest for those who are in need. I offer aid and comfort to those whose needs arise throughout the turning of the wheel. May the Goddess and the God (names) *bless these offerings, the one who gives and the one who receives. So mote it be!*

Ring bell three times.

Cakes and Wine—Ring bell three times. Feet spread and arms upraised, say:

I acknowledge my needs and offer my appreciation to that which sustains me! May I ever remember the blessings of my Lady and my Lord.

Feet together, take up goblet in left hand and athame in right. Slowly lower the point of the athame into the wine and say:

As male joins female for the benefit of both, let the fruits of their union promote life. Let the earth be fruitful and let her wealth be spread throughout all lands.

Lay down the athame and drink from the goblet. Replace the goblet on the altar and pick up the athame. Touch the point of the athame to the cake in the offering dish and say:

This food is the blessing of the Lady and the Lord given freely to me. As freely as I have received, may I also give food for the body, mind, and spirit to those who seek such of me.

Eat the cake, finish the wine, and say:

> *As I enjoy these gifts of the Goddess and the God,* (names)*, may
> I remember that without them I would have nothing. So mote
> it be!*

When all is finished, hold athame in your power hand level over the
altar and say:

> *Lord and Lady, I am blessed by your sharing this time with
> me; watching and guarding me, and guiding me here and in
> all things. I came in love and I depart in love.*

Raise up athame in a salute and say:

> *Love is the law and love is the bond. Merry did I meet, merry do
> I part, and merry will I meet again. Merry meet, merry part,
> and merry meet again! The circle is now cleared. So mote it be!*

Kiss the flat of the blade and set the athame on the altar. Take up the
snuffer and go to the north quarter, raise up arms and say:

> *Depart in peace, Elemental Earth. My blessings take with you!*

Lower arms and snuff the candle, envision the Elemental Power
departing. Go to the east, raise up arms and say:

> *Depart in peace, Elemental Air. My blessings take with you!*

Lower arms and snuff the candle, envision the Elemental Power
departing. Go to the south, raise up arms and say:

> *Depart in peace, Elemental Fire. My blessings take with you!*

Lower arms and snuff the candle, envision the Elemental Power
departing. Go to the west, raise up arms and say:

> *Depart in peace, Elemental Water. My blessings take with you!*

Lower arms and snuff the candle, envision the Elemental Power
departing. Return to altar and set down snuffer. Raise up arms and say:

> *Beings and powers of the visible and invisible, depart in peace!
> You aid in my work, whisper in my mind, and bless me from
> the Otherworld, and there is harmony between us. My blessings
> take with you. The circle is cleared.*

Take up athame, go to the north quarter, point athame down and move widdershins around circle (N-W-S-E-N). Envision the blue light drawing back into the athame and say:

The circle is open yet the circle remains as its magical power is drawn back into me.

When you return to the north, having walked the circle, raise up the athame so the blade touches your forehead, and envision the blue light swirling around back into you. Return to altar and say:

The ceremony is ended. Blessings have been given and blessings have been received, may the peace of the Goddess and the God remain in my heart. So mote it be!

Set down the athame. Put away all magical tools and clear the altar except for candles or any objects that need to burn out or work for a stated time (such as candle magic). The cauldron or libation bowl contents are poured onto the earth (if not out in the yard, then into a flowerpot containing soil and perhaps a hardy, leafy green plant).

Traditional foods for Mabon include squash pies, nutbread, smoked meats, smoked or roasted poultry, bean soup, and wine made of grapes or currants. I like to use a small amount of Cassias (currant) liqueur instead of wine.

Mabon Activities

Here are a few suggestions for Mabon activities that can be incorporated into the Sabbat or done during the day.

- Make a protection charm of hazelnuts (filberts) strung on red thread.

- Hang dried ears of corn on the front door, doorposts, or outside light fixture (hang the corn so it does not come in contact with the heat of the lightbulb).

- Serve a Mabon meal of wine from the God and beans and squashes from the Goddess. I like a hearty multi-bean soup with smoked meats included, such as cut-up mild sausage like mild Italian or Polish.

- Collect milkweed pods to decorate at Yuletide and attract the fairies.

- Call upon the elementals and honor them for their help with (N—earth) the home and finances, (E—air) school and knowledge, (S—fire) careers and accomplishments, (W—water) emotional balance and fruitful relationships.

16

Samhain Sabbat
October 31

Preparing Your Altar

- Altar candles should be orange.

- Incense may be myrrh or patchouli.

- Circle may be decorated with autumn flowers, small pumpkins, branches, Indian corn, and gourds.

- Circle candles remain the usual colors for the elementals (green, yellow, red, and blue).

- Have a piece of parchment with weaknesses or bad habits you want to be rid of written on it.

- Have a black votive candle inside the cauldron.

- Have a white votive candle sitting on the altar.

- Have some heather on the altar and an apple or pomegranate.

Instructions for the Ceremony

Sweep circle area; lay out circle and altar items; bathe and robe. Light incense and altar candles. Ring bell three times and say:

> *The circle is about to be cast and I freely stand within to greet my Lady and my Lord.*

Take center candle from altar, light each candle of the circle moving north, then east, south, and west, and say:

> (N) *I call upon light and earth at the north to illuminate and strengthen the circle.*
>
> (E) *I call upon light and air at the east to illuminate and enliven the circle.*
>
> (S) *I call upon light and fire at the south to illuminate and warm the circle.*
>
> (W) *I call upon light and water at the west to illuminate and cleanse the circle.*

Take athame in upraised hand, begin circle at north and move around the circle north to east to south to west, and say:

> *I draw this circle in the presence of the Goddess and the God where they may come and bless their child,* (name).

Lower the athame at the north, and as you walk around the circle, envision a blue light shooting out from the point and forming the circle boundary, and say:

> *This is the boundary of the circle. Only love shall enter and leave.*

Return to altar and ring bell three times. Place point of athame in the salt and say:

> *Salt is life and purifying. I bless this salt to be used in this sacred circle in the names of the Goddess and the God,* (names).

Pick up salt bowl and use tip of athame to drop three portions of salt into the water bowl and set salt bowl back in its place. Stir three times with athame and say:

> *Let the blessed salt purify this water that it may be blessed to use in this sacred circle. In the names of the Goddess and the God,* (names), *I consecrate and cleanse this water.*

Take the salted water bowl in hand and sprinkle water from it as you move deosil around the circle (N-E-S-W-N) and say:

> *I consecrate this circle in the names of the Goddess and the God,* (names). *The circle is conjured a circle of power that is purified and sealed. So mote it be!*

Return the water bowl to the altar and pick up censer; take it around the circle to cense it; return censer to altar. Take anointing oil, make a Solar Cross ringed by a circle on your forehead, and say:

> *I,* (name), *am consecrated in the names of the Goddess and the God,* (names), *in this their circle.*

If working with family members or a Green-focused coven, open a door in the circle with the athame now for all to enter. Use anointing oil to trace a Solar Cross in a circle on their foreheads as each person enters, having said some kind of greeting, such as the Wiccan, "I come in perfect love and perfect trust." Then close the door with the athame. The text is for solitary use but may be thus altered for family or coven participation. The envisionings are suggestions only.

Take the wand, hold it aloft with both arms open and upraised at the north of the circle (envision a powerful bull arriving) and say:

> *I call upon you, Elemental Earth, to attend this rite and guard this circle, for as I have body and strength, we are kith and kin!*

Lower wand and move to the east, raise up wand (see devas, fairies, or an eagle in flight) and say:

> *I call upon you, Elemental Air, to attend this rite and guard this circle, for as I breathe and think, we are kith and kin!*

Lower wand and move to the south, raise up wand (see a dragon) and say:

> *I call upon you, Elemental Fire, to attend this rite and guard this circle, for as I consume life to live, we are kith and kin!*

Lower wand and move to the west, hold wand aloft (see an undine, a sea serpent, or a dolphin) and say:

I call upon you, Elemental Water, to attend this rite and guard this circle, for as I feel and my heart beats, we are kith and kin!

Return to altar and use wand to draw the symbol of infinity (an 8 lying on its side) in the air above the altar, the sign of working between the worlds. Set wand on altar, raise up athame in both hands overhead and say:

Hail to the elementals at the four quarters! Welcome Lady and Lord to this rite! I stand between the worlds with love and power all around!

Set down athame and pick up goblet of wine. Pour a little into the cauldron. This is a libation to the Divine in which they are honored by offering to them the first draught, then you take a sip. You may prefer to have a bowl specifically for the libation. Ring bell three times and say:

I celebrate the dance of life to death to new life and the balance of the cosmos in my life! The last harvest is gathered and stored for the dark months ahead, and the wheel has turned to the time of the Hunter.

Ring bell nine times and say:

At this time is the veil between the worlds thin, and I welcome thee spirits who have gone before and thee others who pass between two worlds. This is the crone's time and with the Lord of the Shadows, she is the passage from life to life that all must take. They give a refreshing rest in the continuous turning of the spiral dance that goes and returns, yet ever moves on. With the Ancient Ones (names), *I move with the dance unperturbed. Love gives strength; give to gain.*

Take wand, hold it aloft, and say:

Great Lady, (name), *fruitful mother, you have showered me with your bounty, and in this turning of the seasons, I bid you farewell as you walk now as crone with* (name), *the Lord of the Hunt. I know that within you is yet another fruit waiting to be born, and I will bide patient until the mother returns.*

Replace wand on altar. Place cauldron on pentacle, light black candle within it from the center candle, and say:

Here is the cauldron of endings and new beginnings. Into this burning flame do I cast my weaknesses and the habits that keep me from attaining my potential. By the death of these things will I live a better life. So mote it be!

Cast the parchment into the flame to burn. After it is reduced to ashes, ring bell nine times. Take the white candle and pass it through the patchouli incense (or anoint it with patchouli oil if you use a different incense) and say:

With this candle and by its light I welcome you spirits this Samhain night.

This candle will be saved to be lit and placed inside the jack-o'-lantern to light the way for spirit visitors. Because it was used in the Sabbat and was anointed, it will also screen for friendly spirits, which is why I usually do the Sabbat a couple of hours before sunset and do some of the activities listed later during the course of the night.

Take the heather in your power hand, hold it over the altar, and say:

I call upon the power of this herb to bless this house and the spirits that come to visit.

Drop the heather into the cauldron and say:

The air is purified and made pleasant for the spirits and others who may call upon me. Blessed be!

Take up the apple or pomegranate, hold it aloft over the altar, and say:

I call upon thee, Lord and Lady, (names), *to bless this fruit to be the food for the dead. Let any who visit find sustenance in this apple* (or *pomegranate*) *and pass on refreshed. So mote it be!*

After the Sabbat is concluded, bury the apple or pomegranate in the garden or in a pot of soil outside your door.

Cakes and Wine—Ring bell three times. Feet spread and arms upraised, say:

I acknowledge my needs and offer my appreciation to that which sustains me! May I ever remember the blessings of my Lady and my Lord.

Feet together, take up goblet in left hand and athame in right. Slowly lower the point of the athame into the wine and say:

As male joins female for the benefit of both, let the fruits of their union promote life. Let the earth be fruitful and let her wealth be spread throughout all lands.

Lay down the athame and drink from the goblet. Replace the goblet on the altar and pick up the athame. Touch the point of the athame to the cake in the offering dish and say:

This food is the blessing of the Lady and the Lord given freely to me. As freely as I have received, may I also give food for the body, mind, and spirit to those who seek such of me.

Eat the cake, finish the wine, and say:

As I enjoy these gifts of the Goddess and the God, (names), *may I remember that without them I would have nothing. So mote it be!*

When all is finished, hold athame in your power hand level over altar and say:

Lord and Lady, I am blessed by your sharing this time with me; watching and guarding me, and guiding me here and in all things. I came in love and I depart in love.

Raise up athame in a salute and say:

Love is the law and love is the bond. Merry did I meet, merry do I part, and merry will I meet again. Merry meet, merry part, and merry meet again! The circle is now cleared. So mote it be!

Kiss the flat of the blade and set the athame on the altar. Take up the snuffer and go to the north quarter, raise up arms and say:

Depart in peace, Elemental Earth. My blessings take with you!

Lower arms and snuff the candle, envision the Elemental Power departing. Go to the east, raise up arms and say:

Depart in peace, Elemental Air. My blessings take with you!

Lower arms and snuff the candle, envision the Elemental Power departing. Go to the south, raise up arms and say:

Depart in peace, Elemental Fire. My blessings take with you!

Lower arms and snuff the candle, envision the Elemental Power departing. Go to the west, raise up arms and say:

Depart in peace, Elemental Water. My blessings take with you!

Lower arms and snuff the candle, envision the Elemental Power departing. Return to altar and set down snuffer. Raise up arms and say:

Beings and powers of the visible and invisible, depart in peace! You aid in my work, whisper in my mind, and bless me from the Otherworld, and there is harmony between us. My blessings take with you. The circle is cleared.

Take up athame, go to the north quarter, point athame down and move widdershins around circle (N-W-S-E-N). Envision the blue light drawing back into the athame and say:

The circle is open yet the circle remains as its magical power is drawn back into me.

When you return to the north, having walked the circle, raise up the athame so the blade touches your forehead, and envision the blue light swirling around back into you. Return to altar and say:

The ceremony is ended. Blessings have been given and blessings have been received, may the peace of the Goddess and the God remain in my heart. So mote it be!

Set down the athame. Put away all magical tools and clear the altar except for candles or any objects that need to burn out or work for a stated time (such as candle magic). The cauldron or libation bowl contents are poured onto the earth (if not out in the yard, then into a flowerpot containing soil and perhaps a hardy, leafy green plant).

Traditional foods include dark wine (I like blackberry or sangria), banana nut bread, pumpkin pie, squashes, apple cider, taffy apples, and game birds with savory bread stuffing (Cornish hens are very good, and are baked just like a stuffed chicken). A Mute Supper of bread, salt, and cider or beer is traditional if you want to set an extra place at the table during the family meal (this is considered appropriate for visiting spirits of deceased relatives, so you may want to put a name card at the place and prepare something you know the person enjoyed if you want a specific spirit to celebrate Samhain with you).

Samhain Activities

The following are a few suggestions for activities that can be incorporated into the Sabbat ritual or done during the course of the day (and night).

- Drink apple cider warmed and spiced with cinnamon to honor the dead.

- Make resolutions and burn in a candle flame. This is not the same as ridding yourself of bad habits, but is more like New Year's resolutions, as for many Samhain is the New Year.

- Bury an apple or pomegranate in the garden as food for spirits passing by on their way to be reborn. I incorporate this in the Sabbat.

- Do divinations for the next year.

- Make a spirit candle. This is a white candle anointed with patchouli oil. Say:

   With this candle and by its light,
   I welcome you spirits this Samhain night.

   Place it inside the jack-o'-lantern. I have this included in the Sabbat, but if you have many jack-o'-lanterns you may want to do others as well, and perhaps leave the Sabbat spirit candle at the entry to your home (on a table, for example) or in the center of your dining table.

- Set out a Mute Supper.

- Enjoy the trick or treating of the season.

A Parting Note

I write about the Green level of the Craft as I have learned it from my mother, and mostly through her, from my grandmother. The way I practice today is built from those teachings, my readings, historical research, and intuition. As a child I spoke my grandmother's language fluently, and I used to translate back and forth for her and visitors during the year she lived with us when I was three. As time passed, however, and she returned to Brazil and I spoke only English in school, my fluency in Portuguese was submerged. My mother made a point of learning English as soon as she came to America during World War II, and I was always very proud of her mastery of both languages. However, Portuguese was not frequently spoken in my house and as a result, though I could comprehend much of what was spoken when I visited my relatives at age eleven, my grammar was too limited for me to respond well.

The reason I bring up the language differences is to present a clearer picture of when I first began to take notice of the Pagan path I had quietly been raised in. In a sense, my grandmother baptized me into the Craft during my visit to Brazil when I was eleven after I showered in her house. The shower was basically a small room with a tiled floor and drain, and once I had finished with the soap and rinse, she arrived with a large metal basin of cool water, which she splashed over me. I could not really understand at the time the significance of what she did or what she said, and no one else in the family would tell me (they were disinclined to the Craft), but I had the feeling at the time that what had happened was significant and that I had been cleansed. I remember that I was not at all concerned that she had surprised me, but the strangeness of the experience has remained with me.

My grandmother was very canny, and I like to think that she was preparing me for my path. One never questioned her activities and by the next time I saw her, I was fifteen and already into the Craft, and she seemed to approve. My grandmother was very successful with herbal medicines and magic, and I know that she had a lot of knowledge that did not get passed along. The loss of this wisdom is disturbing to me, and one reason that I have written this book is to pass along what I have for others to build upon. This is just one more step towards reclaiming the old ways. May the Lady and the Lord guide you on your own path.

Afterword

I have presented a set of Green Rituals and suggested activities in the previous chapters, but these are only meant to be starting points. Each household creates its own family traditions, and this is how it should be for the Craft. The question of how open one should be about the Craft is a matter that each individual must decide based on that person's situation. I have heard people say that being in the "broom closet" is not healthy for the acceptance of the Craft, and there are indeed many examples of people who are open about being Witches having only positive experiences. But I have also read of numerous cases where people have suffered discrimination and threats because of their Paganism. Religious freedom is a Constitutional right, but enforcing that right may require the individual to go through expensive lawsuits.

Selena Fox of Circle Sanctuary in Wisconsin was targeted by Jeff Fenholt and his associates. The Ashbury Park Press ("Many Witches Still in [Broom] Closet," Janine De Fao, April 7, 1994) covered a number of problems encountered by various other people involved in the Craft. Because they are known to be Witches, there are people who have lost custody of their children, been harassed at work, called names on the street, forced to relocate businesses, and shot at (which happened to a coven in Florida) and were driven out of their neighborhoods. In Georgia, a senator came out against Witches and vowed to force them to leave. In Arkansas, a couple was driven from their shop by fanatical ministers who organized the landlords of the town to not lease store space to them. Surely this is restraint of trade and religious discrimination (and a few other federal crimes) but those people have yet to be charged with any crime at all. Instead the matter has been addressed as a simple civil case.

Christian ministers repeatedly gain national attention by claiming a relation between crime and satanism, and then saying that Witches are Satanists: "What they are doing is promoting witchcraft, which is evil.

Read your Bible" (from the above article). Well, the Bible (as of the sixteenth century King James translation) says, "Suffer not a Witch to live." This kind of rhetoric puts the murder of a Witch on par with that of an abortion doctor in the minds of some fanatics; it's okay because "God" said to do it. This is not a leap in logic since the Fundamentalists have already linked Wicca with abortion issues in Pat Robinson's 1992 flyers denouncing the Equal Rights Amendment, saying it would lead women to kill their children, divorce their husbands, and become Witches. There is no middle ground with such people, and that is why Christianity and other Judaic-based faiths have been at the root of most of humanity's wars and misery for the past two thousand years. A minister quoted in the Ashbury Park Press article said, "They're worshipping Wicca god (sic) and Wicca goddess (sic). There's only one God, and that's the God in heaven. Witchcraft, Satanism, New Age—they're all under the same umbrella." Even Billy Graham said that the best ministers were "not well-educated" and the previous quote certainly proves that. Yet the man is leading people in a congregation and community, and is quoted in the newspaper.

Another minister objected to the Pagan concept of people being able to control their destiny, saying, "The central issue of the Christian experience is that we are not in control, God is in control." What is unspoken here is that it takes ministers and priests to intercede for people and guide them in communicating with God with the hope that the Judeo-Christian God will be benevolent in his control. The Catholic Church condemns the Craft as "superstition," and offers the terror of no salvation for Witches. This is not a threat that can affect Witches, but is meant as a means for keeping people from exploring an alternative to Christianity and Catholicism.

Even in science, the origin of the universe is presented in terms of the Creation of God. It is not until analysis of this notion is made that even a religious leader (an Anglican priest was interviewed on a Learning Channel program about a beginning for the universe— implying a creation of the universe) will admit that the god of science is not the Judeo-Christian god of religion, but Shiva, the Lord of the Dance. In this particular Learning Channel program, an hour was spent on the god/science theme, but the "revelation" that the god of science was Shiva (hence, a Pagan divinity as Creator) was left for literally the last minute of the show, with only a quick view of a statue of dancing Shiva before the credits were rolled (this should have been the beginning of the program, in my view, but my preference for the Dravidic God has already been stated).

Fear over the rising popularity of neopaganism and the Craft is so strong that ministers are compiling studies to say there are only a handful (some 50,000) Pagans in America, with only 90% of them being Witches (Rev. Melton, *The Institute for the Study of American Religion*), but a slightly more accurate accounting puts the number at anywhere from 100,000 to 200,000 (*EarthSpirit*). Even this last number is too small for the reality simply because many Witches are solitaries who are not members of groups or subscribers to newsletters, and many Witches do not fill out surveys such as those from which *EarthSpirit* gathers its data. The membership in *Circle Network News* has quadrupled over the past twenty years, so the indications are that the Christian ministers have good reason to be worried about their job security as more and more Americans turn away from the dominance of the Church and embrace the natural balance of the Lady and the Lord.

The fact that the Craft is attracting increasingly larger numbers of practitioners indicates that a major change in the role of religion is coming, and this sort of societal change always results in fear and extremist behavior by fanatics. In time this will pass, and the influence of the resurgence of the Old Religion is already being established today. Wicca is legally recognized as a genuine religion by the *Chaplain's Guide for the Uniformed Military Services*, the Internal Revenue Service, and numerous state licensing bureaus. All this is good news for neopaganism, and offers encouragement for people to be open in their practice of the Craft.

I present both sides to this issue not to equivocate, but to make the newcomer aware of how society may react. The young college woman who had her shrine dismantled by school officials was certainly wronged, but she may have thought there would never be any objection to what she did—this is America, after all. I like to think that change is in the wind since there are many Witches now with families whose children are not being raised in the Christian system. The growth of the Craft seems to be moving more openly into the next generation, not under the guise of the folklore of mainstream religions as happened with my mother and grandmother (and myself to some degree until I decided to drop the Christian references), but as a self-aware practice.

Other writers, including Scott Cunningham and Silver RavenWolf, have also discussed the pros and cons of this matter, so there are other written views available to the seeker. By being open about the Craft, some people feel that a statement will be made showing that the Old Religion is not evil or something to be feared. Others recommend caution. I feel that to be closeted or open is a decision that only an individual can make based upon the situation and circumstances affecting that person, and criticism by anyone else is irrelevant. Ignoring the realities of daily life will not create changes or prepare an individual for dealing with situations that arise, but each person contributes in their own way for the betterment of their own life and in turn, for the betterment of society.

Appendix A

Aryan and Dravidic Influences on Western Religions

The redefining of Shiva in India as a deity to be avoided and placated occurred when the Aryan invaders of 2000 B.C.E. swept down from Central Asia and commenced a fifteen-hundred-year encroachment into the Indus. There were a number of different Aryan tribes—Hittites, Levites, Luvites, and Vedics, to name a few of the more familiar ones—and the tribes attacking the Indus Valley cities were the Vedics, whose name relates to "fire altars." The Supreme Beings of the conquered Dravidians were changed by the Aryan Vedics through a series of myths intended to diminish their power in the minds of the conquered. This attempt failed and instead, through the succession of myths and Dravidian-inspired counter-myths, the Dravidic deities became recognized in the Vedic pantheon, displacing from the Vedic trinity the warrior god Indra in the process. The great Goddess tagged along as Shiva's wife, but she is the only female in the Vedic Hindu pantheon honored for her power and independence. The Dravidians were able to incorporate their God and Goddess into the conquering religion in this manner. Today, they are still Goddess-centered in their religious practices and matriarchal in their social structure.

The migrations of Aryan peoples during the volatile years beginning four thousand years ago has left an imprint that affects society today. Before the Aryan invasions there was a thriving commerce between the sailors of the Indus and their colony in Sumeria, and there was a movement of Dravidic people and ideas based more on trade than on war. The Bronze Age Dravidic culture meeting head-on with the Iron Age weapons of the Aryans resulted in the Green elements of the Indus culture being integrated with the authoritarian and political deities of the Aryan culture, and created Hinduism. This led to an Aryan backlash to eliminate the Green altogether, giving birth to a Judeo-Christian heritage that looks back to an "Age of Miracles" that never was and forward to an apotheosis of a few "Chosen People" that will never be.

I know of a history teacher who teaches biblical miracles as real-time, historical facts. Imagine the confusion resulting in the minds of young people trying to understand scientific concepts of space and physics paired with people parting the sea, walking on water, and being miraculously assumed into heaven. Yet public schools are often required to present religion integrated into education to satisfy the community leaders and their church pastors. I read a grief-filled school essay from a girl who looked forward to the "Second Coming" of Jesus, but was devastated by the vision of her family and friends perishing after the "Rapture" (when select Christians are taken from the earth prior to the horrors leading up to Armageddon) because they were not born-again Christians like herself. It is traumas like this that compel me to write.

Today's distancing of the people from their God, the subordination of the Goddess into a meek vessel of the God, and the need for an authoritarian priesthood to explain it all and intercede on behalf of the masses reflect more than the early Aryan need for expansion of territory and livestock (the Aryan word for "war" translates as "get more cattle"). Levite Aryanism rejects the Green level that had been accepted by Northern Aryanism (and continued to be so until the birth of the Protestant movement which codified some of the "Aryan heresies" into Christian faith). For the practicing Catholic the distancing is even greater because while the litany states that people can only be "saved" by the body and blood of Christ, only the priest actually partakes of **both** elements of the Eucharist. The power of the priesthood is reinforced throughout the text of the Mass. He gives out one blessing and receives many—one from each member of the congregation verbally blessing him in unison. He gives out the body of Christ and receives himself both the body and the blood of Christ. He calls the congregation sinners, and places the Pope and the clergy (including himself) in the company of saints and angels. In this way the people are kept at arm's length from the true comfort of unity with the Divine.

There may be some people who object to this view of the remoteness of God, saying that they pray daily and expect miracles to happen, but this is not the same as the events of Biblical mythology where deities (both "good" and "evil") are portrayed as taking an active interest in the mundane affairs of humanity. But since archaeology has shown, as an example, that the Jews were never enslaved in Egypt, that the pyramids were built by Egyptians as a religious expression, that Moses was derived from the Assyrian *Mises*, and that any references to a Passover or Exodus are fictitious (John Romer and Neil Silberman have presented this information in the television programs *Testament* and *Archaeology* respectively), the so-called miracles of the Old Testament can be seen as simple mythology, no different from Zeus turning himself into a swan to impregnate Leda with twins (a very popular European art subject from pre-Christian through Renaissance times). Indeed, many of the Bible tales of both the Old and New Testaments came from earlier Egyptian and Babylonian literature. Unless you understand how and when the Bible was constructed, you could be easily misled into thinking it unique and authoritative. The purpose of such Bible stories was to give an identity and sense of exclusiveness to a group of people no different from their neighbors, but ruled by Levite Aryans from Anatolia (see Merlin Stone's *When God Was A Woman*).

The fact is that anyone can expect results that can be interpreted as miracles because when you pray or perform a magical ritual (of which prayer is merely one form), you are engaging in a Green activity by personally tapping into the universal energy to accomplish what you desire. Time, and the events therein, can be altered or manipulated through this energy connection. Modern expression of this is found when people are said to be in control of their own destiny or take responsibility for their own actions. These concepts take power away from an incomprehensible god whose actions are interpreted by an elite clergy, and places it into the hands of individual people. This is why mainstream religious leaders find Humanism, with its premise that humans can be the architects of their own destiny, such a threat. It is more to their advantage to have people believe their lives are pre-ordained (or pre-destined) by a god, and only the anointed representative of this god can intervene on the individual's behalf.

It is all a matter of power and dominance concentrated in the hands of a clergy threatened by independent thinking and personal liberty. That is why the Constitution is so amazingly insistent on personal freedom. The Founding Fathers were Humanists, Deists, and Masons, not radically right-wing in their thinking. Even Thomas Jefferson took scissors to the New Testament of the Bible and cut it down to what he felt was representative of the true message of Jesus—and Jefferson's Bible, which can be purchased these days in some bookstores, is a very thin version of the recognized New Testament. Those are the kind of people who founded America, and we need to recognize and give them the admiration they deserve for independent thinking. We need to reclaim the heroes of the nation's past for the real people they were and reject the mythos surrounding them.

Divination, rejected by mainstream religion as demonic, is not a telling of what will happen, but of how things could occur unless the person involved takes action to direct the future. It offers warnings so the person can take preventative or psychic action. This use of divination negates the predestination aspect of Christianity, which has itself becomes a philosophical quagmire (if God is All Knowing, then he already knows who will go to heaven and who will go to hell, so there is nothing you can do to avoid the latter if you are so fated because the Bible teaches that good works alone are useless and you are only saved by God's grace—hence, life ultimately has no purpose and no direction because although you may frantically seek God's grace, no one really knows who wins in this divine lottery until Judgement Day). The difference with Wicca is that one meets and communicates with the Deities directly and as a result, there is no "belief" required and no "orthodox" dogma. Witchcraft, then, is not a religion of faith so much as a unification with the Divine (without the loss of the person's individuality) and the practice of a Craft.

Among Christians, many who pray for miracles would rather address the Goddess as Mother of God and the lesser gods and goddesses (aspects of the God and the Goddess) as saints, or approach the remote "God Almighty" in the name of a more benevolent aspect, the Son of God—the European Oak King of winter solstice and spring rather than the Holly King of autumn and winter (why else was Jesus nailed to an oak cross—how many oaks do you think grow in the Near East?). While some people object to Virgin Mary being called the Goddess, the historical reality is that all the accolades, pageantries, shrines, holy places (and this includes Lourdes), and titles once associated with the goddesses of pre-Christianized Greece and Europe have been appropriated for Mary over the centuries. All aspects of the Goddess, from giving birth to a God who has impregnated her with himself to being undying (Mary was "assumed" into heaven and then crowned as Queen of Heaven and Queen of the Universe—both are ancient Pagan titles for the Goddess) were given to Mary. She is the Goddess, but in a Christianized form.

My favorite depiction of the Virgin Mary (one which is seen in old churches all over Europe) is as the Queen of the Universe. Long, brown, wavy hair flowing unbound around her, garbed in robes of white and blue, standing with her foot between the horns of the crescent moon and surrounded by stars (and occasionally in the company of a snake). This is the familiar Great Goddess of Paganism taking the position of the blue and white levels of the Northern system. She becomes visually the Law and the Creatrix, with her horned moon symbol (and snakes) making her identity clear to any who can understand it. The artisans of the Church were not divorced from their Pagan heritage, and this union with the prehistoric past is something that is often missing in the religious heritage of a colonial nation like the United States of America.

In the practice of the Green Level, there is no need for intermediaries of any sort—one can go directly to the Goddess and the God. It was the establishment of a priesthood, enforced by warriors under a ruler through civil and church (or temple, in the case of the Jews) laws and punishments for non-compliance that forced most people from the basic path of Green Witchcraft. The surviving Green elements were either adapted into the newer religious forms or discarded and used as a means of identifying non-conformists for punitive action.

Among the many mainstream and Pagan traditions of today there are a number of Green elements which have been adapted to become mainstream ritualized ceremonies, such as the Eucharist and solar holidays. Yet these traditions that are commonly considered Christian come from the symbology adapted by Paul and by later Church Councils many centuries after Christianity began. Ideally, to be unique and true, the Christian faith should have no observations of the Pagan holidays, no venerated saints, and no expansive tales of miraculous exploits by human beings. Recognition of this historical background has resulted in a very strict application of Christian ideals by such recently formed fundamentalist and self-exclusive sects as the Jehovah's Witnesses, who do not celebrate holidays or even birthdays. The sacred Pagan days were usurped into mainstream Christianity under new names, and numerous early saints appear superhuman simply because they have been given the legends of the older gods and goddesses. Charles Squire in *Celtic Myth and Legend* discusses this phenomenon.

Since such traditional aspects of mainstream Christianity are in fact Pagan in origin, then why should any aspect of this "new" religion be accepted at face value? The tradition of deceit is already established. In point of fact, there is nothing "new" in the new faith—not the miraculous birth, not the crucifixion, and not the resurrection. These were all well-known Pagan themes relating to the agrarian/seasonal cycles, and even the name Jesus is merely the Greek pronunciation of the Aramaic Isha, which is the Hindu name "Lord" applied only to Shiva. We have come full circle, and the miracles and stories of Greek Hercules and of Dionysus, the pre-Hellenic deity of Indian origin that even the ancient Greek historians identified with the Indus Shiva, were given to Jesus by the Greek writers of the New Testament Gospels over the first two-and-a-half centuries of the formation of Christianity (Durant, Danielou and Kersten, to name only a few sources).

The only purpose of the new religion, then, was to gain power and authority over people and territory for the clergy. This is the history of Constantine using Christians to secure his position as Roman Emperor against Pagan rivals, and this is the history of Popes involved in wars of conquest and aggression against secular kings. The churches of Europe are filled with the evidence of this power struggle as display cases are filled with the looted jewels and gold of both the European and American Pagan past, melted and re-set into useless chalices and reliquaries, to be seen only by those travelers who bother to investigate the hoarded wealth of the Catholic Church. The only real blessing is that some of the clerical authorities had a sufficient sense of history to preserve some of the Pagan works of art, and thus one may be startled to find unaltered Pagan gold images and items in Christian monasteries and churches.

Appendix B

Mail Order Supplies

The businesses listed here offer a variety of Craft and Pagan goods, as well as herbs and books. If you are interested in what they have to offer, I recommend sending a self-addressed stamped envelope (SASE) with an inquiry as to the cost of their catalog. Most stores will deduct the cost from the first order. This listing is limited because I have screened my collection of mail order resources and selected the ones I felt offered the best in materials, service, and price.

DRAGONWOOD
1211 Hillcrest Street
Orlando, FL 32803
(407) 895-7439

EYE OF THE CAT
3314 E. Broadway
Long Beach, CA 90803
(310) 438-3569

LUNATRIX
P.O. Box 800482
Santa Clarita, CA 91380-0482

MAGIC BOOK STORE
2306 Highland Avenue
National City, CA 91950
(619) 477-5260

ROOTS AND WINGS
980 Winchester
Lincoln Park, MI 48146
(313) 388-9141

WHITE LIGHT PENTACLES/SACRED SPIRIT PRODUCTS
P.O. Box 8163
Salem, MA 01971-8163

The final store had a rather limited selection of Craft items (such as handmade tools and ointments) the last time I got anything from them, but the quality is excellent and you can request materials not listed in the catalog for a tool that is more personal and made to order. I got a lovely bolline from them, and their oils have delicious fragrances.

YE OLDE WITCHES' MILL
P.O. Box 794
Bradon, FL 33509

# Bibliography

Aoumiel. *Dancing Shadows*. St. Paul: Llewellyn Publications, 1994.

Briggs, Katherine. *An Encyclopedia of Fairies, Hobgoblins, Brownies, Bogies, and Other Supernatural Creatures*. New York: Pantheon Books, 1976.

Buckland, Raymond. *Buckland's Complete Book of Witchcraft*. St. Paul: Llewellyn Publications, 1994.

Campbell, Joseph. *The Masks of God: Oriental Mythology*. New York: Penguin Books, 1976.

Campbell, Joseph. *The Masks of God: Primitive Mythology*. New York: Penguin Books, 1976.

Carlyon, Richard. *A Guide to The Gods*. New York: Quill, William Morrow, 1981.

Conway, D.J. *Celtic Magic*. St. Paul: Llewellyn Publications, 1990.

Cunningham, Scott. *The Complete Book of Incense, Oils, & Brews*. St. Paul: Llewellyn Publications, 1990.

Cunningham, Scott. *Cunningham's Encyclopedia of Magical Herbs*. St. Paul: Llewellyn Publications, 1996.

Danielou, Alain. *Gods of Love and Ecstacy, The Traditions of Shiva and Dionysus*. Rochester, Vermont: Inner Traditions, 1992.

Durant, Will. *The Story of Civilization: Part I, Our Oriental Heritage*. New York: Simon and Schuster, 1954.

Durant, Will. *The Story of Civilization: Part II, The Life of Greece*. New York: Simon and Schuster, 1966.

Durant, Will. *The Story of Civilization: Part IV, The Age of Faith*. New York: Simon and Schuster, 1950.

Francisis, Alfonso de. *Pompeii*. Napoli, Italy: Interdipress, 1972.

González-Wippler, Migene. *The Complete Book of Spells, Ceremonies, & Magic*. St. Paul: Llewellyn Publications, 1988.

Green, Marian. *A Witch Alone*. London: The Aquarian Press, 1991.

Kersten, Holger. *Jesus Lived in India: His Unknown Life Before and After the Crucifixion*. Dorset, England: Element Book Ltd., 1986.

Klostermaier, Klaus K. *A Survey of Hinduism*. Albany: State University of New York Press, 1989.

Massa, Aldo. *The World of the Etruscans*. Translated by John Christmas. Geneve, Italy: Minerva, 1989.

Pepper, et al. *The Witches' Almanac*. Cambridge: Pentacle Press, 1992-1993; 1993-1994.

Ryall, Rhiannon. *West Country Wicca: A Journal of the Old Religion*. Custer: Phoenix Publishing, Inc., 1989.

Silberman, Neil Asher. "Who Were the Israelites?"*Archaeology*, March/April 1992.

Squire, Charles. *Celtic Myth and Legend*. Newcastle: Newcastle Publishing Co., Inc., 1975.

Starhawk. *The Spiral Dance, A Rebirth of the Ancient Religion of the Great Goddess*. New York: Harper Collins Publishers, 1989.

Stone, Merlin. *When God Was A Woman*. New York: Dorset Press, 1976.

Thorsson, Edred. *Northern Magic: Mysteries of the Norse, Germans & English*. St. Paul: Llewellyn Publications, 1992.

Williams, Jude C. *Jude's Herbal Home Remedies*. St. Paul: Llewellyn Publications, 1996.

Index

Stay in Touch. . .
Llewellyn publishes hundreds of books on your favorite subjects

On the following pages you will find listed some books now available on related subjects. Your local bookstore stocks most of these and will stock new Llewellyn titles as they become available. We urge your patronage.

Order by Phone

Call toll-free within the U.S. and Canada, **1–800–THE MOON.**
In Minnesota call **(612) 291–1970.**
We accept Visa, MasterCard, and American Express.

Order by Mail

Send the full price of your order (MN residents add 7% sales tax) in U.S. funds to:

Llewellyn Worldwide
P.O. Box 64383, Dept. K690-4
St. Paul, MN 55164–0383, U.S.A.

Postage and Handling

- ◆ $4.00 for orders $15.00 and under
- ◆ $5.00 for orders over $15.00
- ◆ No charge for orders over $100.00

We ship UPS in the continental United States. We ship standard mail to P.O. boxes. Orders shipped to Alaska, Hawaii, the Virgin Islands and Puerto Rico are sent first-class mail.

Orders shipped to Canada or Mexico are sent surface mail. Surface mail: Add $1.00 per item.

International orders: Airmail—add freight equal to price of each book to the total price of order, plus $5.00 for each non-book item (audiotapes, etc.).

Allow 4–6 weeks delivery on all orders. Postage and handling rates subject to change.

Group Discounts

We offer a 20% quantity discount to group leaders or agents. You must order a minimum of 5 copies of the same book to get our special quantity price.

DANCING SHADOWS
The Roots of Western Religious Beliefs
Aoumiel

At last, a contemporary Pagan perspective on Western religious history! Discover the historical roots of neopaganism and its relationship to modern religions.

Learn the fascinating story of how the Pagan deities have been transformed and absorbed into the hierarchy of mainstream religions, and why Pagan beliefs have been borrowed, altered, and refuted by Aryan religions over the centuries. *Dancing Shadows* traces Western religions back 3,000 years to the Dravidian god/goddess beliefs of the ancient Indus Valley (which evolved into the Western Pagan tradition) and the patriarchal sky-god religion of the invading Aryans from Central Asia (on which modern Christianity, Judaism, and Islam are based). This book will show you how the cross-fertilization of these two belief systems—both traceable to a common religious ancestor—is the source of conflicts that continue today.

Aoumiel draws together current research in the fields of history, religion, archeology, and anthropology to formulate a cohesive theory for the origins of modern neopaganism, presenting a refreshing affirmation of the interconnection between all Western peoples and beliefs.

1-56718-691-2, 224 pp., 6 x 9, softcover   **$12.95**

CUNNINGHAM'S ENCYCLOPEDIA OF MAGICAL HERBS
Scott Cunningham

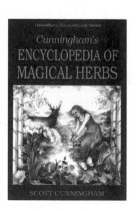

This is the most comprehensive source of herbal data for magical uses ever printed! Almost every one of the over 400 herbs are illustrated, making this a great source for herb identification. For each herb you will also find: magical properties, planetary rulerships, genders, associated deities, folk and Latin names and much more. To make this book even easier to use, it contains a folk name cross reference and all of the herbs are fully indexed. There is also a large annotated bibliography and a list of mail order suppliers so you can find the books and herbs you need.

Like all of Cunningham's books, this one does not require you to use complicated rituals or expensive magical paraphernalia. Instead, it shares with you the intrinsic powers of the herbs. Thus, you will be able to discover which herbs, by their very nature, can be used for luck, love, success, money, divination, astral projection, safety, psychic self-defense and much more. Besides being interesting and educational it is also fun and fully illustrated with unusual woodcuts from old herbals. This book has rapidly become the classic in its field. It enhances books such as *Green Witchcraft* and is a must for all Wiccans.

0-87542-122-9, 336 pp., 6 x 9, illus., softcover   **$14.95**

JUDE'S HERBAL HOME REMEDIES
Natural Health, Beauty & Home-Care Secrets
Jude C. Williams, M.H.

There's a pharmacy—in your spice cabinet! In the course of daily life we all encounter problems that can be easily remedied through the use of common herbs—headaches, dandruff, insomnia, colds, muscle aches, burns—and a host of other afflictions known to humankind. *Jude's Herbal Home Remedies* is a simple guide to self care that will benefit beginning or experienced herbalists with its wealth of practical advice. Most of the herbs listed are easy to obtain.

Discover how cayenne pepper promotes hair growth, why cranberry juice is a good treatment for asthma attacks, how to make a potent juice to flush out fat, how to make your own deodorants and perfumes, what herbs will get fleas off your pet, how to keep cut flowers fresh longer ... the remedies and hints go on and on!

This book gives you instructions for teas, salves, tinctures, tonics, poultices, along with addresses for obtaining the herbs. Dangerous and controversial herbs are also discussed.

Grab this book and a cup of herbal tea and discover from a Master Herbalist more than 800 ways to a simpler, more natural way of life.

0-87542-869-X, 320 pp., 6 x 9, illus., softcover **$12.95**

THE COMPLETE BOOK OF SPELLS, CEREMONIES & MAGIC
Migene González-Wippler

This book is far more than a historical survey of magical techniques throughout the world. It is the most complete book of spells, ceremonies and magic ever assembled. It is the spiritual record of humanity.

Topics in this book include magical spells and rituals from virtually every continent and every people. The spells described are for love, wealth, success, protection, and health. Also examined are the theories and the history of magic, including its evolution, the gods, the elements, the Kabbalah, the astral plane, ceremonial magic, famous books of magic and famous magicians. You will learn about talismanic magic, exorcisms, how to use the I Ching, interpret dreams, construct and interpret a horoscope, read Tarot cards, read palms, do numerology, and much more. Included are explicit instructions for love spells and talismans; spells for riches and money; weight-loss spells; magic for healing; psychic self-defense; spells for luck in gambling; and much more.

No magical library is complete without this classic text of magical history, theory and practical technique. The author is known for her excellent books on magic. Many consider this her best. Includes over 150 rare photos and illustrations.

0-87542-286-1, 400 pp., 6 x 9, illus., softcover **$14.95**

BUCKLAND'S COMPLETE BOOK OF WITCHCRAFT
Raymond Buckland

Here is the most complete resource to the study and practice of modern, non-denominational Wicca. This is a lavishly illustrated, self-study course for a solitary or a group. Included are rituals; exercises for developing psychic talents; information on all major sects of the Craft; sections on tools, beliefs, dreams, meditations, divination, herbal lore, healing, ritual clothing, and much more. This book unites theory and practice into a comprehensive course designed to help you develop into a practicing Witch, one of the "Wise Ones." Raymond Buckland, a famous and respected authority on Witchcraft, was the first to go public with the Old Religion in the United States.

Never before has so much information on the Craft of the Wise been collected in one place. Traditionally, there are three degrees of advancement in most Wiccan traditions. When you have completed studying this book, you will be the equivalent of a Third-Degree Witch. Even those who have practiced Wicca for years find useful information in this book, and many covens are using this for their textbook.

If you want to become a Witch, or if you merely want to find out what Witchcraft is really about, you will find no better book than this.

0-87542-050-8, 272 pp., 8 ½ x 11, illus., softcover   **$14.95**

THE WITCHES TAROT KIT
Ellen Cannon Reed, illustrated by Martin Cannon

Previously sold separately, *The Witches Tarot* book and deck are now packaged together as a complete kit. Also included are a 32 pg. instruction booklet and a layout sheet.

This tarot deck has become a favorite among paganfolk who enjoy the presentation of the mystical Kabbalistic symbolism from a clear and distinctly Pagan point of view. Creator Ellen Cannon Reed has replaced the traditional Devil with The Horned One, the Hierophant with the High Priest, and the Hermit with the Seeker. Each of the Magical Spheres is included, in striking color, on the corresponding cards. Even non-pagans have reported excellent results with the cards and appreciate their colorful and timeless beauty.

In the book, Reed defines the complex, inner workings of the Kabbalah. She includes a complete section on divination, with several layout patterns. In addition, she provides instruction on using the cards for Pathworking, or astral journeys through the Tree of Life. An appendix gives a list of correspondences for each of the Paths, including the associated Tarot card, Hebrew letter, colors, astrological attribution, animal, gem, and suggested meditation.

1-56718-558-4, 320 pg. book and 78 full-color cards   **$34.95**